The Historic Inns of Frome

SCOTTISH WIDOWS FUND
CROWN
CROWN
HOTEL
W.R. BOWN
HUMBER
CYCLES

The Historic Inns of Frome

Mick Davis & Valerie Pitt

AKEMAN PRESS

Published by AKEMAN PRESS
www.akemanpress.com

© Mick Davis & Valerie Pitt 2015

ISBN 978-0-9560989-9-3

All rights reserved. No part of this publication may be reproduced, stored in a retrieval system, or transmitted, in any form or by any means, electrical, mechanical, photocopying, recording or otherwise, without the prior permission of Akeman Press.

Front cover: The White Hart in Cheap Street, closed in 1924

Back cover: Frome inn signs past and present

Title page: Three of Frome's grandest inns – the George, the Crown and the Bull – around 1890. Only the George remains open today.

Printed by Ashford Colour Press. Gosport

Contents

Introduction vii

A Plan of Frome in 1774 viii

Albion, Cheap Street 1
Anchor Inn, Eagle Lane 2
Anchor, Catherine Street 3
Anchor, Stony Street 4
Angel, King Street 5
Angel & Crown, Vallis Way 8
Apollo Tavern & Welshmill Brewery 11
Archangel, King Street *(see Angel)*
Artisan, Christchurch Street West *(see Ship)*
Bath Arms, Palmer Street 12
Bear, Cheap Street 15
Beehive, Keyford 16
Bell, Christchurch Street East 19
Bell, Church Forecourt 20
Bell, Fromefield 21
Bell, Trinity Street 22
Bird in Hand, Nunney Lane 24
Bird in Hand, Portway *(see White Horse)*
Black Boy, Wallbridge 24
Black Swan, Bridge Street 25
Blue Anchor, Behind Town 28
Blue Boar, Market Place 28
Boar's Head, Vicarage Street 33
Boot, Albion Place, Paul Street 33
Bridge Hotel, The Bridge 34
Bull Hotel, Market Place 37
Carpenter's Arms, Milk Street 40
Castle & Arch 40
Castle, Catherine Hill 40
Cat, Cole Hill 41
Champneys Arms, North Parade 41
Clothier's Arms, Milk Street 42

Cornerhouse, Christchurch Street East *(see Lamb)*
Crooked Fish 44
Cross Keys, Back Lane 45
Cross Keys, Blatchbridge 45
Crown, Keyford 46
Crown, Market Place 50
Crown & Sceptre / Jolly Butcher, Trinity Street 55
Crown & Thistle, Market Place 57
Dolphin, Market Place 58
Dolphin / Farmer's Arms, Spring Gardens 58
Dr Andrews, Milk Street 59
Eagle, Eagle Lane 60
Farmer's Arms, Spring Gardens *(see Dolphin)*
First & Last, Wallbridge *(see Railway)*
Fleur de Luce, corner of Stony Street & Palmer Street 61
Forester's Arms, Locks Lane 63
Fox, Blatchbridge Lane 63
Fox & Hounds, Tytherington 64
Full Moon and Golden Lyon upon the Bridge 65
George, Market Place 65
George in ye Woodlands, Marston Bigot 74
Globe, Back Lane 75
Globe, Vallis Way 75
Golden Lyon upon the Bridge *(see Full Moon)*
Great Western / Live and Let Live, Portway 76
Greyhound, Milk Street 78
Griffin, Milk Street 79
Jolly Butcher *(see Crown & Sceptre)*
Half Moon, Castle Street 81

Half Way House, Clink Road   83
Horse & Groom, Portway   84
Horse & Groom, East Woodlands   84
Horse & Jockey, Mattocks Lake, Silver Lane   85
King of Prussia, Naishes Street   86
King's Arms, Milk Street   87
King's Head, The Butts   87
King's Head, Trinity Street   88
Lamb / Cornerhouse, Gorehedge and Christchurch Street East   89
Lamb & Fountain, Castle Street   93
Lamb & Lark, Woodlands   96
Lion, Broadway (see Wheelwright's Arms)
Live and Let Live, Portway (see Great Western)
Mansford & Baily (see Wheatsheaves)
Masons Arms, Marston Gate   97
Masons Arms / Queen's Head, Whittox Lane   100
Mechanics Arms / Roebuck / Antelope, Water Lane   101
Murtrey Inn, Orchardleigh   103
Nag's Head, King Street   104
New Inn / Weaver, The Butts   104
Old Bath Arms, Palmer Street (see Bath Arms)
Olive Tree, Christchurch Street West (see Ship)
Pack Horse, Christchurch Street West   107
Packsaddle, Broadway   110
Plume of Feathers, Keyford Street   110
Portway Hotel, Portway   112
Prince of Wales, Vicarage Street   112
Queen's Head, Badcox   113
Queen's Head, Whittox Lane (see Queen's Head)
Railway / First & Last, Wallbridge   114
Red Lion, Broadway   115
Red Lion, The Butts   115
Red Lion, Feltham Lane   117
Rifleman's Arms, Murtrey   117

Ring O'Bells, Broadway   119
Rose & Crown, The Butts   122
Royal Oak, Broadway   124
Royal Standard, Horton Street   126
Selwood Inn, Clink Road   129
Ship / Olive Tree / Artisan, Christchurch Street West   131
Ship, Oldford   136
Somerset Arms, The Butts   137
Spread Eagle, Castle Street   139
Star & Garter, Coward's Batch, Milk Street   140
Sun, Catherine Street   141
Swan, Badcox   144
Talbot, Trinity Street (see Bell)
Tandem, Locks Lane   147
Three Swans, King Street   147
Three Wheatsheaves, Bath Street (see Wheatsheaves)
Trinity, Vallis Way (see Globe)
Trooper, Trinity Street   151
Unicorn, Keyford Street   152
Victoria, Christchurch Street East   154
Vine Tree, Berkley Road   157
Waggon & Horses, Gentle Street   159
Weaver, The Butts (see New Inn)
Wheatsheaf, Catherine Hill   163
Wheatsheaves / Mansford & Baily / Three Wheatsheaves, Bath Street   164
Wheelwright's Arms / Lion, Broadway   166
White Hart, Market Place and Cheap Street   168
White Hart, Vallis Way   171
White Horse / Bird in Hand, Portway   171
White Swan, Vallis Road   173
Woolpack, Badcox   174
Woolpack, Culver Hill   175
Wyredrawer's Arms, Portway   177
Bibliography   179
Photo Credits   180

Introduction

This book is the result of the happy coincidence of both authors, who were researching the subject separately, meeting in the archives at Frome Museum and deciding to combine their efforts, and is the product of a three year research project. In addition to archival research, it has been informed by many interviews and correspondence with residents of Frome past and present, and to those willing informants we should like to express our thanks. The authors would also like to express their gratitude to those inhabitants of both extant and ex-pubs who have allowed us into their homes and businesses and to the many kindly souls who have provided us with photographs.

Special thanks are due to Diane Rouse, with whom we co-curated the successful 'Lost Pubs of Frome Exhibition' in 2013, and to David Lassman & Sandy Usher who ran the local history course through Frome Community Education. A huge debt is also owed to Brian Marshall, Treasurer of Frome Museum, without whose forbearance this book would have faltered long ago. Finally, we are very grateful for the research of earlier Frome historians, most notably Derek Gill, whose transcriptions and notebooks fill the shelves of Frome Museum, and who broke new ground with his investigations into local pubs in the 1980s.

Had we included every iota of information unearthed for this volume we could have extended our work into decades of investigation. As with family history, there will always be new avenues to follow, but a line had to be drawn. Nevertheless, all the data upon which this book is based will now be compiled into an ongoing database, available for anybody to consult at Frome Museum in the hope that it will prove of use and interest to genealogists, house historians and social historians alike. We invite people to add to this resource themselves, and any information, photographs, anecdotes, or details of publicans' families will be gratefully included and acknowledged.

In terms of layout, we have gone for the simplest option and listed the pubs alphabetically according to the name by which they are most commonly known, but cross-referenced with name changes or aliases.

The aims of this book are many, but not least of these is to enhance the pleasure of a visit to any of Frome's existing public houses with a little bit of history!

Mick Davis & Valerie Pitt
c/o Frome Museum 1, North Parade, Frome BA11 1AT
info@frome-heritage-museum.org; 01373 454 611

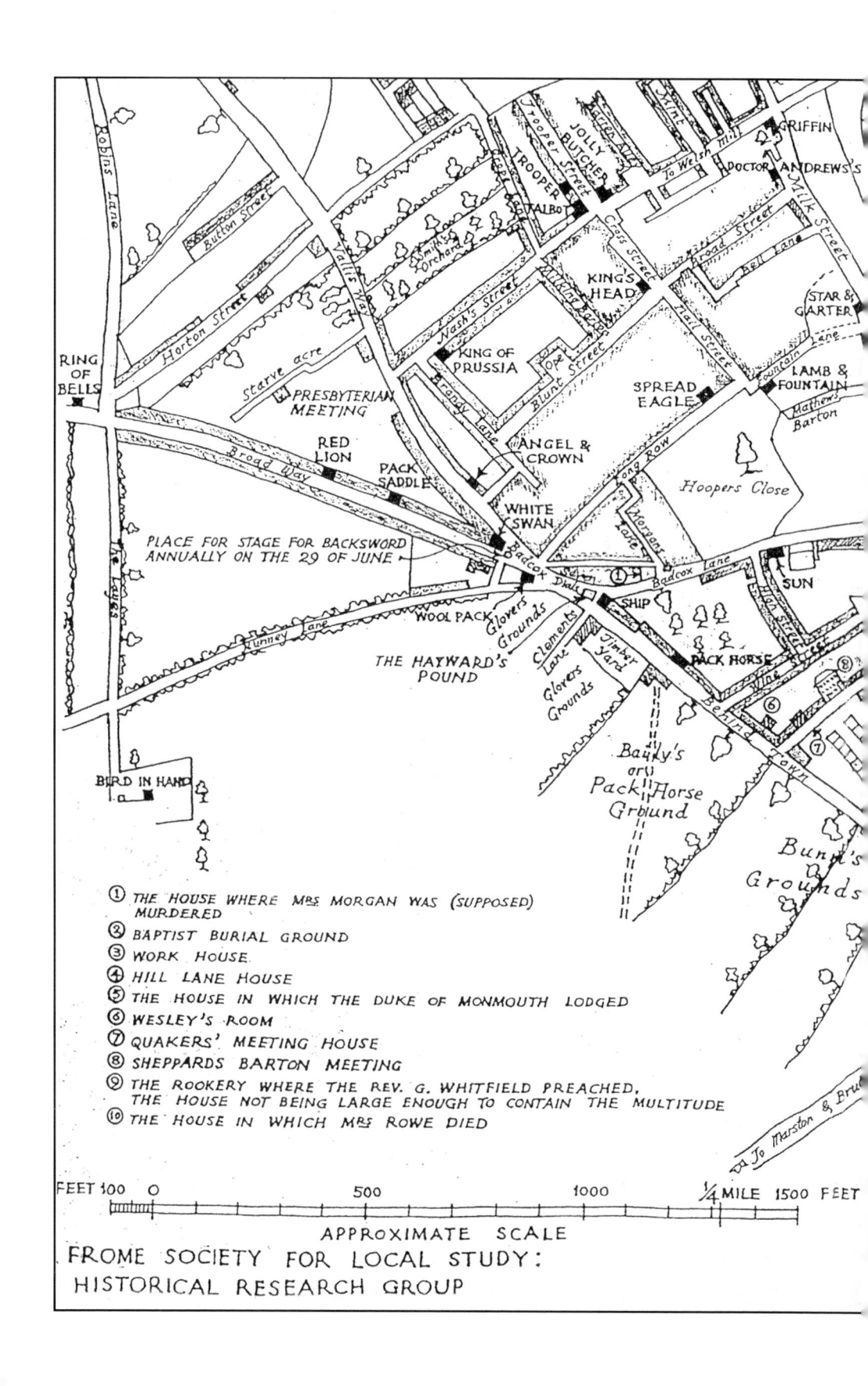

① THE HOUSE WHERE MRS MORGAN WAS (SUPPOSED) MURDERED
② BAPTIST BURIAL GROUND
③ WORK HOUSE
④ HILL LANE HOUSE
⑤ THE HOUSE IN WHICH THE DUKE OF MONMOUTH LODGED
⑥ WESLEY'S ROOM
⑦ QUAKERS' MEETING HOUSE
⑧ SHEPPARDS BARTON MEETING
⑨ THE ROOKERY WHERE THE REV. G. WHITFIELD PREACHED, THE HOUSE NOT BEING LARGE ENOUGH TO CONTAIN THE MULTITUDE
⑩ THE HOUSE IN WHICH MRS ROWE DIED

APPROXIMATE SCALE

FROME SOCIETY FOR LOCAL STUDY: HISTORICAL RESEARCH GROUP

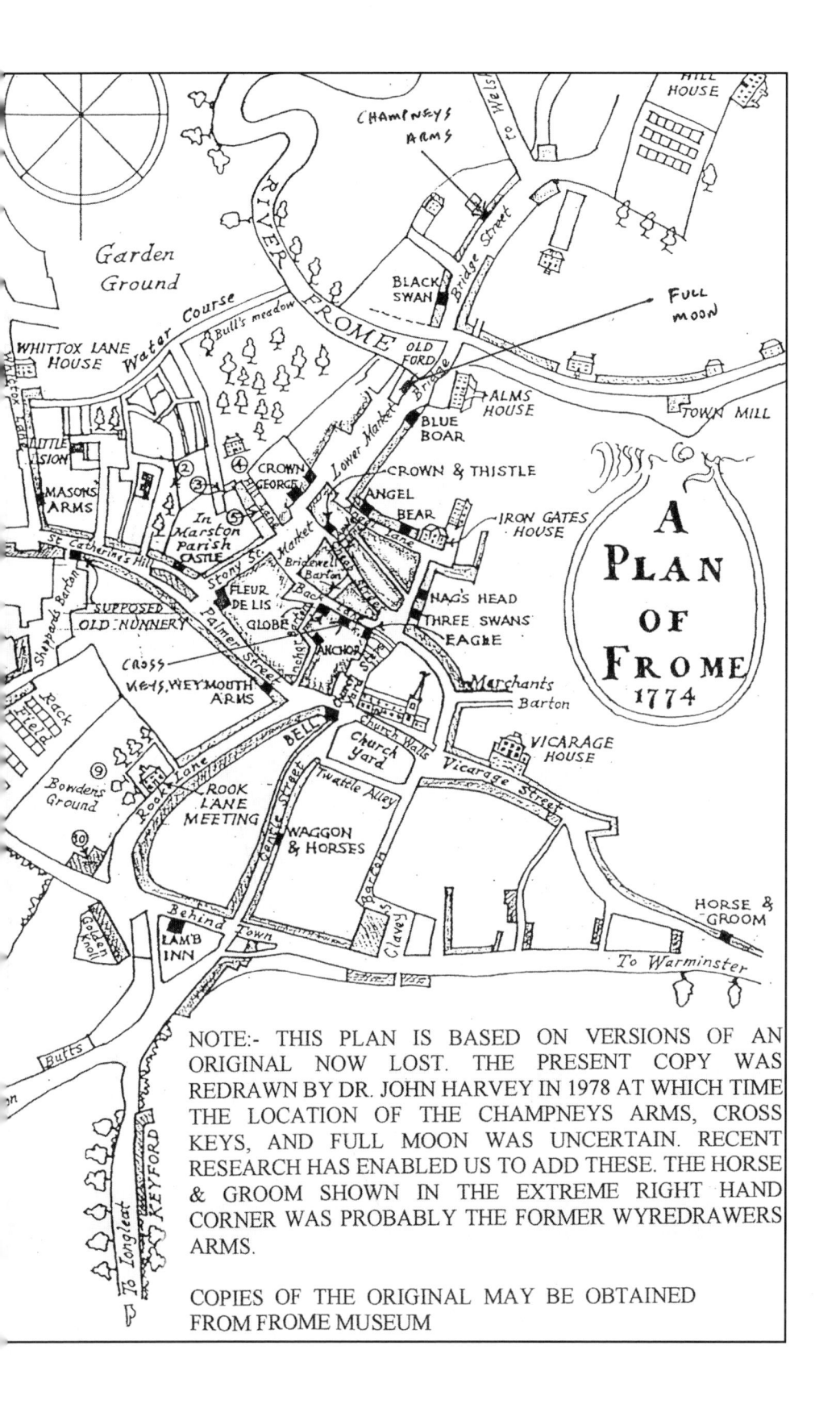

NOTE:- THIS PLAN IS BASED ON VERSIONS OF AN ORIGINAL NOW LOST. THE PRESENT COPY WAS REDRAWN BY DR. JOHN HARVEY IN 1978 AT WHICH TIME THE LOCATION OF THE CHAMPNEYS ARMS, CROSS KEYS, AND FULL MOON WAS UNCERTAIN. RECENT RESEARCH HAS ENABLED US TO ADD THESE. THE HORSE & GROOM SHOWN IN THE EXTREME RIGHT HAND CORNER WAS PROBABLY THE FORMER WYREDRAWERS ARMS.

COPIES OF THE ORIGINAL MAY BE OBTAINED FROM FROME MUSEUM

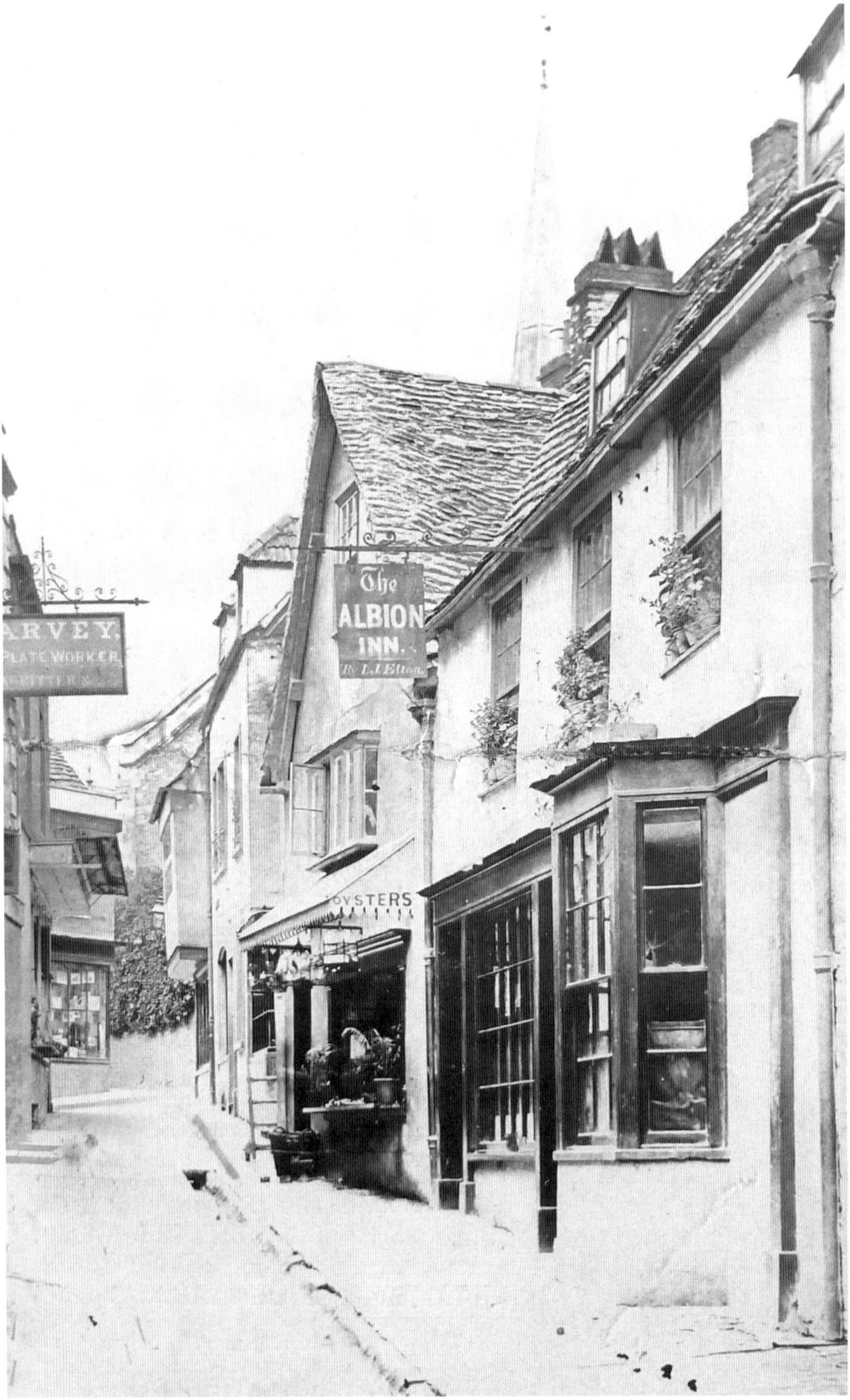
ARVEY,
PLATE WORKER,
The
ALBION
INN.
OYSTERS

Albion, 16 Cheap Street

A licensing application in 1884 states that the Albion beerhouse opened around 1859 and the census of 1861 gives the landlord as local lad Alfred Butcher, blacksmith and victualler. In 1863, new landlord Henry Williams applied for a full licence on the grounds that his house was more of an inn for travellers than a beerhouse, and that he often had between five and seven people staying there. The application was refused with no reason given, but possibly because the White Hart was just across the road. A year later the freehold was put up for auction and sold to the Bailys, the local brewers and pub owners, for £260.

In 1871, Alfred Coombs, 'house painter & beerhouse keeper', was landlord. A conveyance of 1873 describes the rear of the premises in Eagle Lane as having been the auction rooms of Charles Taylor, but now incorporated into the pub. In a brewery prospectus of 1893, the former auction rooms were described as a store house for the pub.

Above: The Albion in 2013
Opposite: The Albion around 1884

This little beerhouse never seemed able to keep a landlord for long and must have suffered from having to compete with the White Hart across the road. Among those who tried to make a go of it were Samuel Lusty, a shoemaker, and Isaac Elton, who in 1884 applied for permission to install a billiard table. From reading press reports, it would seem that such an application would equate today with an application for live rock bands every night. Despite Isaac Elton being bailiff to the Market Company, and the house being owned by J&T Baily, reputable and established brewers, the magistrates

> thought that the multiplication of billiard tables would be an evil and therefore had, in its wisdom, restricted their increase. Any fully-licensed house could put up a billiard table without coming to the bench and the fact that only two had put up tables showed that no more were required. The Albion had had five tenants in the last eight or nine years and the house did not pay as a beerhouse and the table was not intended to be a place of recreation but simply as an adjunct to a beerhouse to make it pay better.

The fact that the Bailys had, due to a 'misapprehension of the law', already gone to great expense in building and fitting up a billiard room probably got up the collective noses of the bench and the application was refused.

Things did not improve. In 1885 Isaac Elton was arrested for 'forcibly ejecting' Albert Joyce from the premises with such enthusiasm that he fell and fractured his skull on the watercourse in the street. Joyce was in the Cottage Hospital on the critical list for some time and the case was adjourned several times because of this, but it seems that things went in Elton's favour, as in August he was once more able to apply for a billiard table licence, which was again refused.

By 1887 he had had enough and the Lamb Brewery advertised The Albion to rent. James Ruddock was the new landlord and seems to have made a go of it for a while as he was still there in 1903. This period of stability did not last and, in June 1913, 16 Cheap Street was put up for auction as a 'former beerhouse, now void', marking the end of its short and unhappy life as a pub.

By 1918, it had become the Flora Grill & Tea Rooms, and it continues in much the same vein today as the Settle, a very successful restaurant and bakery with an international reputation, having expanded into the fish shop next door and appeared in an early episode of one of Keith Floyd's TV cookery programmes. The original wrought-iron sign bracket is still there, however, with the chains that once held the sign hanging from it, maybe hoping to be useful again one day.

Anchor, Eagle Lane (formerly Back Lane)

Before Bath Street was built in 1810, if you had walked along Eagle Lane from Eagle Inn towards the Wheatsheaves, you would have passed the old Anchor Inn on your left.

In 1677 William Whitchurch owned 'the Anker, Cheapstreete'. He was still there in 1683 but later sold the inn to a dyer, Henry Allen, who also owned the Swan. In his will of 1724, Allen left the pub to 'my wife Mary Allen, my brother Samuel Allen, my friends William Hendry and John Harris'. Henry Allen died in 1728, and his widow Mary took over. In 1759, Samuel Allen assumed ownership and installed a series of tenants. Henry Rogers was landlord in 1771 and rented out post-chaises and saddle horses from the inn. The Anchor later became a coaching inn, and during the 1780s a post-coach to the Cross Keys on Wood Street in London stopped there every Monday, Wednesday and Friday at 3pm, returning every Sunday, Tuesday and Thursday at 6pm, carrying four passengers inside and one outside. By 1785, the inn was occupied by Jerome Joyce, although Samuel Allen still owned it.

In 1808 the building was described as warehouses owned by Sampson Payne and Roger Thomas, and occupied by Sampson Payne. This fits in with the lease being granted to George Porch in 1813 upon the life of his wife Elizabeth, then aged 30. Porch was described as an upholsterer, so presumably he used the redundant pub for storage, along with several adjoining buildings which were described as 'lumber rooms'. Derek Gill, in his book on Bath Street, states that the site of the Anchor is now occupied by No 4 Bath Street, refronted and adorned with two ionic columns dating from around 1830. In 1835 the lease was taken over by Luke Perman and expired with the death of his daughter Eliza in 1896.

Almost certainly the reason for the end of the Anchor was the construction of Bath Street, which effectively swallowed up most of the inn, leaving a much smaller building unsuitable for use as a coaching inn.

Anchor, 29 Catherine Street

The Anchor in Catherine Street was a typical nineteenth-century beerhouse. The building dates back to at least 1785 when it was owned by the Earl of Cork but occupied by Robert Hinton, a peruke or wig maker. He was succeeded by William Hinton, a hairdresser. When William Hinton died in 1831, the property was purchased for £190 by carpenter John Mizen who added a front extension before opening it as a beerhouse.

Following Mizen's death in 1873, John Chivers took over as landlord, followed by Daniel Rendall. The latter was succeeded by his widow, Maria Rendall, who held the licence from 1878 to 1883. As for the character of the Anchor Inn, it was possibly one of the less salubrious of Frome's beerhouses. In June 1879, Alfred Yerbury committed a particularly nasty series of assaults there. One night he had been gambling with dominoes, in the course of which he inexplicably broke his watch. When his wife tried to take the watch from him, he promptly beat her mercilessly. Another customer, James Thorn, intervened on the poor woman's behalf and received a thorough thrashing from Yerbury in return. James Thorn's wife then stepped in, whereupon Yerbury savagely assaulted her too. For his trail of destruction, Yerbury was fined £1.

Dreadful behaviour was no stranger to the Anchor. In August 1883, landlady Maria Randall was herself fined £1, this time for permitting drunkenness and 'knowingly permitting her premises to be the habitual resort of reputed prostitutes'. There were no less than nine prostitutes on the premises at the time! Maria left four months later. Her successor, Charles Timbury, fared no better, for the following year he too was summonsed for harbouring prostitutes. Timbury also departed within a few months.

The former Anchor beerhouse as it looks today

His successor, Sidney Long, lasted four years before Harriet Voyse came on the scene in January 1889. She was granted an interim licence for three months but failed to provide satisfactory testimonials, so a permanent licence was denied. In April, John Coombs acquired the licence, but only briefly, for James Gerrett, a former silk worker, took over soon afterwards. He moved in with his second wife and large family and remained there until his death in 1898, at which point his younger son Arthur Jesse Gerrett took over.

Arthur Gerrett was the Anchor's longest serving landlord, holding the licence from 1898 to 1949. During World War Two, it was a popular haunt for American soldiers and their sweethearts. On occasion it would get so rowdy that Gerrett had to employ a bouncer to eject the riotous soldiers.

Gerrett died in 1950 and John George Robinson took over. The last landlord was Frank Benger, who was there from 1955 to 1957, and was best known for his pet monkey which used to sit in the bar and 'do despicable things'. In the 1970s, the former beerhouse became a second hand furniture shop run by Mrs A L Markey. Today it is a private house.

Anchor, 15 Stony Street

Although the Anchor beerhouse here only opened in the nineteenth century, the building is much older. A rain hopper at the back is dated 1688, and in the 1700s there was a butcher's and slaughterhouse here, initially owned by Richard Sockett of Worcester and then by William Lacy of Frome. Thomas Starr was the butcher from 1783 until the late 1790s, and he was succeeded by William Sparks and Nathaniel Selwood.

In 1805, William Lacy sold the building to John Gregory, a baker, for £145, and he converted the slaughterhouse at the back into a bakehouse. After John Gregory's death in 1823, it passed to Charles Gregory, trustee for Henry Gregory. Four years later, Henry himself took it over, and, after the passing of the Beerhouse Act, opened it as a beerhouse.

Henry Gregory was the Anchor's most infamous owner. His involvement in the 1832 Frome Election Riots led to his appearance at the Somerset Lent Assizes in April 1833. William Giles, special constable, testified that Gregory, though unarmed, was at the head of the rioting mob and by his gestures and manner was evidently defying the constables. Another special constable, surgeon Henry Britten had seen Gregory opposite the George Inn door between nine and ten o'clock, addressing a crowd. Major Richard Werr testified that Gregory had pointed him out to the mob, who then surrounded him and beat him with sticks. Many of the rioters were seen taking sticks from Gregory's back yard and going into the Market Place.

A rainwater hopper on the former Anchor, dated 1688

The jury found Gregory and his co-defendants guilty and sentenced them to eight months' hard labour. The *Times* of 6 April 1833 included a long report of the trial, in which Gregory was described as 'a baker [who] keeps a beerhouse or an inn – one of the new houses under the new act ... He has borne the character of a sober, honest and industrious man. He likes a little beer in the evening and is in a large way of business, exclusive of his beerhouse.' He was also described as an old inhabitant of Frome and a supporter of the Tory candidate, Sir Thomas Champneys.

After his release, he had to 'enter into his own recognizance in the sum of £50' to keep the peace for two years, but he was a broken man, and died in November 1835.

The Anchor remained in the ownership of the Gregory family, however, eventually passing to Henry Gregory's son-in-law, Andrew Diesch, who bequeathed it to Horatio Channon in 1868. However, from 1837 the actual *occupier* of the building was Samuel Hodder, who was both publican and baker. He was a pillar of the community, and in 1838 laid on a meal at the Anchor for Frome's surviving Waterloo veterans. After nearly a quarter of a century at the beerhouse, he sold off his stock in trade – casks, beer, furniture, brewing equipment – for £108 in October

1860. He was succeeded by Thomas Smyth, albeit briefly. In March 1861, Smyth's personal effects were put up for auction as he was 'leaving town', and the building was advertised for sale. On offer was

> a freehold for many years known as the Anchor Inn in Stony Street, together with shop, bakehouse, cellar and offices adjoining. The premises combine the business of a Beer House with that of a Bakery and an extensive business has been transacted thereon in both trades for 24 years and upwards by Samuel Hodder.

It was sold to a Mr Howard for £325, and 30-year-old James Baker from Milborne Port took over as licensee, running the business with the assistance of his wife Louisa and sister-in-law Frances Joef. He soon encountered problems and in June 1861 was summonsed for possessing five quart-measures deficient in quantity. Baker claimed the measures had come with the business, but this was no defence. He was fined £1 and the measures were confiscated. Three months later, in September 1861, Baker quit, and his brewing plant, casks, beer, porter engines, furniture and tools-in-trade were auctioned. It was an ignominious end for the Anchor, which had seen three publicans leave within the space of eleven months.

Following its closure as a pub, the building was occupied by William Jervis Jelly, a pastry cook. It then became the London Coffee Tavern, and in 1891 was renamed the Anchor Dining & Refreshment Rooms. In 1999 Jon Evans opened the Garden Café, a top quality vegetarian restaurant, in the former Anchor.

The Garden Café, formerly the Anchor Inn, in 2013

Angel (now Archangel), 1 King Street

Quite possibly the oldest building now used as a pub in Frome, but much altered in the eighteenth and nineteenth centuries. Claims that it dates back as far as 1312 are based on stories of an old book produced in 1320 and once in possession of the Frome Literary & Scientific Institute, though this may be a bit of a myth as no one seems to know anything about it today. Frome architect and historian, Rodney Goodall, however, believes that the building is 'certainly the right size and layout' to have fourteenth-century origins.

Be that as it may, the first provable record of a pub named the Angel comes from 1659, when William Pobjoy was making a new door for the church, and mention is made of an inn on Church Slope opposite the churchyard. Other records of building work at the church from the same period use 'ye Angell' as a reference point. Edward Fry, for example, was engaged to make 'a gutter under the churchyard next the Angell'.

By 1665 the Angel Inn seems to have moved to its present location, with Back Lane being renamed Angel Lane after it. The probability is that it moved around the corner to bigger premises nearer to the Market Place where there was easier access for carts and coaches. Records from this period are patchy and those that do exist are happy to give names and dates but seldom an exact location. The freehold was initially owned by the Stourton family, but had been acquired by the Longleat estate with Frances Yerburie as tenant by this time.

The Archangel in 2014

For an inn this old and prominent, we have discovered surprisingly few stories or events of interest. By 1668, it had passed to Edmund Baylie, possibly a forebear of the Bayly family which was to have a huge impact on the drinking life of the town in years to come. They seem to have been in partnership with the A'Court family who owned various properties about the town, including the Swan at Badcox.

In August 1775, perhaps to break the monotony, a singing competition was held for a silver cup valued at two and a half guineas, 'no catches, glees or duets allowed and dinner to be on the table at one o'clock precisely' – serious stuff!

> TO be Sung for, on Monday the 14th day of August next, at the Angel inn, in Frome, Somerset, a handsome SILVER CUP, value two guineas and a half, by any company of Singers, that will attend. The company that sings the best of Two Three-Voice Songs, and Two Two-Voice Songs, to time and tune, will be entitled to the said Cup. Each company to produce their music in score to the umpires, by eleven o'clock in the forenoon. Regard will be paid by the umpires to the goodness and merit of the songs produced. Not less than three companies will be allowed to sing, as the second-best company will be entitled to a handsome silver punch-ladle. No catches, glees, or duets to be allowed. Each company that sings, to dine at the aforesaid house.
> Dinner to be on table at one o'clock precisely.

Ten years later, in 1785, Stephen Middleton took over, followed, as so often happened, by his widow. The census of that year shows Edith Middleton as publican and proprietor employing one man and four women. She was there until her sudden death in 1798, her tenure having resulted in 'much reputation to herself and satisfaction to her guests', according to the *Frome Directory* of that year. A second generation of Middletons took over and ran the place until 1837.

In 1834 it was announced that a coach called 'The Hero (Improved)' would start from the Angel Inn on Tuesday, Thursday, and Saturday afternoons and travel to London via Warminster and Salisbury, and that the operators would not be accountable for any parcel or luggage above the value of £10.

In the mid-nineteenth century, things got a little more exciting, with press reports of drunks and fights, and in August 1859, if you were in need of a gun, the Angel would have been the place to go:

WJ SINGER PRACTICAL GUN MAKER, WARMINSTER

Begs to inform Sportsmen that from the great patronage he has received from Frome and its neighbourhood he intends to visit Frome Market every Wednesday, from the first of August, at the ANGEL INN, MARKET PLACE, where all orders or repairs intrusted to him will meet with punctuality and good workmanship.

WJS will have a Stock of Guns with him for inspection. Old Ones taken in exchange and New Ones allowed for a fortnight on trial.

In 1890, the Longleat Estate sold the freehold at auction for £860 to the Holcombe Brewery. A couple of years later, the local bench became alarmed when a Walter Bolas applied for a licence. The police strongly objected on the grounds that Walter was a 'professional betting man' and no stranger to the County and Bankruptcy courts. His application was refused but, as luck would have it, he had a brother named Frank, a professional cricketer by trade. Frank was a single man of good character who lived with his brother but had nothing to do with gambling. Superintendent Williams was not silly enough to fall for that one and again objected on the grounds that it would be Walter who called the shots. The magistrate was inclined to agree and asked how the pub would be run when he was away cricketing. Frank replied that his wife would run the inn for him and, although he did not yet have a wife, he was prepared to marry before taking on the house. He was also prepared to give a formal undertaking that his brother would have nothing to do with the business.

Perhaps surprisingly, the licence was granted. The final exchange between Mr Ames, Frank's solicitor, the court clerk, and Major Tucker, the magistrate, is priceless:

> Mr Ames observed that the agreement was drawn up so that Walter could not go inside the doors.
> Major Tucker, 'Yes we make a strong point of that.'
> Mr Ames, 'Not as a customer?'
> The Clerk, 'I think you had better not raise that point.'
> Mr Ames, 'Very well.'
> The parties then withdrew.

It seems the magistrates made the right decision after all. Frank Bolas played briefly for Somerset but seems to have given up when he took over the pub and continued successfully as landlord until around 1898.

1n 1916 the Angel was the first pub in the district to be taken to court under the draconian Defence of the Realm Act (DORA). The landlord's wife, Pearl, was accused of selling whiskey and soda to three farmers after hours, and, even though he was not there, landlord Joseph Weeks was arrested as well as he was legally responsible. Despite what, by any stretch of the imagination, was a very trivial matter, the case took up over half a page in the *Somerset Standard* – and they had very big pages and small print in those days! It was not just consumption that was the issue here but 'treating' as well – under the terms of the act buying rounds was illegal and the man who bought the drinks received an extra fine.

The Angel was again up for auction in 1919 as a 'fully-licensed freehold hotel' but failed to reach its reserve and was bought in at £740. After the sale a deal was done with Joseph Weeks, who had been licensee since 1911 and stayed at the inn until 1936.

In the 1930s, local architect Percy Rigg was asked to draw up plans under the 'Frome and District Town Planning Scheme' for completely remodelling the corner of the Market Place which, had it gone ahead, would have been a catastrophe worthy of the 1960s. The drawings in Frome Museum – one of which is reproduced below – show a building so out of scale, proportion and style that it is tempting to believe that he had a different town in mind. Luckily, disaster was averted.

ELEVATION TO KING STREET

In 1959 the Angel's owners, Georges' Brewery of Bristol, were carrying out building works when they 'uncovered three small rooms which were sealed off. In several of these rooms they had found ... the ceilings ... of the original building – wattle and mud', along with old coins, including spade guineas dated 1725 and 1802, and a long-case clock in pieces. The *Somerset Standard*'s report of this discovery, published on 1 May 1959, includes the information that, 'as far as is known, the inn had been licensed since 1312 – the first record in a book dated 1320, which is to be seen in the library of the Frome Literary Club'. This is the only reference to this mysterious book, which seems to have disappeared.

The Angel acquired a bit of a rough reputation in later years, when it became the haunt of seasoned cider and lager lovers. At one point, the menu was seen pinned to the ceiling – 'cheese roll, crisps, or nuts'. It is unfair to poke fun at someone's local, and no doubt many a good time was had there, but the building was worth more and deserved to have some money spent on it. For this it had to wait until 2008 when money was not only spent but positively lavished on it, creating an upmarket hotel with refurbished bars, kitchens, en-suite rooms and an excellent restaurant.

Angel & Crown, 39 Vallis Way

Still an impressive range of buildings, this inn was first mentioned by name in the church rates for 1770. The Angel & Crown, then known simply as the Angel, was owned by Richard Treasure, who had a number of other Frome properties at that time. By 1771 it was known as the Angel & Crown and appeared on a 1774 map of Frome under that name. Possibly the original Angel in the Market Place objected to their name being copied or they just thought they would go one better and add a crown to their angel – we will probably never know. By the time of the 1785 census, it was being run by John Ford, publican, who had gone bankrupt by 1793.

The Angel & Crown undergoing restoration in 2012

It is unclear when the building was first used as an inn, but there is part of a datestone in the fireplace which bears the '16' part of a seventeenth-century date. When it was surveyed by the Royal Commission on Historical Monuments, the building was dated to around the 1680s, but of course it may have been a private house initially and remodelled later.

Mr Treasure continued to pay the rates until 1802 when William Wiltshire took over. When it was sold at auction in 1825, it was described in the *Salisbury & Wiltshire Journal* for 23 May as 'long established, convenient and roomy, with malthouse, brewhouse, three cellars, two stables, outbuildings, large yard and appurtenances, now occupied by John Bishop'. The new occupier was Charles Bishop, presumably a relative of John Bishop who had been publican there from around 1814, but he went bankrupt soon afterwards, despite advertising the place 'for sale or rent' in March 1826.

In June 1830 there was a fight between a party of four Irishmen and the locals. Two brothers named Butcher, one a saddler and one a wheelwright, had 'their skulls literally beat in; and no hopes were entertained for their recovery, the lower part of the house was completely drenched in blood. All four Irishmen were detained the same evening.' An inquest was held at the George later that month. One of the brothers had survived and one of the Irishmen admitted that he had struck the blows. Michael Tekin was charged with murder and committed to Shepton Mallet gaol.

Despite its age and size, the Angel & Crown seems to have drawn little attention from the media through the years (which is a face-saving way of saying that we were unable to find out much about it), but there was a bit of a rumpus in 1862 when a soldier named Francis Lee was given a month inside with hard labour for being drunk and riotous, throwing a policeman down and kicking him. There was another 'misunderstanding' the same year when licences were due to be renewed. Superintendent Deggan planned to say a few things to the bench about drunkenness and the 'harbouring of prostitutes' but the landlord, Mr Houlton, nipped in quickly and had his licence signed before anything could be said. He was nonetheless called back and told to put his house in order before the next session or his licence would be forfeit.

Above: The fireplace in the main room in 2013

Below: The Angel & Crown on the 1886 Ordnance Survey map

Bottom: Council plans for a new fire station in 1960

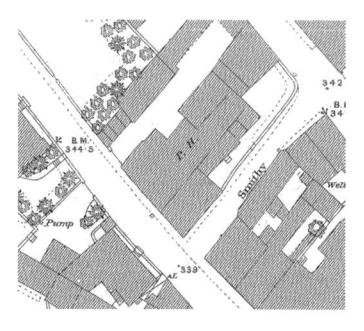

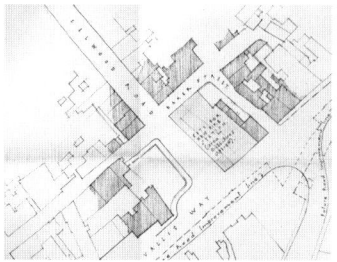

Soldiers from the 4th Battery of the Royal Artillery were billeted in the towns pubs during the spring of 1892 and a dishonest local dealer was fined £3 or one month's hard labour for getting Bombardier William Smerton drunk and conning him out of two half sovereigns.

In 1889, a John Sticker put the Angel & Crown up for auction. It was bought for £1,820 by the Lamb Brewery, and was described in their 1893 prospectus as 'fully licensed with yard and stables'. The 1901 census shows the landlord as Albert Barnes from Christchurch in Hampshire. He was there with his wife Florence until 1916.

In 1959 the Lamb Brewery sold the freehold to Walter Brooke, former landlord of the Swan across the road. Within a year, he had sold it on to the local council who considered knocking it down to build a new fire station or, failing that, a car park. After a lot of discussion, they decided to knock down the Unicorn and build the fire station there instead, and sold the Angel & Crown to Bruce Grimes, an antique dealer and furniture restorer. Today, the listed building is being restored as a private house.

Apollo Tavern and Welshmill Brewery

Very little is known about this. On 24 October 1808, an advertisement appeared in the *Salisbury & Wiltshire Gazette*:

> TO MALTSTERS
>
> To be Lett, and entered upon immediately – a convenient DWELLING HOUSE, together with the Out-houses, a walled garden and large MALT-HOUSE adjoining; situate at Frome. Apply Miss Newport, Welshmill Lane Frome.

This may be an early mention – it is certainly in the right area – but the church rates provide us with a name and show Luke Perman as the owner of a 'house, brewhouse and the Apollo Tavern' from 1832 until 1837. George Porch is shown as the occupier from 1832 until January 1834, when the brewery and the contents of the house were auctioned off. The catalogue in Frome Museum lists the stock in trade of the Welshmill Brewery along with the entire contents of his house, from furniture, paintings and books to the copper coal scuttle, auctioned by Mr Harrold on the premises. Included was lot 133: 'two full length plaster figures' – perhaps statues of Apollo – adornments from the tavern? It is possible that the lots were sold after Porch's death; he had a wife and two children, so maybe they sold up and moved away or possibly he was made bankrupt. His family have not been found in the 1841 census for Frome.

After the auction, the church rates show that Perman was still the owner, with the brewhouse and Apollo occupied by Allen Carr until 1837, but there is no mention of the place after that.

Census returns for 1841 show Perman aged 40 and of independent means living in North Parade with wife Sarah and 15-year-old daughter Eliza. In the census of 1861 he is described as the proprietor of land and houses originally from Silton, Dorset and living at Welshmill. He died in Frome aged 73 in 1868.

Interesting that they should choose the word 'tavern' for their establishment as this name was usually applied to an upmarket urban house, not quite a gentlemen's club but a cut above the common ale house or inn. Obviously ahead of its time for Frome as it did not last long.

Catalogue from the 1835 auction now in Frome Museum

Bath Arms / Old Bath Arms, 1 Palmer Street

One of the original Frome pubs shown on the 1774 map. It changed its name slightly but fairly often in the early days, appearing as the Lord's Arms in the census of 1785, the Marquis of Bath's Arms in 1783 and Lord Weymouth's Arms by 1800, before adopting its current name of the Bath Arms in the 1830s. This was used alongside the Weymouth Arms before settling down in modern times as the Old Bath Arms. All its names, however, were variations on the titles of the Thynne family, owners of Longleat and much of the town of Frome and its environs.

The earliest known leaseholder (according to a deed of 1889 listing former occupiers) was Susannah Lock. By the time of the town census of 1785, however, Zachary Baily was the owner and Ann Vigor the publican. Baily still held the lease in 1811 when the remainder of it was put up for auction at the George Inn. We have no precise record of the outcome but it seems to have been bought by William Hagley, a local surgeon, perhaps making an investment outside of his normal occupation.

In 1814 local constable Gregory was called out to a sordid and unusual case. In his journal for 18 January he records that 'a married woman came with her husband to get redress against a married man for an assault and ill-treatment of her person.' She gave evidence as follows:

> I was at Mr Bayley's at the Weymouth Arms ... having a pint of beer when I had occasion to go the privy your honour. This man came after me and said he would come in ... He pushed me about and used me very ill your honour and I left the place without doing what I went to do. After a while I went to the privy a second time to do what I could not do the first time and he followed again your honour. Now your honour could I not sware a rape against this man?

The man was asked for his version and replied,

> Sir she compelled me to do it ... As my witnesses will prove she went out on purpose for me to follow her. And when we came back here is a witness that asked her whether he had done it and she said he had, and should again, and then we had a quart each together.

The magistrate was having none of it and gave the husband a stern lecture on not looking after his wife and 'letting her go to Public Houses drinking'. The woman was disbelieved because she did not cry out and 'should have resisted his coming in and with the noise which he must have made forcing an entry added to the shrieks which you ought to have made would have made people in the house hear you'. The accused was given a severe reprimand for carrying on in this fashion, even though he was married, and the case was dismissed.

The woman's husband then asked the magistrates to get his wife to swear that the man did not violate her person in the privy, because if she did not swear it he would think that he did and he could not live happily with her. Eventually, the woman swore on oath that the man tried to do it but did not and Champneys the magistrate told the husband that he 'should now live happy for he thought his wife was a virtuous woman'. Gregory's final comment was, 'Ah, you poor fool, though art a fool of the lowest order'.

Edmund Baily, aged 50, was landlord in 1841. An advertisement in Langford's *Directory* of 1854 described him as 'Brewer, Maltster & Hop Factor'. The Baily family

EDMUND BAILY,
BREWER,
MALTSTER, AND HOP FACTOR,
PALMER STREET, FROME.

Agent for the

CELEBRATED

OAKHILL, INVALID, & DOUBLE STOUT

PORTERS,

AND

PALE INDIA ALE.

Malt and Hops of the best quality,

WHOLESALE AND RETAIL,

ON THE MOST LIBERAL TERMS.

GENUINE HOME-BREWED ALES,

In Casks of Five Gallons and upwards.

E. B. particularly solicits the attention of the Nobility, Clergy, and General Public, to the great excellence of the

OAKHILL PORTER,

Of which he is the Sole Agent,

and begs respectfully to observe that this healthful beverage has received the highest commendations from the most distinguished medical authorities in the Kingdom.

An advertisement from Langford's 1854 *Directory*

continued to lease the pub and brewery from the Longleat estate, with 99 years being granted to William Baily in 1828, and a similar term being granted to EW Baily in 1871, when the deeds record him carrying out building work to the premises.

In 1886 the small breweries of Badcox, Bath Arms and the Castle amalgamated as the Frome United Breweries Company Ltd, and in 1899 Lord Bath sold the freehold of the pub that had long born his name, along with the brewery site, to the company for £5,000, which they financed by issuing shares.

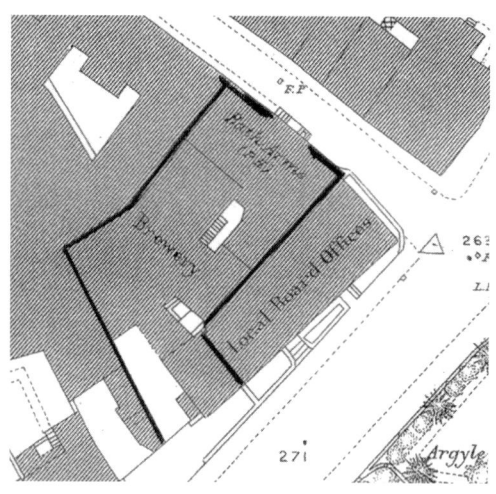

OS map of 1886 showing the extensive brewery behind the pub

Henry Fricker from Bradford on Avon was landlord from around 1891 until 1902. A little later it passed to Herbert Hughes, a grocer, who became landlord during the World War One. In 1916, at the age of 40, he applied for exemption from military service on the grounds that he had already lost two of his men to the war effort and both his businesses would fail if he had to leave as well. Conditional exemption was granted on the understanding that he would carry on his grocery business which was seen as an essential service, and he continued to run the pub until 1931.

Things chugged along pretty well for the next few years, with various landlords hosting meetings of the chess club, darts matches, angling association meetings, and RAF and football association dinners, but in mid-June 1959 the old pub closed its doors for what was thought to be the last time.

There are stories of it becoming a sort of gift shop for a while, and it was probably empty for some of the time, but

The Bath Arms around 1900 when Henry Fricker was landlord

in 1975 Mrs Paula Knight opened it as an upmarket restaurant serving traditional food with advance bookings only and a maximum of 40 covers. It continued as a restaurant under different owners, with varying degrees of success, until 2012 when it was taken over by Richard Findley, who completely transformed what is a very awkward building, full of stairs and odd rooms, back into a pub. It has rapidly become one of the most popular pubs in town. In 2013 it won the *Frome Standard* pub of the year award, and the following year won Channel 4's 'Three in a Bed' competition.

The Bath Arms in 2012

Bear, Cheap Street (and surrounding area)

An inn known as The Bear is shown in the church rates of 1753 as owned by Thomas Lacy on a lease from the Earl of Cork. By 1770 it was described as being in 'Back Lane', formerly known as Cox Street and renamed Eagle Lane in the 1820s. The property was referred to as 'Late Nappers' which may refer to a John Napper who was in possession of the Three Swans across the road from 1755, having married into the Whitchurch family who owned it.

Then things get complicated. In 1773, Thomas Horner recorded the granting of a licence to John Lester for an ale house called the White Bear, which had been void since the last licensing day. The map of 1774 shows the Bear in Angel Lane between Iron Gates (now the pet emporium) and The Angel – pretty much where No 7 King Street now stands. The 1886 OS map shows that it also had access to a large yard at the rear – by then used as a timber yard – which would have been essential for stabling. Angel Lane had become King Street by the census of 1785 and John Lister is shown as publican of the Bear, with the Earl of Cork as owner.

The possible site of the Bear – 7 King Street – seen here around 1910

It seems likely that the Bear moved from Angel Lane to King Street, possibly at the time John Napper moved. Church rates for the period 1786 to 1799 read 'Earl of Cork & Orrery, Bear Inn & stables', but do not give a location.

Things are then further complicated by a series of leases examined by Derek Gill, beginning with one in 1821 which refers to 'that tenement in Cheap Street formerly known as the Sign of the Bear', although it seems that Cheap Street was sometimes used to describe that general area.

So, either there were three pubs called the Bear within a few hundred yards of each – which seems unlikely, and frankly rather silly – or it kept moving. Another possibility is that, as Cheap Street backs on to Eagle Lane, the establishment had an entry in both streets and that the later deeds refer to the original Bear, not the King Street one. Wherever it was, it seems that it had closed by 1799 and more research will need to be done to establish the sequence.

Beehive, Keyford

The Beehive was a nineteenth-century beerhouse, but evidence suggests that another pub, the Castle & Arch, existed on the same site around 1757. If this is true it probably occupied the old Beehive building, pictured below and taken during the tenure of Charlotte Webb in the early 1900s.

Frederick Elliott is a great example of a publican with a dual occupation. Throughout the 1870s he ran the Beehive whilst simultaneously selling groceries there, assisted in later years by his teenage sons Frank and Walter. In July 1878, Frederick had a nasty encounter with drunken customer, Edward Millard, who threatened to take his brains out with a scythe. Mercifully there were few such instances at the Beehive. At some point after 1882 young Walter took over the helm but it was not to be a happy experience for him.

Early in 1886, he became embroiled in a legal dispute with Dr FE Pearse over the sum of £14 10s 6d. On the day the matter went to court a telegram was read

The Beehive in the early 1900s

out to those assembled: 'Please adjourn; Elliott is ill in bed.' On enquiring who was attending the ailing Mr Elliott, the judge was surprised with the response – Dr Pearse, the plaintiff. 'This is very singular,' exclaimed the judge and went on to ask what ailed Mr Elliott. According to the doctor – not that he had any kind of axe to grind – Elliott was simply suffering from the effects of alcohol and was not seriously ill. The case was adjourned, but Walter Elliott died a few days later.

Following Walter's demise, the licence was transferred to Bristolian Richard Osgood, whose sojourn was brief, for Harry Barnes took over the licence in 1887. Barnes also ran a grocery business out of the pub, but ultimately did not have a particularly long or happy association with the place. The trouble began in August, when 34-year-old artilleryman Andrew Raynor, billeted at the Beehive, died there. He was buried with military honours at Christ Church, with crowds numbering several hundred in attendance.

Two years later, young George Parrott was summonsed for being drunk, riotous and refusing to quit the premises. PC Lovell had to eject Parrott by force, for which he was subjected to a tirade of verbal abuse, culminating with the suggestion that he was a '******* monkey'! Barnes, keen to ensure he lost as few customers a possible, testified that Parrott was 'not particular drunk'. Parrott was fined 2s 6d and costs; Barnes left in early 1891.

Life took a downturn for Harry Barnes after he left, and in August 1891 he was summonsed for being drunk and disorderly. Evidently he directed some particularly fragrant language towards PC Sargent as he wended his inebriated way along Keyford Street one night and refused to go away when requested. According to the police, he had been trying to pick a fight with them ever since they had fined him when he was landlord – he was fined again!

In April 1891, the licence was transferred to an ex-policeman, John Webb, although he too would have his troubles at the inn. The following year he was up before the magistrates himself, charged with assaulting his wife. He had punched her, knocked her to the ground and held her down with his foot in front of their daughter. Webb was fined £1 and the chairman of the bench advised Charlotte to have him arrested if he did it again. John Webb died in 1899 and the licence was transferred to his widow Charlotte. She continued running the inn with the assistance of her daughters – her two sons by now had joined the army and were fighting in Boer War.

On 24 January 1900 Trooper Willie Webb of the 2nd Life Guards wrote to his mother from Naauwpoort, South Africa:

> Just a few lines to let you know I am alright … the fighting is nothing compared to the inconvenience we have to put up with … When we have been out scouting we have been fired on several times, but they cannot hit us … I feel no fear, and I feel certain I shall come home to you again. I hope by the time you get this I shall be in Kimberley and see my brother … My horse is all right so far that I had in London. I sleep close beside it under the tree with my blankets to cover me and the saddle for a pillow. I am writing this under a tree with my horse saddled ready to turn out at a moment's call … We can hear the booming of the guns all round us all the time … We are expecting an attack in the morning, but we are well prepared. You must not expect to hear from

me for a long time, as we will be on the march ... From your loving son, W L Webb, 2nd Life Guards.

The following month, Charlotte received a telegram from her other son, Herbert, who had been in Kimberley during the siege: 'Met Willie. Well, Herbert.'

In April 1900, she received another letter from Herbert describing how he had endured the siege of Kimberley and what happened when his brother William arrived there:

> [His] column camped on the same side of town as ours was camped, and Willie and I slept so near each other without knowing it, being only about half a mile apart. The next day as soon as he got up to leave he came and found me out, and I suppose no two brothers ever met under more unique circumstances. We stayed together until his leave was up ... Next morning I got special leave myself and went across to see him, but to my mortification I found they had struck camp and gone away to the Free State. You can't imagine my feelings to have him snatched away like that after a separation of over eight years ... I hope you do not fret about us. We are all right. The danger is comparatively small.

In April 1900, she received another letter from William:

> I am still safe and well up to now, but I have had some very narrow shaves ... What do the people of England think of the relief of Kimberley? ... It was something grand to me as I relieved my own brother ... At present we are all in good health and spirits. It is no good feeling down on our luck. All I hope is that I shall be able to go right through with it.

A few days later a telegram arrived:

> I regret to inform you that information has been officially received from the War Office that your son, Trooper W L Webb, 2nd Life Guards, has been reported missing.

Fortunately, it later emerged that William Webb had been taken prisoner.

With one crisis narrowly averted, Charlotte Webb was left to face another. In November 1901, the Beehive was robbed. The burglars, William George Deacon, Basil Simon Farant and Hebert Frank Payne were aged 15, 14 and 13 respectively. They had already broken in to the Woolpack at Culver Hill earlier that night and the total value of their cache was £4 1s, a few cigars and a bunch of keys.

Charlotte Webb finally retired in 1923. She died in Bath in 1930 and her body was brought back to Frome where many of her old friends from her days at the Beehive attended her funeral.

After Charlotte left, Arthur Halliday ran the Beehive for five years, followed by the extraordinarily named Sebright William Jones, who took over in 1929. He had only been there a few months when, on 8 January 1930, the *Western Daily Press* reported that the Lamb Brewery had agreed to demolish and rebuild the Beehive further back so that the road could be widened.

Sebright Jones stayed on as landlord of the newly-built inn and was still there, aged 77, in 1946, when tragedy struck as he climbed the stairs to bed one night. Overcome by a dizzy spell, he plunged backwards down the stairs and fatally fractured his skull. Jack Bardon took over, and two years later the Lamb Brewery carried out further structural alterations to the pub.

Jack Bardon ran the Beehive with his wife Annie until his death in 1956, after which Frank J Johnson, who had been awarded a Distinguished Conduct Medal in World War One, and his wife Winifred became licensees. Winifred ran it single-handedly after her husband's death, and when she retired in 1967 was Frome's 'only remaining woman licensee'. For decades – centuries even – Frome's pubs had been run by just as many women as men and it was ironic that in the 'liberated' 1960s there were to be no female licensees. Frome resident Trevor Biggs recalled that, when Mrs Johnson was at the Beehive, 'the bar was on the right and the lounge was on the left as you went in. It also had a Jug and Bottle. It was quite a popular pub then.' Popular or not, the Beehive's days were numbered, and by the 1990s it had been converted into flats.

The Beehive in 1992

Bell, Christchurch Street East

The Bells of Frome are a confusing cacophony. There were at least four and any potential confusion arising from this has been ably assisted by the tendency of clerks of yore not to specify to which Bell they were referring in their various scribblings.

The Bell Inn in Christchurch Street East – once simply referred to as 'Behind Town' – is one of the earliest recorded public houses in Frome. Its history is complicated, but it can be traced back to 1577, when a lease for the Bell was granted to widow Joan Alford, 'late wife of Richard', by the Longleat Estate. It was described as a 'four-bayed tiled house and stables surrounded by pasture of eleven acres with a pigsty cottage and shop'. It seems likely that Joan Alford's parents, Robert and Edith Poley, had held the inn before Joan. Little is known over the next century, but by 1679 William Chapman, cloth-drawer, held the lease. The rent was 30s 4d per annum plus 'a fat capon at Christmas', along with an obligation to annually plant three apple or pear trees, and three oak, elm or ash trees. In addition, the lessee was required, 'on reasonable request, [to] keep and nourish for the lessor one hound or spaniel'.

Such clauses seem to have been *de rigueur* with Longleat tenancies, for when Joel Barber leased the Bell in 1707 it was for £1 0s 4d half yearly plus a fat capon at Christmas and 'the best beast or goose of the owner or occupier of the premises or £3 6s 8d'. In 1763, when the lease was advertised, it was described as 'an inn at Frome, in the county of Somerset, well known by the name or sign of the Bell, belonging to the Right Hon Lord Viscount Weymouth'. The lease was transferred from William Barnes to John George, who was probably the Bell's last landlord, for in 1772 the inn was recorded as 'void' in the church rates. Three years later it was described as 'a messuage formerly used as an inn known as the Bell'. The name lingered on, and as late as 1799 the site was still being referred to as 'the Old Bell'. The remains of the inn are believed to have been incorporated into the building now known as Fairlawn House.

Bell, Church Forecourt

The 1774 map shows this pub standing on the south side of the churchyard. It seems likely that it was occupied or even owned by Samuel Dymock in the early 1700s, followed by Thomas Dymock from the 1740s until at least 1767. It then moved from the control of the Dymock family to the Gifford family. In 1770 Benjamin Gifford was the owner with John Gifford as occupier. Fifteen years later Jane Gifford took over ownership although John was still the publican.

He was replaced in 1791 by Benjamin Gregory and his teenage wife, Mary. Gregory died in 1799 and his young widow took over for just one year, before she remarried Lebbeus Barber in 1800. He became landlord, but in 1811 acquired another inn, the Talbot in Trooper Street.

Above: The site of the Bell in 2014

Below: Wyatville's sketch of the proposed gateway

Bottom: The gateway around 1900

Lebbeus was still running the Bell in 1812, but its days were numbered, and by 1814 the inn was no more. Both the Bell Inn and several nearby cottages were in an advanced state of decay and a committee of parishioners was formed to get rid of them. The Vestry Minutes for 9 September 1814 record that 'we availed ourselves of the opportunity of Sir Jeffry Wyatville being employed to restore and improve Longleat House. The ruinous hovels which stood before the West Front were removed, a spacious area opened, and a handsome gateway erected.'

However, when one Bell closes another opens ...

Bell, Fromefield

The will of William Kingman, gentleman, of Frome Selwood, dated 28 March 1762 (which survives in the Somerset Record Office) states that:

> I give and devise unto Sarah my wife.... all that messuage or tenement in Fromefield now in the occupation of James Flower victualler with the Tennis Court, Bowling Green & all outhouses, buildings, stables, court yards, backsides, appurtenances thereto adjoining & belonging and also that acre of pasture ground (be it more or less) which appurtenant now called Touy's Piece situate in Frome Northfield lying in the common with lands of Mr. Haynes and now in the tenure of John Cooper Brewer unto my nephew John Sedgefield.

This, although it does not say so, was the Bell Inn at Fromefield. It is first referred to as the Bell in an advertisement in the *Bath Chronicle* in 1762, which indicated that it had been open for about 40 years, and mentions the names of Mr Kingman and John Allen. In 1785 Thomas Box was the publican and ownership rested with the Rev John Kingdom who had come to Frome in 1762 and was a pastor at Badcox Lane Baptist Church until his death in 1806.

In June 1792 an inn 'known by the sign of the Bell at Fromefield' was put up for auction at the Blue Boar. It was described as having a tennis court, bowling green and stables, and was bought by John Billingsley, who founded the Oakhill Brewery in 1761. Billingsley was a noted agriculturalist, involved in turnpike trusts and canal building as well as brewing, and the author of *A General View of Agriculture in the County of Somerset* (1794). He retained ownership until his death in 1811.

The former Bell Inn at Fromefield in 2014

As for the publicans, Joseph Mussell was there from 1793 to 1803, followed by H Wheeler from 1805 to 1809. The latter was possibly the Henry Wheeler who hired post-chaise horses from the top of Bridge Street in the 1820s. From 1810 to 1812, the inn was run by Mr H Hooper.

The last mention of the Bell at Fromefield is in the 1818 church rates. In more recent times the building has operated as an antique shop and, from 1989, as the

Café Noir. In 1990, the owner, Peter Davies, was granted a full licence to enable him to serve brandies and liqueurs, reminiscent of the good old days of the Bell Inn. Later it became Crofts. Today the Bell is disguised as a Chinese takeaway – still retaining its links with the hospitality industry.

Bell, 7-8 Trinity Street

Some inns in Frome seem to draw tragedy and financial ruin. Happily, this was never so with the Bell – originally known as the Talbot – in Trinity Street, for many of its landlords were blessed with extraordinary prosperity.

Before the building of Holy Trinity Church in 1838, Trinity Street was known as Trooper Street. The Talbot appears on the 1774 map, and in 1785 James Hiscox was both publican and proprietor. He also held the licence of the Fleur de Lys at what is now the junction of Stony Street and Palmer Street. Hiscox remained there until at least the mid-1790s when he was replaced by William Davis.

On 23 January 1811, when it was put up for auction, it was described as 'that well-established and good-accustomed inn, called the Talbot, desirably situated in the manufacturing town of Frome, and now occupied by Mr Robert Sweet, as tenant from year to year'. It was bought by Lebbeus Barber from Horningsham, who owned the Bell in the churchyard, which was scheduled for demolition. He changed the name of the Talbot to the Bell, but kept Robert Sweet on as landlord.

Lebbeus Barber died on 7 May 1824 and was laid to rest in his native Horningsham. His widow Mary joined him there the following year. Lebbeus's tomb is an impressive monument, and is prominently placed near the church door, as befitted his wealth and status. His will reveals just how wealthy a man he was, for in addition to leaving all his real estate jointly to his wife Mary and eldest son Robert, he left 'six hundred pounds to my son Charles ... twelve hundred pounds to my son (illegible) ... twelve hundred pounds to my son Lebbeus ... twelve hundred pounds to my son James ... twelve hundred pounds to my son John [and] six hundred pounds to my daughter Mary'.

Son Charles went on to run the nearby Masons Arms in Frome, and it was the eldest Barber boy who took over the Bell. William Baily was by now the tenant landlord, and the Baily family would remain there for the next six decades. Various branches of the Baily family at times owned and/or ran countless inns in Frome, including the Lamb, the Swan, the Crown & Sceptre, the Roebuck and the Somerset Arms, to name but a few. There was, in addition, the expansive Lamb Brewery.

By 1831 Henry Baily had taken over from William Baily, and, when the inn was sold on 6 June 1833, it was described as 'that well-accustomed inn, called the Bell Inn, in Trooper Street, with the brewery and offices thereto belonging, now in the occupation of Mr Henry Baily, under a running lease'.

Henry Baily, his wife Henrietta and their children were still there in January 1863 when James Yerbury Sr was brought up on remand for stealing one half-crown, two shillings and three sixpences from the till drawer at the inn. Baily had seen Yerbury take the money and the case was pretty clear cut, which did not, however, stop Yerbury from pleading not guilty. He was sentenced to two months' hard labour and was removed from the court room exclaiming his hope that both he and the bench 'would have to stand before God that night to prove the truth of what he said'.

In December 1870 Henry Baily Sr died a very wealthy man and was replaced by his younger son, also called Henry, and his wife Emma. By now the inn and attached brewery were lucrative enterprises, the latter alone employing three men in addition to Henry Baily. Within a decade, Henry had expanded even further. He was now the proprietor of the Bell Inn, the Crown & Sceptre Inn and the Bell Brewery and lived at Parbury House in Frome. He died in 1884 and his executors passed the licence to Edward Morgan, a wool cutter, who was still there in 1889.

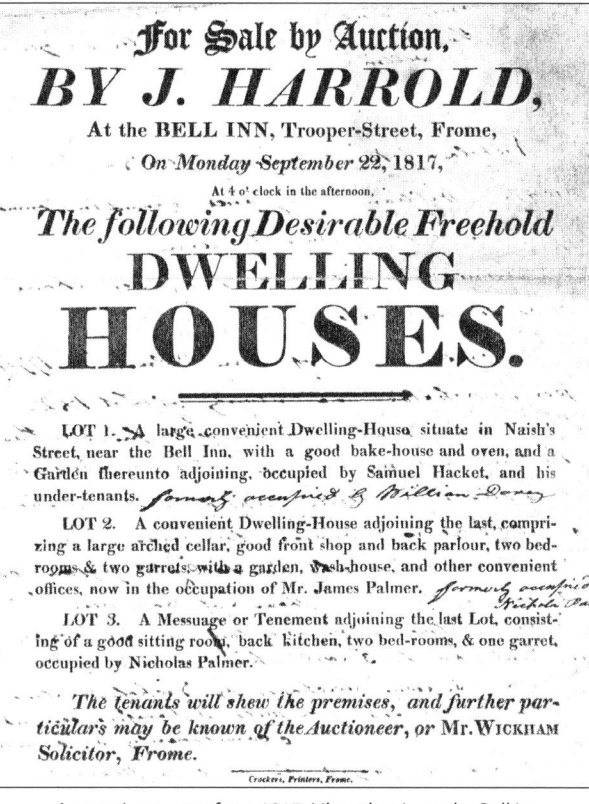

An auction poster from 1817. Like other inns, the Bell in Trinity Street was often used as a venue for auctions.

In August 1890 the Bell was put up for auction. This 'highly important sale of a very valuable freehold fully-licensed and free inn, and a ten-quarter malthouse' took place at 6pm on 3 September 1890. The particulars described the property as

> those very valuable freehold fully-licensed premises, known as the Bell Inn, situate at the junction of Trinity Street and Naish's Street, comprising modern fitted bar and smoking room, with Jug & Bottle department. Excellent dwelling house (with private entrance) consisting of three sitting and seven bedrooms, with the usual offices, brew-house with reservoir well; large hop and malt stores, and most extensive cellarage ... The premises are of great extent, having a frontage on Trinity Street of 52 feet, and on Naish's Street of 82 feet, and the situation is the best in town for commanding a large and lucrative business. An extensive and increasing trade has been carried on for many years past, and there is every facility for re-fitting the brewery in the rear of the premises; the water is especially adapted for brewing purposes, and the house, up to a recent date, was famous for its sound, heavy beers brewed on the premises.

The lease was held by Frome United Breweries, who paid £60 a year, but, as the lease was coming up for renewal, the brewery quite wisely bought the freehold at the auction for £2,150. Edward Morgan remained as landlord after the transfer of ownership until he retired to live at Portway in 1900, when his son Russell Morgan took over. In the 1920s, Russell was succeeded by ex-butcher Silas Berry who stayed at the Bell until his death in 1952.

In 1961 the Bell closed and was scheduled for demolition as part of the Trinity Area Redevelopment project. Nothing happened immediately and in 1964 the inn, though now unoccupied, was described as structurally sound with the sign still hanging above the door. Remarkably, the building survived the developers' schemes and was ultimately converted into flats in the 1970s, complete with new façade.

The former Bell in Trinity Street in 2013

Bird in Hand, Nunney Lane

First mentioned in the church rates of 1770 as belonging to Dr Alexander Houston and occupied by Daniel Townsend, the Bird in Hand is shown on the 1774 map as lying in a meadow to the south of Nunney Lane, in what is now Dommett's Lane, on the site of Phoenix Court retirement flats.

An extract from a lease of 1777 suggests that it had already closed by then:

> Mary Prowse, spinster, conveys a number of properties to Charles Clavey of Frome including ... all those messuages at Nunney Lane formerly the Bird in Hand with stable, yards, garden and appurtenances measuring 2 roods 24 perches formerly in tenure of Henry Cook, after Robert Greatwood which fell into the hands of Lyppyatte Bodmin together with all houses etc. then passed to Janet his wife and purchased by Mary Prowse.

'Fell into the hands of Lyppyatte Bodmin' is an interesting way of putting it, implying that there might be more of a story here, but as yet we have not been able to trace him.

In succeeding years it was often referred to as 'formerly the Bird In Hand', and in 1787 an advertisement appeared:

> To Be Sold at the George Inn one piece of pasture ground by estimation six acres in Nunney Lane called The Bird in Hand now in the occupation of Mr Thomas Houstoun as tenant at will.

A Charles Clavey is shown paying the rates from 1783 until 1798, when William Dommett took over – hence the name of the road. The site was used as a nursery by Mr Cuzner from 1825, and has been largely built over in recent years.

Black Boy, Wallbridge

Multiple entries in the church rate books refer to various properties in Frome as 'near the Black Boy', which indicates it was a prominent landmark. There have been several suggestions as to how it got its name, including spurious references to chimney sweeps, miners and servants. The most likely explanation is that it referred to King Charles II, nicknamed 'the Black Boy' by his mother, Queen Henrietta, on account of his swarthy appearance. He no doubt acquired his dark looks from his Italian maternal grandmother Marie de Medici, and, during his flight after the disastrous Battle of Worcester, 'wanted' posters described him as a 'tall, black man'. In other words, the Black Boy Inn was another name for the King's Head.

The earliest reference to the Black Boy at Frome is the payment of church rates by Henry and Walter Marchant in 1679, some 18 years after Charles II had been restored to the throne. The Marchants were still there in 1693 as tenants, the pub being a part of the immense Longleat Estate holdings. In 1702 a lease was granted to Richard Rose, cordwainer, for the property 'called or known by the name of the figure of The Black Boy'. In the lease, the Longleat Estate retained their rights to the timber from all trees on the property. In addition, Richard Rose had to plant three apple or pear trees and three oak, ash or elm trees each year.

John Wayland took over the lease in 1710, and in 1732 we find him paying fourpence in the church rates for 'Ye Blackboy'. Wayland remained there until 1733, when a lease was granted to John Young, who died in 1748. The pub is clearly marked with its extensive orchard on the John Ladd 1744 map, now held by the Longleat Estate.

William Kellow, or possibly Kells, was in occupation in 1766, and seems to have been convicted for selling beer without the necessary licence in 1785. The last known reference to the inn is the rate book entry for 1805.

Approximate site of the Black Boy, 2014

As to its precise location in modern terms, the Black Boy Inn proved a slippery character, but its site has now been identified as beneath a discount store or petrol station in the area in front of Frome railway station!

Black Swan. 2 Bridge Street

The name 'Black Swan' is alleged to refer to a mythical beast, as black swans were not thought to exist until discovered in Australia in the late seventeenth century. The name was adopted by inns that their owners claimed to be exceptional, although in most early records and church rates the one in Frome is described simply as 'The Swan'.

It is shown on the map of 1774 but is thought to be much older. The site, at least, is recorded as belonging to the Smith family of Combe Hay as early as 1699 when a great deal of Frome property formerly belonging to Robert Smith, a clothier, was disposed of. The Smith family had managed to run up debts of £16,000 and an Act of Parliament was required to sort it all out. The pub lies in one of the oldest streets in the town, which, before North Parade was cut in 1794, was the main road out of town to the north. This section was known as Pig Street and today's elegant façade is a refronting from around that time, with the rest of the building probably being around a century older. The fine-looking buildings to its right were all destroyed in the mid-twentieth century and, as we shall see, the Black Swan nearly shared the same fate.

The pub was certainly in existence by 1763, for on 4 August that year the *Bath Chronicle* reported that a Frome clothier, Daniel Neale, had borrowed the Black Swan landlord's mare at various times on the pretence of 'going journeying for gentlemen' and was away for up to a fortnight at a time. He had recently shown watches and considerable sums of money to his shop mates, saying that there were far easier ways of making money than working. That 'easy way' was operating as a highwayman, and at the time of the report he was 'in the care of the constable' awaiting trial. The report added that his wife ran a shop in the town. He was executed at Gloucester on 27 August. According to the following week's *Bath Chronicle*, 'Neale expressed great terror at the approach of death, and seemed to think that his sins had been too great to be expiated by so short a repentance; and prolonged the moment in which he was to be turned off to the very last.'

In 1813 parish constable Isaac Gregory and the landlady seemed intent on rubbing each other up the wrong way, as his journal indicates:

> December 5th: 'I caught my own apprentice, Bartlett, at The Swan over the bridge. Gave the landlord a reprimand for his conduct. Mr Butcher's wife was extremely saucy – said she would give any person two or three quarts of beer at any time she thought proper... I told her if ever I was insulted so again I would report it to the magistrates but she would not keep her saucy tongue still, although insisted upon by her husband.

They were still going at it five years later in 1818:

> Mr Candy sworn in as a special constable, took him round with me to the public houses – I was ill used by Mrs Butcher at the Swan.

In 1829, Joseph Pitman took over the lease, and in 1834 purchased the freehold from Mary Balne. He died 'of a brain fever' three years later at the age of 43, leaving a wife and six children. In 1839, his widow Mary married Edward Organ from Painswick in Gloucestershire, and he held the licence until his death in 1863. On Christmas Day 1856, he was nicked for entertaining 40-50 people after 11.00pm. When asked to clear the house he replied that he was 'not going to fling my customers out on to the street' and told the officer to go away. The magistrates were lenient as it was his first offence and he was fined one shilling plus costs.

Early in 1859 one of the serving girls almost died after taking an injudicious amount of sulphate of zinc believing it to be Epsom salts. One of the residents had left the unlabelled packet lying about and 'the servant acting as her own Esculapius took it in her head that a dose of salts was just then needed by herself and thereupon mixed up a dose of what she little imagined was a deadly poison'. Luckily, Dr Slade was called for in time and she recovered.

Another interesting case occurred in 1867 when barmaid Elizabeth Grist found £20 in notes on the pub floor, which must have seemed like a fortune. The loser, a farmer called Thomas Phippen, missing them after visiting the pub, placed an advertisement in the *Frome Times* some while later, asking for their return. Sadly, this escaped the attention of Ms Grist. Phippen went in search of his notes and naturally asked at the pub if anyone had found them. Grist said that she had found four £5 notes on the floor that day but would not give them up unless Phippen could prove they were his, pointing out that she had found them in the morning and he had lost them in the afternoon.

Phippen decided to sue her for the return of the money and the case went to court. The learned judge pointed out that it was rather unlikely that two people would lose the same large amount of money in the same place on the same day and the jury retired. Fifteen minutes later they were back with a verdict – in Elizabeth Grist's favour! A retrial was ordered, this time to be held in Bath, when the jury found in Mr Phippen's favour, though it must have cost him far more than £20 in costs to prove his point.

The Black Swan became one of the main houses of refreshment for the old Frome Market under the Rebbeck family from 1882 until around 1914. Albert Rebbeck was a cricketer of some renown who played for the Mechanics' Institute Club and also helped revive football in Frome, acting as secretary of the town club; he died of a heart attack on 7 February 1914.

It is difficult to see why such an established inn at the centre of the cattle market should fail – maybe people only went there on that one day a week. Anyway, fail it did and closed its doors for the last time as a pub in 1955.

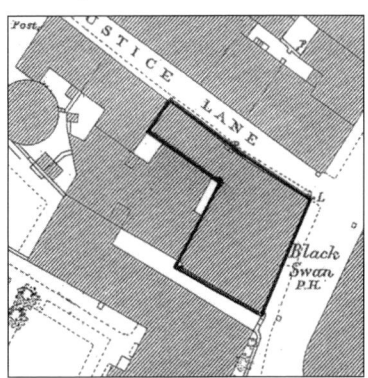

Above: The Black Swan lying derelict in the 1970s
Below: The Black Swan on an OS map of 1886
Below right: The Black Swan Arts Centre in 2014

The building had been listed in 1946 as being of historic interest but was none the less allowed to fall into dereliction after being purchased by Frome UDC in 1961. In 1974 the council applied for listed building consent to demolish it on the grounds that it was in such a bad state of repair as to be dangerous! (perhaps hoping for a even bigger car park.)

It survived the bad years and in 1986 was turned into the Black Swan Arts & Crafts Gallery, an innovative enterprise which continues today with a popular café, exhibition centre and craft shop.

Blue Anchor, Behind Town

'The Anchor' as a pub name was often an ecclesiastic emblem and the addition of 'Blue' had no real significance except to distinguish it from any other inn called the Anchor. No doubt this was the case with the Blue Anchor in Frome, where there was more than one Anchor Inn. As to its exact location, the only clue is that it was 'behind Frome Town', an area we now know as Christchurch Street.

In 1737 the Longleat Estate granted a lease to John Paise, husband of Elizabeth Paise and father of Richard Paise, for the Blue Anchor. John Cullen, victualler, obtained a 99 year lease in 1759 for 'the Inn on the Wast Land [sic] behind Frome Town known as the Blue Anchor'. One of the conditions of his lease was that John Cullen had to 'keep and nourish for the lessor one hound, greyhound or spaniel dog bitch or pay 15s in lieu'. The lease was cancelled in 1781 and a new one granted to Richard Paise, shoemaker.

The lease passed to John Hancock in 1784 and formed part of the estate of Charles Clavey, carrier, the following year when his will described 'all that dwelling house and smith's shop sometime in possession of John Budd but now a brewhouse, Behind Town opposite the farmhouse on the other side of the road'. John Middleton was there in 1786, but the Blue Anchor seems to have closed soon afterwards, as no further mention has been found.

Blue Boar, 15 Market Place

It is unusual to know when a pub this old was built, but in the case of the Blue Boar we know that it was built by Theophilus Lacey, mercer, following a lease granted to him for 99 years on 3 November 1691. We know little else about Lacey, except that he was succeeded by his widow Elizabeth, and then by Robert Hayward, maltster, who was granted the premises by Richard Fownes (or Flowers) of Stapleton, Dorset on 7 September 1722 at a yearly rent of ten shillings.

Fownes was successor to the Cabell family who owned the land at the time of the original lease. A Sun Fire Insurance Valuation of September 1724 has Thomas Lewis as victualler and occupier with Haywood as owner. The premises, which included a dwelling house valued at £150, goods

The Blue Boar in 2013

in the same at £90, and malthouse and stables with stock at £120, had a total value of £600. Robert Hayward is shown as the tenant until around 1767 when it passed to his widow Ann and through her to the Bunn family.

William and Elizabeth Bedbury were the next occupiers, and the lady of the house was not one to be trifled with. In 1771, when a customer behaved insolently towards her she seized his hat and refused to return it. He took out a summons against her and the magistrate ordered her to hand it back. Her husband didn't fare much better in court. The following year, two men complained about being assaulted by a sergeant in the 11th Regiment of Foot. William was summoned as a witness and ended up being reprimanded for 'not being so active as he should have been in suppressing the disturbance'.

When Constable Gregory was called to the inn in March 1818, he was clearly in no mood for petty squabbles, recording that he had been 'sent for in haste to the Blue Boar two men was fighting in the parlour one of the men lost his hat and had his cloths much torn, it served him right as he had no business there and he had no pity from me'.

There was more violence afoot in 1823 when a man was killed in the roadway a short distance from the pub. The *Bath & Cheltenham Gazette* for 2 September carried the following report:

> On Friday last an inquisition was held by Peter Laying Esq, coroner, on the body of John Crees who died in the town of Frome on Wednesday 27th of August. It appeared in evidence that the deceased, with his brother and two other friends, had on Saturday 23rd August drunk a pint of beer each at a public house in Frome, and were going home perfectly sober, when they were followed out of the inn by seven or eight young men who were calling on them to come back and challenging them to a fight: the deceased was a few yards behind his companions and was overtaken by the other party from the public house, when an affray took place and the deceased was knocked down on the pavement, and received on the back part of his head a wound, of which he languished till the following Wednesday when he died. A most minute investigation which occupied two days was entered into before the coroner and jury, and no pains were spared to elucidate all the circumstances of the case by a long examination of more than 20 witnesses. On Saturday night last at 11 o'clock the jury consisting of 16 most respectable gentlemen returned a verdict of manslaughter against Timothy Turk, Thomas Adams and Edward Noble as principals; and against John Richmond and Charles Snelgrove as aiders and abettors who were all committed for trial at the next assize for this county.

At the trial it emerged that

> in the same company there was a person named Coombs, in whose temporary absence the prisoners and the deceased played some tricks with his beer which occasioned a wrangling. All the party left the house nearly at the same time and as soon as they got into the Market Place a quarrel was raised in which the deceased and his brother, *who had reap-hooks* [our italics], took part … Turk received a wound from the hook of the deceased and also received a blow in the back part of the head from Adams which made him fall insensible. Crees was taken to the guard house as it was supposed, in a state of intoxication, and remained there until the following morning when he was visited by a surgeon and removed to a private house where he lingered in great pain till the

following Wednesday when he died. The evidence did not press against any of the prisoners except Adams and he alone was found guilty and sentenced to four months imprisonment.

We not only have the newspaper report of this tragic incident, but also a remarkably detailed and copiously annotated sketch of what took place, published at the time and reproduced below. It is a vivid evocation of how easily a Saturday night out could turn nasty – and, looking back, it seems that Crees's assailants were very lucky not to have been convicted of murder and hanged.

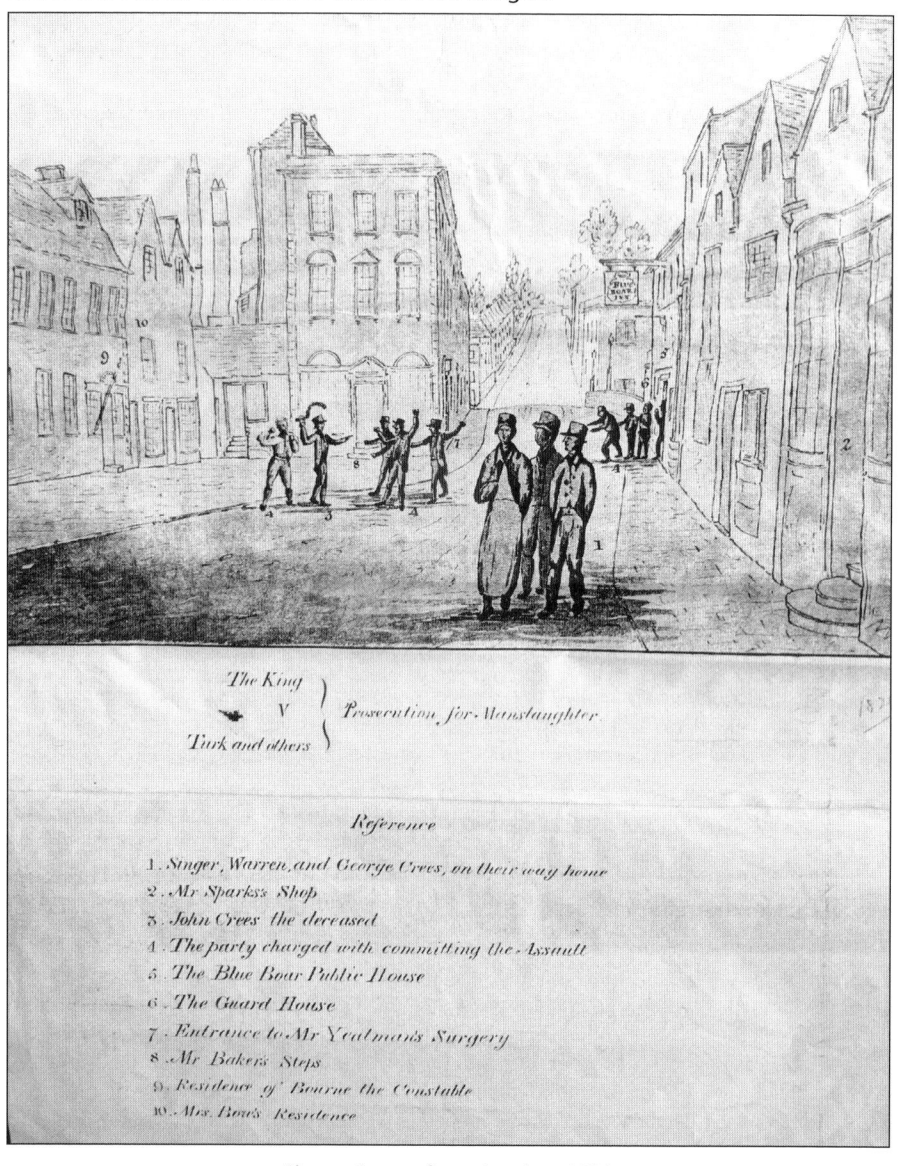

Above: A case of manslaughter, 1826
Opposite: The auction of 1851

Four years later, on 18 August 1827, the *Exeter & Plymouth Gazette* reported that two lads had observed three men taking timber from Mr Oxley's timber yard. When they called him up, he came out with a lantern and carving knife, but the culprits had made off. Hearing a rustle in the bushes nearby, he jumped over the fence rails and was faced with 'a very powerful ill-looking fellow with a drawn sword in his hand. The rascal endeavoured to escape [and] gave Mr O a tremendous blow to the head and stabbed him in the side'. Oxley fought back with the carving knife 'till the fellow cried out for mercy and delivered up his sword'. He was taken to the guard house next to the Blue Boar, where he was found to be a local millwright named Howarth. When the police searched his house, they 'found it literally crammed with stolen articles of every description: among which are elegant female dresses, books, barrels of gunpowder and pistol bullets, Bath stone grates, a dog's house, bar iron, new beams and scales, new board of every description, chains, bags of hops, casks, velvet pulpit cloth and cushions, nails, screws, blocks, every kind of labouring and gardening tools, silver spoons, a tanned cow hide, ladders, earthen ware, new brooms, servant's liveries, bags of feathers etc etc'.

The culprit was taken to the Blue Boar for medical attention, from whence he escaped during the night 'by leaping out of a window 20 feet high into the water and gaining the opposite bank'. With one bound he was free, but not for long. After a few weeks he was recaptured and sentenced to death, later commuted to transportation for life.

Still, at least the constables had learnt that locking a prisoner in a room with an open window was not the most secure of arrangements – for a few years anyway, because in August 1844 a Mr Batt tried to sell a stolen horse at well below market value, arousing suspicions that it was stolen. He was arrested and imprisoned in an upstairs room at the inn – the very same room in which George Howarth had been imprisoned. On Sunday night the padlock was secured and 'all was right', but come Monday morning when breakfast was taken up, 'an open casement and about thirty yards of bed cord hanging outside the window, told the fact of how the constables were regularly done'.

After all this excitement things were fairly quiet, with a William Batchelor behind the bar until his death in 1843. In 1851 the freehold was put up for auction. We have no record of who bought it but Giles Pike was landlord in January 1857 when a Superintendent Summers carried out a raid to catch after-hours drinkers. He claimed that he heard a great noise coming from Pike's house and upon investigating found 40 or 50 people inside, many of them drunk and some unable to stand – not a sober man there.

The floods of 1888

Summers was backed up by his constable, PC Pike. Also on the scene was the Parish Constable, Mr Newport, who was asked to take down the names of those present, but, when asked for his version of events, claimed that 'there was no noise or improper conduct that I saw nor was there anyone drunk.' Not surprisingly, those present backed up his evidence, while, to make things worse, some of the defence witnesses claimed that there had been a band playing while others said there had been no band at all. Despite the police bringing a complete dog's dinner of a case, the bench assumed that something must have been going on and, 'the evidence for the defence being contradictory, defendant was fined 40s and 6s 10d costs'.

By the 1861 census the Blue Boar was being run by Joseph Singer and his wife Elizabeth, and was the scene of one of the town's most incompetent attempts at theft. James Ruddock, having 'possessed himself of the pub curtain unperceived', nips over the road to the Black Swan and tries to sell it. Having no luck, he takes it back to the Blue Boar and – gets arrested! Some people are just not suited to a life of crime.

Some people are similarly unsuited to starting fights in pubs. In 1868, the local constable was called to a disturbance and found Silas Goddard, a tailor 'whose garments were out of repair and who was the possessor of a wooden leg', swearing and wanting to fight someone. He eventually pushed Mr Harvey, the landlord, over. When PC Watts went to assist, 'he received a poke in the side from the prisoner's wooden leg. Prisoner flourished his timber member violently and boasted of its various uses and the advantages derived from it compared with its predecessor. Some broken heads would have been the result had not PC Watts unscrewed the leg and took it away.' He was fined £20 or two months' hard labour.

In 1875 the freehold was again auctioned, and was bought by Jonathan Drew, a brewer and maltster, for £1,040.

One of the disadvantages of living by a river is the risk of flooding, and this was a constant feature of life at the Blue Boar as the photograph above shows. Serious floods also occurred in 1900, when 'a steady stream of water poured through the premises and into the street', causing everyone to move upstairs, and again in 1909, when the pub was flooded to a depth of two feet. As late as 1976, Mrs Ruby Perrett, who

The Blue Boar Inn
FROME (opposite Car Park)

Pleasant Room available for Meetings and any Social occasion.
Excellent Buffets at Moderate Prices
"Wedding Receptions a Speciality"
Coach Parties Catered for (by appointment)
Also outside catering undertaken for Dances, etc.
Comfortable Lounge — Fully Licensed

Proprietors : LOU and RUBY PERRETT
Telephone : Frome 2436

An advertisement from the 1960s

had been at the pub for 43 years, was given a reduction in her rates due to the river flowing through her pub. Flooding seems to have been such a regular occurrence that it makes you wonder why buildings were placed so close to the river in the first place, unless later developments upstream were causing it.

The Blue Boar is still going today, hardly changed externally and offering bed and breakfast, karaoke, a big telly, real ale and olde worlde charm.

Boar's Head, Vicarage Street

All that is known about this pub comes from entries in the church rates, starting with Samuel Watts in 1753, followed by James Watts in 1757 and Thomas Lacy in 1763. These are the ratepayers – the only occupier mentioned is John Thick, in 1763.

Joseph Webb took over in 1772, when the entry reads 'house, late Boar's Head'. From 1781, however, it is referred to as the 'Boar's Head' again. Mrs Webb took over in 1790, and had become Widow Webb by 1794. The first mention of it being in Vicarage Street comes in the entry for 1792 and continues until the final entry in 1799.

And there the trail goes cold. There are certainly existing buildings old enough to have been a pub from that time but we shall just have to await further research

Boot, Albion Place, 14/16 Paul Street

Established before 1863. The first known landlord of this small beerhouse was Joseph Plank, a cordwainer or shoemaker from Shepton Mallet. Given his occupation it seems likely that it was he who named and opened it, probably with his workshop out the back. In August 1863 he moved to the Spread Eagle, but was only there for a short time, and ended his days in the workhouse at Westbury on Trym, where the 1911 census describes him, aged 80, as a 'former hotel keeper'.

By 1871, Henry Trimby of Penselwood, an 'engine smith', was the licensee of the Boot. His son, Thomas, was an apprentice wheelwright, and lodging with them was Henry Brooks, an engine fitter and turner. In 1876, when the pub was put up for auction by Harding & Sons, it was described as 'the Boot Inn formerly two houses in Albion Place, Paul Street occupied by William Knight, together with house adjoining occupied by Jabez Eames with garden ground in rear'. It failed to meet its reserve of £390 and was unsold at £350.

The former Boot in 2012

By 1884 Henry Trimby, now described as a 'blacksmith', aged 45, had had enough and decided to quit, auctioning off his furniture and effects at the Auction Mart in Vicarage Street. The Boot struggled on for a few more years after Trimby left but its licence was not renewed at the licensing session of 1891 and it closed.

Later information is sparse but in the 1980s the place seems to have been run as a restaurant, possibly by the granddaughter of artist Arthur Rackham and wittily renamed 'The Wellington'! It is now a private house.

Bridge Hotel, 3 The Bridge

In 1821 the bridge over the river in Frome was rebuilt, but retained its rare feature of three-storey buildings along one side. Initially, No 3 was a private home occupied by retired currier Richard Strong, who died in 1856. His son John then sold off all his father's possessions – the tools of his trade and his personal furniture – and applied for 'a licence for a house on the Frome Bridge, to be called the Bridge Hotel'. Two magistrates opposed his application, the rest were in favour, so the opening of the new hotel was delayed for a fortnight. John Strong finally got his licence in August 1857 but was made bankrupt less than a year later and Charles Adams took over as landlord.

Adams advertised the establishment widely, boasting that it was 'replete with every comfort' – there was even a 'private room for ladies'. Unfortunately, Charles Adams' pub was not quite as civilised as anticipated. Within weeks he was fined for Sunday trading. A year later, in early 1859, he was in trouble again – no less than a hundred people had been crammed into the tiny tap room, singing, dancing and disturbing half the town. Amongst the crowd were several well-known prostitutes. And where was the landlord? Ill in bed – or at least that's what his customers told the police! The magistrate was having none of it – he'd often seen dubious-looking ladies hanging around the door of the pub and was determined to rid the town of such menaces. 'The house is put down as a bad one by the neighbours,' he declared, and 'whatever is done there a curse seems to rest on it.'

In 1860 young John Grant took over the Bridge with his wife Eliza and sister Sarah. Yet, despite this feminine influence, the bad behaviour continued. In 1861 local magistrates ordered the police to keep it 'under surveillance'. The licence was suspended and only reissued under caution. To no avail – prostitutes were still being arrested there in 1865.

Not that John Grant himself had an easy time of it. He was the victim of constant theft – money, glasses, his boat and even his dog! The toy terrier had been purloined whilst Grant was busy chasing a lost goat. His pilfered pooch was subsequently found, hidden in a cart in the yard of the Lamb Inn.

William Carey took over from Grant, but nothing changed. In April 1872 the police reported that the Bridge Hotel was 'the worst conducted house in Frome'. The pub's owner, Mr Trotman, evicted his tenant and explained to the magistrates that the reason 'things had been going on unpleasantly for some time [was] owing to quarrels between Carey and his wife'.

The next landlord was Charles George Tucker. He tried to clean up the pub but still faced the age-old problem of customers refusing to leave when they had had too much to drink. One such customer, Robert Coleman, was prosecuted for overstaying his welcome. 'Very sorry and won't do it again,' Coleman declared in court, but was fined nonetheless. This was not the only occasion when Tucker encountered troublesome customers. When George Wilcox was ejected for disorderly conduct, he took the slight badly and returned a few minutes later with a pickaxe to smash most of the Bridge Hotel's windows. Tucker rushed out only to come face to face with Wilcox's axe, raised up ready to deal him a fatal blow. The quick-thinking Mrs Tucker grabbed Wilcox's arm causing the axe to crash to the ground.

> **BLUE ROCKET No. 3.**
>
> Would the red poet were in better fettle,
> Then he might put us more upon our mettle!
> His efforts grow still weaker every time,
> Devoid alike of wit, and point, and rhyme.
> Squib follows squib, and rocket follows rocket.—
> *Harvey* will have a fortune in his pocket
> If this goes on. And *Sage* will take Fromefield,
> And live in splendor on the golden yield.
> *Le Gros* must figure to complete our ditty—
> "Room for the chairman of the Red Committee!"
> Though for his mincing ways we feel great pity;
> He's on the Bench, and so we won't be witty.
> Go to the Bridge, where *Tucker* daily d——s!
> And pours out liquor for the Banbury lambs,
> Who drain so deeply that they will—we fear
> Bring into use their landlord's "Shillibeer!"
> Go to the Antelope—see *Alfred Showering*,
> Showering forth beer his landlord puts such power in!
> Where *Sam* on Monday evening spouts again,
> And *Dunn* his ballot dodges will explain,
> If you would wish Republicans to meet,
> Go to the Inn "King's Head," in Trooper Street,
> Where builder *Whiting* hoists his liquor in;
> And *Tanner's* hordes of Radicals begin.
> *Bradbury*, the mayor of Frome, cries "Caution, please!
> "Though from the Blues I get my bread and cheese,
> "I'm Red. But if I stated all my views,
> "My eight appointments I should quickly lose!"
> Now we must stoop to shoot at smaller game,
> And sing *Bartholomew*, the barber's fame,
> Who with dire anger in his sallow gills,
> Picks up the filth to fling at Tory bills.
> *Vincent* is Liberal? Yes, I suppose!
> Ask the poor man who wants to pledge his clothes;
> Cheap Street is very dear to working men;
> And *Gregory* howls within his narrow den!
> We've been from top to bottom you will see,
> Up to Lord Cork and down to *Letheby*.
> A further list of names we fear may tire;
> But more are ready if our friends desire!

A political broadsheet from 1876 referring to Charles Tucker of the Bridge Hotel and his Shillibeer

Worse was to come for the Tuckers. On New Year's Eve 1873 a young labourer, Samuel Dartnell, stabbed fellow drinker Samuel Hinton six times following a quarrel at the pub. Dartnell went on the run, trudging alongside the railway line to Wiltshire and then on to Hampshire. He eventually gave himself up and was sentenced to seven years' penal servitude. Hinton recovered.

Throughout his time at the Bridge, Tucker and his wife supplemented their income by running a 'Shillibeer' or hearse hire company as a sideline, a fact referred to in a political ballad of 1876. They finally gave up the trade in 1877. Tucker died in middle age leaving his widow Sarah Ann, who had so bravely fought off an axe-wielding drunk, to end her days in Frome workhouse.

In the decade after Tucker left, the Bridge had eight different landlords and petty crime continued to dog the pub. Local man William Osment ran the place for a year in 1877 before opting for an easier life working in the Welsh mines! In 1880 Henry and Mercy Payne took over the pub for four years and then left to run the Black Horse at Walcot in Bath. It was difficult to find a good man willing to take on the Bridge Hotel long term. In February 1889 an application for a licence by George Miles was opposed by the police on the grounds that he was 'not a fit person' and was suspected of being involved in criminal activity. The court ordered the pub to be closed until a respectable person could be found to run it.

In 1890 John Mylchreest, a soldier with 25 years service, took over, but his stint there was no quieter – on one occasion he was attacked by a customer and stabbed with broken crockery. Mylchreest himself caused quite a stir in Frome when he was accused of refusing to admit the police to the premises in 1891. This was not Mylchreest's last appearance in court. In April 1894 he was charged with drunkenness after being found lying on his back in the road opposite the Blue Boar. A large crowd gathered and it took two policemen to guide him up to the police station. Mylchreest kept the Bridge for almost a decade, but in 1899 he was summonsed yet again for being drunk on the premises. The case was not proved but he left soon afterwards.

From 1900 the Bridge began a more stable existence, for this was the year Charles James Stockting, a former printer's manager, took over. With the coming of World War One, several of Stockting's sons enlisted. Youngest boy Reginald joined up as a private in the Somerset Light Infantry before transferring to the Machine Gun Corps. He served in Mesopotamia, where he died on 1 November 1917. His father had left the Bridge the year before.

Above: The Bridge Hotel in 1959

Below: The back of the Bridge Hotel in the early twentieth century, where landlords could still moor their boats

Frank Meaker took over for a few months before moving on to the Britannia in Wells and leaving the Bridge in the safe hands of the Crockford family. Frederick Crockford, a former coachman, ran the pub for nearly three decades. In April 1919 he held a concert for demobilised soldiers, highly appropriate considering the fate of one of its former occupants. Following Frederick Crockford's death in 1943, his widow Florence took over as licensee for six years. She was followed by landlords Percy Bond and Trevor Byfield. In 1957 the Bridge witnessed behaviour redolent of the previous century when a customer leapfrogged over the bar and stole £3 from Trevor Byfield.

In the early 1960s the Bridge Hotel was in the capable hands of Howard and Isabelle Watts, and it became known for its lively atmosphere and music. With Isabelle, an ex-ENSA member, in residence, things were bound to liven up as these fabulous pictures clearly show.

In 1973, owners Watney Mann sold the property to John Clarke and the pub closed in August that year. Until recently, the premises were shared by the Halifax and Age UK, although the latter has now left. Most of the original features of the old pub are now lost – either hidden behind modern fittings or removed entirely, although some architraves remain and the ironwork designed to hold the original inn sign is still in situ.

Bull Hotel, 9 Market Place

In 1865, the Misses Eliza and Maria Bull opened a restaurant on the Bridge. Their catering proved so appetising that demand soon outgrew these small premises and they relocated to the Market Place. In 1871 they obtained a wine licence and in 1873 extended into the building next door, which had previously been occupied by the Frome Church Union. These new premises proved equally popular and had to be added to again and again as their fame spread. There were 20 rooms there, making it one of the largest establishments in Frome. It also had a livery and posting premises nearby. Thus began the hostelry later known as the Bull.

In 1874 they applied for a spirit licence. A petition in favour was signed by 179 people, including all the residents of the Market Place (except other publicans!), and

The Bull in 1906

curates and vicars from local churches. The Frome Licensed Victuallers' Association, however, opposed it, questioning 'whether unprotected females should be entrusted with a public house licence', and claiming it was unnecessary as there were eleven public houses within 250 yards. There was also opposition from the Earl of Cork, owner of the George Hotel. Despite this, the Misses Bull won the argument and a licence was granted.

The Bull retained its respectable reputation, as can be judged from the services it offered: hot baths, stabling, facilities for clubs, food for outings, dinners for clergymen, etc, prepared by their own 'experienced chef'. During the 1890s it was a regular meeting place for groups such as the chess and swimming clubs, and the granting of the licence did nothing to alter the genteel character of the establishment. Admirably conducted, it was a place where the clergy, gentlemen travellers and the gentry could go to socialise. The crowning glory came when the Duke of Norfolk, Lord Loudoun and the Ladies Howard paid a long visit to the hotel, His Grace forwarding a charming letter of thanks to the sisters Bull.

Eliza and Maria were an interesting pair. Their origins were humble – daughters of a Mells agricultural labourer, their story was a classic Victorian tale of rags to riches. It was Eliza who moved to Frome first and worked as a servant. Maria joined her later and the pair set about building up their hospitality empire. It was enough to ensure that they would later retire in comfort to a house on Weymouth Road.

In 1891 they renamed their establishment the Bull and in 1896 handed over the reins to Edward Sidney Ogburn, son of a wealthy farmer. Within five years he was bankrupt. In court he attributed his failure to 'money expended on the premises, loss on horses, robbery by servants, ill-health, depression in trade during the past two years, and want of capital'. It can hardly have helped when the hotel flooded in the winter of 1901.

Walter Edwin Yerbury took over in 1902. He was already landlord of the Crown and remained there whilst his wife ran the Bull, which 'attracted a different class of customer, being largely used by tourists'. Such an arrangement was unusual, but the houses were no more than 30 or 40 yards apart.

At Christmas 1902, Mr Yerbury gave up the Crown to concentrate on the Bull. In the early 1900s he laid on an omnibus to meet all trains at Frome station, and supplied carriages for 'daily hire, weddings, picnic parties and funerals'. Sadly, in 1907 Yerbury went the same way as his predecessor – bankruptcy.

Next came Richard Haynes Nelson Mintorn, the most unlikely of men to find running licensed premises in Frome. Both his father and his grandfather were established artists and moved in London circles. His sojourn in Frome was brief, but at least he did not fall into bankruptcy like so many others. Perhaps it was his spirit of adventure which led him to Frome – the same spirit that led him to volunteer for the army in World War One despite being well over the age for conscription. Private Richard Mintorn died in April 1918, aged 54.

The last landlord was Charles Herbert Kell who ran the Bull from 1911 until early 1914 when the premises were sold to the General Post Office, and the entire contents were auctioned off in a sale lasting several days.

Above: A photograph from around 1900 showing how close the Crown was to the Bull

Below: The omnibus used to collect guests from the railway station

Bottom: The Bull in the floods of 1917, shortly after its conversion to GPO use

Eliza Bull had died two years earlier and Maria followed her in 1917, aged 84. Both women left sizable estates, not bad for two humble country girls – the only people who had ever made a profit from the Bull Hotel. At Maria's death the local press commented that

> one is almost tempted to say that she and her sister belonged to a past generation, but they continued in the business of caterers to the public at so

good and stately an age that they are still very widely remembered amongst a wide circle of former clients and friends and the mention of their name recalls many a happy meeting and association at the Bull's Hotel in the Market Place.

The building is currently shared by a pharmacy and a coffee shop.

Carpenter's Arms, Milk Street

In the 1785 census, Thomas Hughes is shown as the licensee of the Carpenter's Arms, while a Mr Phillips, who also owned a shop in the same street, was the proprietor. There are no other references to it, although it may have been renamed to become one of the other pubs recorded in Milk Street.

Castle & Arch

The only known mention of this pub comes from the 1757 Act 'for repairing and widening several Roads leading to, through and from the town of Frome in the county of Somerset'. This refers to 'roads leading from the town of Warminster through Locks Lane and Keyford towards Shepton Mallet as lies between an alehouse in the parish of Frome called the Castle & Arch and a lane in the same parish called Water Lane'. Local historian Michael McGarvie suggests that it may have occupied the site of the Beehive in Keyford.

Castle, 32 Catherine Hill

First shown on the Frome street map of 1774, by the time of census of 1785 the Castle was owned by William Allen, and the publican was William Bull, who employed three men and two women. In 1786, when it was put up for rent, it was described as 'a good accustomed inn with stables, garden and convenient offices adjoining, known by the name or sign of the Castle and with a malthouse adjoining'.

In February 1818, Constable Gregory recorded that during 'a general turnout of the public houses in the evening [he] had a desperate scuffle at the Castle with two country fellows and was beat very much – another of their party attempted a rescue at the blind house. We secured him likewise.'

From 1837, the Castle was owned by William Knight of the local brewing family, who bought it from the ubiquitous Baily family, and had a sizeable brewhouse out the back known as Knight &

The former Castle in 2013

Gunning's Castle Brewery, a partnership which was dissolved in 1875. The census of 1841 shows Knight, aged 30, in occupation with his wife Maria, four children, three servants and a lodger called John Harris, who was a hawker. In 1858, he took a stand 'so praiseworthy that the example may speedily be followed by others in the same trade' – he closed all day on Sundays!

By 1861, the Castle was being run by William's son, Francis. At the time of the 1881 census, Jonathan D Knight, aged 43, was recorded as the master brewer, employing ten men. In 1889, however, he amalgamated with the Badcox and Bath Arms Breweries to form the Frome United Breweries Company, and the brewery was dismantled as production was concentrated at the Badcox Brewery. Much of the old building is still there, and the large arch through which the beer-laden wagons trundled is worth seeing, but the site is now residential.

After the brewery went, life at the Castle was fairly quiet and uneventful. The local press has very few mentions of the house, suggesting that it was well run. However, highlights include a woman being drunk on the premises in 1895 and refusing to leave, the darts team beating the Bell at Buckland Dinham in 1949, and in 1957 a man being found drunk in charge of a motorcycle near the pub. By 1961 it had closed and become a hat and scarf shop. It later became a store room for antiques, a printer's, and a shop selling collectables. At the time of writing it is the outlet for Truly Sopel, fashion designer.

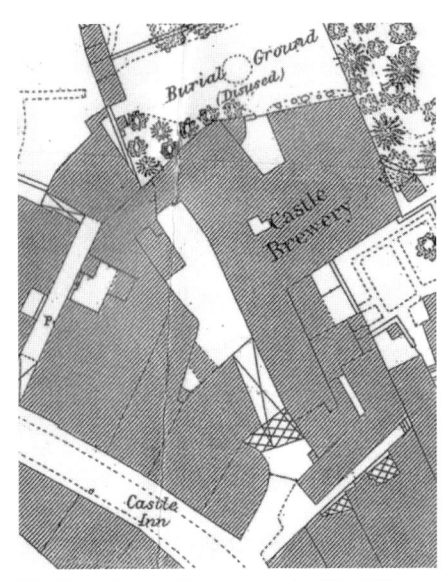

The Castle Inn and Brewery on the 1886 OS map

Cat, Cole Hill

First mentioned in the church rates for 1742, when 'Thomas Whittington late Bridges' paid 'for the Catt 2d'. Entries for Nicolas Whittington appear from 1744 to 1747, followed by Richard Whittington in 1753 – thus linking the Cat with Dick Whittington!

From 1759 until 1767, Nicholas Whiting is shown as the ratepayer and an unverified report places the Cat at Cole Hill in the Crowmarsh area of East Woodlands, possibly near the Horse & Groom or in that general area.

This is another pub that needs further investigation.

Champneys Arms, North Parade

In 1739 a new inn was built on Bridge Street to serve as the London Coach Office. It was named the Champneys Arms – or the Sir Richard Champneys Arms – after the owner of the land upon which it was built. Now it is simply No 2 North Parade, this particular route having been cut under a 1797 Act to provide a safe, direct and handsome entrance to Frome from the North.

The Champneys Arms was an impressive structure in its heyday – three floors, each comprising three rooms, in addition to a brewhouse, tower and even a tennis court. The first tenant was William Baily, a joiner who had helped build the inn. He was followed by Samuel Paine. By 1771 Benjamin Coulston – a man prepared to do anything to draw in custom – was landlord. In July 1771 he hosted a flower festival there. A prize of one guinea was offered to the person showing three of the best carnations, with a large silver tablespoon for second place. The caveat to this was, however, that the prize-winners had to contribute five shillings each towards the following year's prizes!

John Scott took over as landlord later that year and by November was already having trouble with his customers. As was customary at the time, guests staying at the Champneys Arms often had to share rooms with complete strangers. The result was sometimes vexatious. On 21 November 1771, Sarah Salter was apprehended on suspicion of stealing from a Mrs Tippit after both women had lodged in the same room. Mrs Tippit explained to the magistrate how she had heard Sarah Salter walking about the room during the night. She also heard the clink of money and, when she arose the next day, found her money had gone. Sarah was kept in custody until landlord John Scott made his deposition the following day.

The former Champneys Arms in 2013

When Hannah Tippit had arrived at the inn, Scott explained, she was already drunk and Sarah Salter had implored him not to put them in the same room. Share a room they did, however, and, when she arose the next day, Hannah Tippit began drinking again. She did not mention the 'stolen' money for several hours, however. After she had left, her husband arrived at the inn and was told of the theft. His response was unexpected – he warned the magistrates 'not to believe a word the old bitch says'. It was far from the first time his spouse had falsely accused somebody of theft! Not surprisingly, the case against poor Sarah Salter was dropped.

When the Champneys Arms was sold in 1790 by order of the Court of Chancery to pay the debts of its then owner, Sir Thomas Champneys of Orchardleigh, it was referred to in the documents as 'late an inn'.

Clothier's Arms, 45 Milk Street

Originally a private dwelling, this fine Georgian house was once known as the Bellhouse, and, before Milk Street was renumbered, was at No 6. It was occupied by Lewis Cockey, who made church bells and later set up a cast-iron foundry in Frome. It was opened as a beerhouse by Thomas Porter, a clothier – hence its name – who installed Robert Baily as landlord.

In 1859, the *Somerset & Wiltshire Journal* – which described it as 'newly opened' – reported that Robert Baily had been fined 40 shillings for allowing prostitutes on the premises. They were amongst a party of about 20, singing, playing the tambourine and drinking after hours. The magistrates commented in the same year, concerning a different matter, that 'any person who has premises rated at £15 can open a beerhouse and this one is not wanted'.

Wanted or not, it carried on for many years. Robert Baily, aged 36, was still landlord in the 1861 census, and was living there with his wife Eliza, their two young children, and two lodgers in their sixties, Thomas and Sophia Kite, farm labourer and washerwoman. A few months later a more colourful character moved in, and in November 1861 the following advertisement appeared in a paper called *The Era*:

> TO THE MANAGERS OF THEATRES
>
> JEROME LIONEL, Pantomimist, wishes to make arrangements for the ensuing Christmas, for either Harlequin or Clown. Mrs LIONEL can also be engaged as Columbine. The above artists are well up in their business, having played nine years in England successfully. First-class testimonials if required. Terms moderate.
>
> Address J Lionel, Clothier's Arms, Frome, Somersetshire.

In 1866 Thomas Porter sold the beerhouse to William Knight, the brewer, for £430 in an auction at the George. When Knight got into trouble with the bank and had to auction off all his properties, it was sold again by Harding & Sons in June 1881 and purchased by WS Baily of the brewing family for £440.

There was a nasty incident in 1882, when landlady Maria Read answered a bang on the door at 11.15pm and was confronted by a very drunk William Webley demanding beer. She refused, as it was well after hours, whereupon he became violent, eventually throwing a stone at her head, with the result that she lost three pints of blood. Webley was in bed drunk when arrested and claimed to have no memory of the incident – he got four months' hard labour.

When not fighting off drunks, Maria was a dressmaker, while her husband Alfred was a cloth finisher and presser. The following year, he was arrested for allowing games of cards in his house, and, although a further charge of attempting to bribe PC Hawkins was dropped, he left the pub within a couple of months.

The former Clothier's Arms in 2013

The owner, William Shore Baily, died in 1889 and the pub was put up for auction along with his other pubs, the Crown, the Red Lion and the Roebuck. It was sold to another member of the Baily family for £650. In 1893 a Charles Cook was granted an interim licence but warned 'as to the future conduct of the house'. In 1900 Elizabeth Weyman stole a tin box of 50 cartridges from a shop in town and took them down the pub, which would have been fine, as the owner had not missed them. Incomprehensibly, she then placed them on the pub's hob and would have been responsible for an even longer piece in the local paper had not a lodger spotted them and got her to throw them away. Chances are that she didn't even know what the box contained, but she got seven days' none the less.

On census night 1901, the landlord was Charles Randell, and whoever listed the occupants had his work cut out. As well as his wife Bessy and eight other family members, there were no less than 16 lodgers. According to a pencilled note in the margin, 'these were only lodgers for the night and consequently designated lodgers'.

They included four travelling musicians from Italy, another from Texas and a sixth from Warwickshire, plus an estate agent, six general dealers, two children and one unspecified. Maybe this was the night of the first Frome Carnival.

By March 1922 the County Licensing Committee had had enough and would not renew the licence despite pleas by Mrs Jesse Carter, who held the lease from Frome United Breweries, that she was making a living, had lived there for sixteen and a half years and had over 400 customers a week. The pub closed for good and she was awarded £975 9s 4d in compensation.

Crooked Fish

The Crooked Fish holds a special place in the hearts of the writers. Very little is known of this pub and maybe it is this hint of mystery which intrigues us. Perhaps it is simply the rather daft-sounding name. Other than a couple of references in the church rates between 1757 and 1767 and one tragic episode in 1753 when John Adams of Yeovil was found hanging in the stables, there is little to tell of this historic inn. We do not even know its location and it does not appear on the map of 1774, so perhaps it had closed by then, or it may have been beyond the range of the map like the Black Boy Inn.

> Bath, Jan. 1. Laſt Saturday ſev'night one John Adams, of Yeovil, in the County of Somerſet, was found hanging in a Stable at the Sign of the Crooked Fiſh at Frome. Tueſday laſt the Coroner's Jury ſat on the Body, and brought in their Verdict, *Felo de ſe.*

From the *Derby Mercury*, 5 January 1753

Equally amiss would it be not to mention those very early innkeepers of Frome, the *spiritual* forebears of other publicans mentioned in this book, for whom we can find no precise location. Herewith, a modest sampling of their doings:

John Danyell was an innkeeper in Frome between 1537 and 1556, paying three pence yearly for the privilege of his licence. At this period inns were often known by the delightful term 'tippling houses' and we find that Richard Marten was also a tippling house keeper during the 1500s. However, he ran into trouble for using his tavern for other purposes, as this report from October 1550 indicates:

> Richard Marten supports in his home a certain unknown woman as is thought of ill life. Therefore he is ordered to remove her by the next [court] under pain of 6s 8d.

In 1568 John Wympoy was also in trouble, in his case for illegal gaming at his inn:

> Anthony Treherne Constable there of his office presents upon his oath that John Wympoy keeps unlawful games called 'table pley' in his house.

It is worth pointing out that the constable who reported Wympoy was also an innkeeper!

Naturally, there were landladies in Frome too, although the innkeeping business may not have been as profitable as Emma Stourton wished, for in 1569 she ran into a spot of bother concerning the state of her property:

> The stable of Emma Stourton is in decay by defect of roofing [and] she is ordered to repair the premises sufficiently before the feast of All Saints on pain of forfeiting 10s.

Other sixteenth-century innkeepers include William Edmondes who ran an illegal tippling house in 1568.

Of course, with all this early tippling, somebody needed to ensure that standards were maintained, and Frome, along with many other towns, employed official ale tasters. Appointed annually, they were responsible for ensuring the quality, strength and fair price of the town's ale. It was a hard job, but in 1553 John Waterman took it on, having been elected by innkeepers Nicholas Edgill, John Danyell, Richard Saunders, Richard Marten and John Aprice. He was succeeded in 1568 by William Barber.

Cross Keys, Back Lane, now Eagle Lane

Before Bath Street was cut through, the area known as Anchor Barton was a maze of small streets and pubs. The Globe was first mentioned in the church rates for 1770 as owned by Henry Austin and standing in Back Lane, West Woodlands. Austin is also shown as paying the rates of the Packsaddle in Broadway from 1781 to 1791. The Cross Keys is the unnamed pub marked on the map of 1774 standing in the centre of what was then Back Lane – now known as Eagle Lane – between the Globe and the Eagle. By 1775, it was owned by Joseph Cook. His family also paid rates on the Unicorn from 1781 until 1803, when it can be assumed that his widow sold it. The last mention of the Cross Keys in the church rates is in 1799, when it was in the hands of the executors of Cooke's estate. It probably closed as a pub shortly afterwards.

It was definitely redundant by 1804 when Cook's widow and son put the building up for auction with other properties at the Angel, and advertised it in the *Bath Chronicle* as 'all that messuage or dwelling house formerly a public house called the Cross-Keys situated in Back Lane, near the Market Place, and now in a state of repair almost finished'.

Probable site of the Cross Keys in 2014 Could the render on the end of the building show its original outline?

Today the outline of a very old building with a mansard roof can be seen on the end wall of the adjoining building marked out in render as the photograph above shows.

Cross Keys, Blatchbridge

The first record of this beerhouse is on Christmas Day 1856, when Joseph Harvey, a farmer of 40 acres and landlord of the Cross Keys, was charged with opening before time. Luckily, he was able to call witnesses to say that those being served were travellers and was acquitted. An article in the local paper in 1985 stated that the building was originally a farmhouse on the Longleat estate and was shown on a map of 1720. This fits in with the census returns of 1841, which show a John Harvey as a farmer and father of Joseph in Vinney Lane Blatchbridge.

In 1871 Joseph Harvey, who was described as having 'kept the Cross Keys for 20 years', asked to remove the licence to new premises on the other side of the road a little higher up, with good stables and set back from the road. The application seems to have been unsuccessful, and by 1879 George King was landlord. The last we hear of Joseph Harvey is as a retired farmer and widower, aged 78, living at 8 Summerhill with his niece.

In 1875 William Knight the younger, a brewer of Keyford, rented the pub off the Longleat Estate for a period of 21 years at £14 per annum. He sold the lease on to a JP Bartholomew in 1881. In 1891 the licence was transferred to Richard Morgan, who moved in with his wife Martha and two sons, and stayed until his death in 1944. In the 1911 census he is described as a farmer and inn keeper, so he must have taken over at least some of the farm from the King family. In 1919, the Longleat estate put the pub up for auction, but it failed to sell. It did not obtain a full 'on' licence until 1947. An Ushers house at one point until absorbed by Courage, the pub struggled a bit from being isolated and from the drink-drive and smoking bans. It closed in 2008, but, after a major refurbishment, reopened in April 2009, with new landlords from the nearby Masons Arms.

The Cross Keys at Blatchbridge in 2013

Crown, 24 Keyford

The Crown at Keyford dates back to a period when Keyford and Frome were still separate. Sitting on the busy route to Longleat, it would have been much visited by passing trade. If the eminent Pevsner is to be trusted, the pub dates back to at least the 1600s and the discovery in its garden of a coin dating from the reign of Charles II lends credence to this suggestion.

Research into the Crown's early history is complicated by Frome having two inns with the same name and the unfortunate tendency of clerks of yore not to specify to which they were referring. We do know, however, that in 1785 the Keyford Crown was owned and occupied by publican Richard Pobjoy (1712-1797). Between 1800 and 1816 it was owned by Richard's daughter Ann, whilst being occupied by landlord John Joice (or Joyce) who had married Hannah Pobjoy in 1795. By 1835 it was owned by Thomas Jarvis of Edington, Wiltshire, who sold it to John Knight, owner of the nearby Unicorn. He died in 1847 and it was inherited by his son, William Knight. Although the Knight family owned the Crown for many years, however, they never ran it themselves. During the 1800s, most of its landlords had other occupations besides running the inn. These included a carpenter, a horse dealer and a tailor.

By 1822 Lucy Joyce held the licence, but she became bankrupt at the end of the following year. In 1830 the inn went to John Batchelor and in 1839 John Stevens took over. He had been working as a carpenter in Blatchbridge for almost 20 years before moving to Frome in the mid-1830s. After taking over, he continued running a construction business alongside his duties as a publican. Following his first wife's death, John retired from the pub trade and concentrated on carpentry.

John Surger held the licence briefly in 1844, followed by tailor Joseph Singer, a widower from Rodden who ran the inn with the assistance of his older children, Alfred and Ellen. Singer was landlord in 1851 when a hideous murder took place in the town. The four men connected with the crime had visited the Crown on the afternoon of the murder, and Singer later testified to this. Singer's occupancy coincided with another piece of bad press for the Crown. In 1853 the *Wells Journal*, with a barely disguised hint of condescension towards its neighbour Frome, reported that 'most flagrant cases of Sabbath desecration are continually occurring in this town', citing the Crown in Keyford as a prime offender. Evidently one Sunday afternoon Constable Nicholls attended the Crown, having received a tip-off, and discovered 25 people, including some of the 'worst characters in the town', drinking and carousing. The landlord was duly hauled up before the authorities whereupon he produced witnesses in his favour and had the case dismissed – to the astonishment of all, not least the *Wells Journal*!

The Crown at Keyford in 1958

Benjamin Butcher took over in the late 1850s, and in 1859 was forced to summon the police when drunken John Barber refused to go home, and assaulted both the landlord and PC Rowe. Butcher left in the 1860s, and a horse dealer called Richard Lifely took over and ran the inn with his wife Hester. She was well placed to assist at the inn having been raised in a public house. Her father was Henry Williams of the Victoria Inn, her brother Joseph had been landlord of three other houses in Frome, and her older sister Sarah was also in the trade.

In 1872, when Lifely returned to horse dealing and moved to Nunney Lane, James Yerbury, a coachbuilder, took over. He hardly had an easy time of it. A customer called Charles Mills attacked an old man named Charles Smart there in 1874, punching him in the eye, wrenching his arm around and injuring his chest. Fortunately PC Milton was on hand as a witness and reported seeing Mills attempting to throw a hand truck over the old man, who had copious quantities of blood cascading from his eyes. Mills was drunk at the time and subsequently claimed to have taken the pledge! He was still fined though. Later that year Emma Wheeler was summonsed for being drunk and refusing to leave. PC Milton reported that Emma was completely inebriated and 'using disgusting language'. He was compelled to physically throw her out of the pub!

Yerbury had had enough by 1881, and returned to his old trade of carriage building. William Davis took over briefly, followed by Joseph Burton in 1874. The link between the public house and politics was never more evident than it was in Frome. This occasionally led to spurious and defamatory rumours about the conduct of political events in and around particular inns. In November 1876, William Knight, who still owned the Crown, and Joseph Burton, the landlord, were compelled to write an open letter to the editor of the *Daily Post*:

> I saw in your edition of today a most lying, scurrilous, and libellous report respecting the meeting held at the Crown Inn, Keyford. I was present, and could bring any amount of witnesses of both shades of politics to say that they never attended a more orderly meeting ... PS There was not a single female present at the meeting either in the room or the yard. The respectable tenants and neighbours of the Crown Inn, at Keyford, more than 40 in number, both Liberals and Conservatives, have volunteered their evidence to substantiate the meeting as most orderly and quiet ... The Crown Inn is one of the oldest, if not the oldest, licensed inn in Frome, and there has not at any time ever been the slightest charge made against the house.

There was even talk of Knight and Burton taking legal action, although this appears to have been more a case of sound and fury. There was, however, a political broadside circulating in Frome at the time – quoted in full on the opposite page – which also targeted Knight, and the Crown Inn, along with other Frome worthies.

In 1880, James Yeoman acquired the licence but his incumbency lasted a matter of months, and in January 1881 the licence was transferred to Samuel Pickford. He failed even to last the year, for in December 1881 it was the turn of Samuel Turner from Nunney to take over.

Samuel Pickford, meanwhile, moved to Cottle's Oak to run the Royal Oak with his wife Ann and their 'servant' Rose Tyler. Ann died, but Rose remained faithful to her employer, who was also the father of her daughter Gertrude, and stayed with him when he retired to live in Trudoxhill, first as his housekeeper and then as his 'wife'.

Samuel Turner, unlike so many of his predecessors, remained at the pub for many years. His wife Emma died in 1891 and the following year he married again. Both Charlotte, his second wife, and his granddaughter, Lily Bishop, helped Turner continue to run the Crown as his once robust health began to fail.

After a lingering illness, Samuel Turner died in March 1902 at the age of 68. He had held the licence for over 20 years and was well known and highly respected. In the days when the local company of Volunteers furnished the Battalion band, Turner was the bandmaster whilst simultaneously holding the rank of Staff Sergeant. He served as band leader for over 20 years, but due to a discrepancy in record keeping was unable to substantiate this, and thus could not claim his Volunteer long-service medal. In addition to all this, for ten years he conducted a brass band of his own. He was an enthusiastic and capable musician, excelling as a cornet player, and, before his health began to fail, his services were in demand for miles around. He played in numerous concerts in Frome and elsewhere and always played free at charitable events. He was active in local politics and a member of the Frome and District Licensed Victuallers' Association from its formation.

> A SQUIB
> Published at the Time of the 1876 Election
>
> Whene'er I take my walks abroad,
>   What funny sights I see;
> How shall I thank my Tory friends
>   For all their gifts to me?
>
> There's Mr Baily with his beer
>   For Tory lambs to drink,
> And Mr Knight and his son Will
>   Invite the crowd to take their fill.
>
> The Crown will shower its coppers too
>   Promiscuously to Red and Blue,
> When Scottish Jimmy steps inside,
>   His snuffy coloured bags to hide.
>
> Tom Parfitt claps his brawny hands,
>   And cries 'we're sure to win,
> For see – we've Cruttwell's ragged band
>   With whistle, noise, and din.'
>
> Big Mason thinks it fine to head
>   This Grand Extempore band;
> And little Olive tramps in front,
>   With Bennett hand in hand.
>
> John Lewis and poor little Philp
>   Are in the noisy clan,
> And swear to vote for Fergusson,
>   He's such a nice dear man.
>
> Let Jimmy nurse his cold in bed,
>   He'll never stand in Lopes' stead;
> He'd better take a shay and pair,
>   And seek a healthier clime, in Ayr.
>
> In spite of Blue Election tricks,
> On Samuelson our hopes we fix.
> Assured that he will ever be
>   A faithful, honest, true MP.

Charlotte Turner ran the inn briefly until Edwin Say and his wife took over. By this time the Crown was owned by the East Street Brewery of Warminster who, in 1909, carried out alterations to the inn. Edwin Say moved to the Somerset Arms midway through World War One and Henry Riddle took over. In June 1917 the Crown was in need of new bar staff, but war had been raging for nearly four years and labour was in short supply. Hence, somewhat pragmatically, the advertisement in the 'Situations Vacant' column read:

> Person (respectable) WANTED, for general work in public house and willing to assist in bar when required. Soldier's widow not objected to. Mrs Riddle, Crown Inn, Keyford, Frome.

Henry Riddle had been born at Rode and was a builder before moving to Frome. A keen musician, he played the euphonium for the town band and was fond of the violin. He and his wife ran the Crown Recreation Club, organising excursions to places like Wells Cathedral and Gough's Cave at Cheddar, which aimed to be both educational and enjoyable. He died suddenly in 1935 aged 59 and his widow Rosa took over.

In March 1938 Frome Urban District Council decided to schedule the Crown for preservation. Mr and Mrs Martin took over in the 1940s when they married and were still running the Crown 25 years later. The Crown is still there today as a quiet 'locals' pub and retains its old world charm.

Crown, Market Place

Murder, robbery, royalty incognito, slave auctions – the Crown in the Market Place witnessed it all during the four centuries it operated as an inn.

The earliest part of the building dates from the 1600s. Over the following two centuries it was substantially extended outwards in stages, so that the earlier parts now lie to the rear of the property. In written records, it first appears in 1668 when John Thomas was paying the rates there. There is further mention of the building in 1681 when it was called Garret's House. There is a datestone above a fireplace in the bar, which reads EIM 1697, and includes what appears to be a representation of a crown. It was around this time that a three-storey extension was added, all of which seems to suggest that this is when it became an inn. The Georgian-style façade which is visible today was added much later, probably after the two halves of the Market Place were united in the early 1800s.

A datestone above a fireplace

The first reference to the Crown Inn by name comes in 1727 when John Morgan is mentioned in the parish rates as paying 'for ye Crown Inn 6d'. The Morgan family were substantial landowners in Frome and John had inherited property from his father Edward, who is listed as paying the rates there in 1697. The 'M' on the date stone probably stands for Morgan, and the 'E' and 'I' may refer to Edward and John. By 1715 it was owned by Mrs Jane Morgan. Subsequent proprietors included Richard Rundall in 1745, Daniel Fryer in 1776, and later Daniel Fryer's widow.

When the Sun Insurance Company valued the contents in 1730, the household goods and stock in trade alone were estimated as worth £200, whilst the stock in the cellars and stables were valued at £300. The landlord at this time was John Young.

The Crown during the 1700s was clearly a prestigious establishment, as can be seen from the type of entertainment it offered during Easter week in 1764, when landlord Benjamin Coulston hosted a singing contest, the prize being a silver bowl worth two guineas.

By 1785 the owner was Edward Fryer, whilst the tenant publican was Samuel Holmes, who had taken over in 1783. He continued to maintain the high standards, running post chaises and even refitted the house to make it more 'commodious'. Sadly, such investment provided scant return, despite many creative attempts to turn a profit. In October 1789 Samuel Holmes was declared bankrupt, the tenancy having already been advertised a few months earlier:

> To be let, and entered on immediately, or at Midsummer next, for the remainder of a term, of which eight years are yet to come – The Crown Inn, in the town of Frome, in the county of Somerset. The said inn is most commodiously situated in the Market Place, and possesseth every requisite for the accommodation of travellers and others. The stock and furniture to be taken at a fair appraisement ... About 40 ton of very good hay to be disposed of.

1789 also saw the effects of another bankrupt being auctioned off at the Crown. Frome had long-standing links with the West Indies, so we should perhaps not be surprised to learn that the estate owned by this bankrupt was in Jamaica, and that, amongst the 'goods' on offer was the ownership of 'negroes and other valuable properties'. Holmes's successor was William Finall who died in 1812 and was succeeded by his widow Eleanor.

Throughout the eighteenth century, there is barely a whisper of scandal at the Crown. It is only in the nineteenth century that things begin to go awry. The entry in Constable Isaac Gregory's diary for 18 May 1814, for example, reads:

> Sent for to quell an affray at the Crown … A farmer took a buckle to Mr Hill to get repaired. He was a considerable time about it and because he charged twopence for it the farmer began abusing him for overcharging. Mr Hill then offered to do it gratis which did not please the farmer and so they went on – he being joined by half a dozen more farmers, quite drunk, it was utterly impossible to restore order among such a set as they were.

Constable Isaac Gregory was later summoned to the Crown again:

> Half past eleven at night an alarm of Murder was cried in the street. The person who cried murder so dreadfully and frightened many of the inhabitants in their beds … said he was a dyer by trade, that he was attacked and beat by several men who had followed him from the Crown, that he had not molested either of them and he thought they would kill him if he had not cried Murder – several persons told me he had been very abusive at the Crown and had beat a young man there which was confirmed by the watchman … He was Drunk and I thought it highly proper to confine him for the night … but in the morning he was very penitent, dreaded the idea of being had before the Justice and said that if he was not permitted to go to his work he should lose his place, he very much begged me to discharge him – which I did.

Eleanor Finall died in 1822 and her daughter Susan took over. She died on 8 December 1830, aged 45, and there is a memorial to her and her parents in St John's church.

The Market Place c1860, with the Crown on the right

The memorial to William, Eleanor and Susan Finall in St John's church

In December 1832 Frome voted in its first MP – the Whig Thomas Sheppard. The supporters of Tory candidate Sir Thomas Champneys of Orchardleigh were somewhat displeased. Rioting – which lasted for three days – ensued, and

> a large body of the Mob wearing White Ribbons ... shouting 'Champneys for ever' made a most furious attack on the Crown Inn ... and proceeded to demolish the Bar ... The Magistrates then ordered the Special Constables, about twelve of whom were armed with Carbines, to make a sally from the George through the Crown.

James Knight was the next landlord and was still there in May 1840 when the owner, John Langley Fryer, died. The inn was put up for sale, but Knight remained until 1842 when Henry Taylor took over. He was succeeded by William Baily Mees, who played host to the Crown's most prestigious guest – if only he'd known it at the time!

One Friday in mid-October 1853, a twelve-year-old boy arrived at the Crown to stay for the night. He was, in fact, the future King Edward VII travelling incognito. The poor waiter, unaware of his young customer's real identity, provided a napkin for the Royal tutor but failed to do so for 'the little boy'. Prince Edward reportedly demolished the best part of a joint of beef before attending a service at the parish church. He slept the night in room 7 – which was referred to as the Prince's Room thereafter. On Saturday morning he went for a walk through the rain-soaked streets of Frome before returning to the inn where a fly and two horses were waiting to take him to Warminster.

Mees was succeeded by the Gough family, two generations of which ran the Crown from the 1850s to 1884. Their time there was witness to the inn's most tragic event. In May 1874 the Goughs engaged a new servant, 24-year-old Emily Spencer, who had previously been working across town at the Bath Arms. Within days, the Goughs began to suspect their new employee was pregnant, but Emily stoutly denied it. When she was taken ill, surgeon Mr Cockey confirmed the landlord's suspicions, and later that day she became worse. Emily's room was searched and the body of a baby was found under the mattress with a cord around his neck. Emily was committed for trial on a charge of 'wilful murder' but was convicted of the lesser crime of 'concealment of birth'. She was sentenced to twelve months' hard labour.

William Bown, from Bristol, was licensee from 1884 to 1899, when he moved next door to the George. During his time there, in 1889, the trustees of the late William Shore Baily put the inn up for sale, the auction particulars describing it as

> all that well-accustomed and very old established full-licensed freehold hotel, together with the Yard, Stables, Coach-houses and Garden in rear of same, known as the 'Crown Hotel', occupying a most commanding position in the Frome Market Place, now let to Mr W R Bown on a lease expiring 29th September, 1889.

It was sold to William Garton, a Southampton brewer, who sold it on to the Anglo-Bavarian Brewery Company in April 1894 for £1,800. In April 1899, Walter Edwin Yerbury took over as landlord. He had a reputation for getting things done and was clearly a man of ambition. In Yerbury's day the inn was known as 'the Crown Commercial Inn, complete with coffee room and guest rooms'. He was respected as an experienced landlord, having kept the Lamb Hotel for many years, and started a omnibus service from the Crown which met every train at the station.

Yerbury also specialised in catering for picnics and social gatherings and was the proprietor of the Keyford Livery Stables. This was still not enough for the ambitious Mr Yerbury, however. In 1902 he applied for the licence of the neighbouring Bull Hotel, a very different sort of establishment. The Bull, which catered mainly for tourists, would be run by his wife, while he would continue to manage the Crown, but have overall supervision over both. A few months later, however, he gave up the Crown to concentrate on the Bull, and in 1907 was declared bankrupt.

Newcastle-born George Angus took over from Yerbury, both as licensee and omnibus proprietor. He died in 1911 and was buried in Christ Church cemetery. His widow, Clara, succeeded him and maintained the inn during the wartime period. It was during her time as landlady, in 1915, that a young Wilf Brake began drinking at the Crown. Seventy years later, still loyal to his local, Wilf was presented with a tankard on his 87th birthday to commemorate his custom at the inn for over 70 years. Mathematicians will rapidly deduce how old Wilf was when he began frequenting the pub. Clara Angus left in 1919, by which time the Crown had been sold by the Anglo Brewery Company ('Bavarian' having been dropped from its name during World War One) to George Samuel Knibbs. Now it was the turn of Henry Court to make his mark. This he surely did, despite only being in residence for a matter of months.

The outbreak of war in 1914 had had an immediate impact on the British pub. When Lloyd George announced that, 'we are fighting Germany, Austria and Drink; and, as far as I can see, the greatest of these deadly foes is Drink', it was only a matter of time before things tightened up for publicans as the wartime authorities secured

George Angus's name appears on the signboard of the Crown in this photograph of the Market Place. He was its landlord from 1902 to 1911.

Above: The Crown in the late nineteenth century, when William Bown was the landlord

Below: The Crown in the 1920s, when the stables had been converted to a garage, advertised by a large sign on the side wall

new powers under DORA, the Defence of the Realm Act. DORA was the bane of many a licensee's existence. One of its main aims was to restrict opening hours, so that alcohol could only be served between the hours of 12-2.30pm and 6-10pm. Pubs could still stay open all day, however, even though they were not selling liquor (in theory), which made it notoriously difficult for the police to enforce the law. Often, plain clothes policemen from outside the district would be brought in to detect breaches by posing as customers.

Unfortunately, for Henry Court, the restrictions imposed under DORA continued into peacetime, and on 10 September 1919 two plain clothes policemen came into the Crown and witnessed Dorothy Knibbs, the owner's wife, serving whiskey to a soldier at 4.10pm. Henry Court was not even in the bar at the time, but as licensee he was summoned before the local magistrates. He was a respected licensee who had held a licence for a total of 16 years, eight of which had been spent at the Ship in Frome, and he had never been in trouble with the authorities. Despite his protestations that Mrs Knibbs had not even charged the soldier for the drink, he was still fined for this breach. Unfortunately his troubles were only just beginning.

Just one week later Henry Court was up before the authorities again. He had been arrested at his pub during the week and taken off to Bath, charged with receiving stolen goods – in this case a large number of military boots. He was released on bail. Within days, yet another case involving the pub was before the authorities – this time the Crown was the victim of theft. Terence Brian, an Australian soldier, was charged with stealing two glasses from the bar. In court, the soldier pleaded absent-mindedness. He had already missed his ship home because of the court case and thus lost £28. The magistrates found him guilty but imposed only a small fine. The following week, Court himself was back in court on the matter of the stolen footwear. Over a period of twelve months, some 6,000 pairs of boots had gone missing from the stores of the Australian Imperial Forces at Warminster and Henry Court was sentenced to six months' hard labour as an accessory.

In Court's absence, the landlord of the Crown at Keyford, Henry Riddle, was granted an interim licence for the Crown in the Market Place too. The application for the licence was made by Fussell's Brewery of Rode who were purchasing the Crown from Mr Knibbs. Riddle ran the Crown for several months until a full-time replacement could be found and then returned to running the Crown at Keyford.

During the 1940s Freda Davis was landlady, and in 1946 was granted a music licence to 'relay wireless music to the lounge only'. Superintendent Hiscox stressed that it should be to the lounge only as 'we don't want it too noisy'. She was succeeded by a former head waiter from the Pump Room in Bath, Fred Peaty, and his wife, who ran the Crown from 1948 to 1970, by which time the owners were Bass Charrington.

In February 1999 the Crown was sold to a London developer, but proposals in 2000 to transform it into a betting shop were opposed by Frome Town Council. Finally, in 2004 it was sold again and given a facelift to render it usable as a pub once more. It had been empty for seven years. Unfortunately it subsequently closed again – this time for good.

When the authors began preparing the work for this book, the Crown was a rather sad, neglected and vacant building. It was subsequently transformed and reopened as a clothing store in July 2013. Whilst it may no longer be a pub, it has at least resumed its place as a vibrant, working part of the Market Place.

The Crown in 2012 awaiting its fate as a clothes shop

Crown & Sceptre (formerly Jolly Butcher), 38 Trinity Street

The Jolly Butcher, as it was originally known, first appears on the map of 1774. At the time of the 1785 Frome census, when the street on which it stood was known as Trooper Street, it was owned and run by Edward Culverhouse.

Later owners include James Pobjoy and a William Sheppard of Bath. It was during the latter's tenure, in November 1813, that constable Isaac Gregory had 'a very dangerous day'. The publican at the time was James Stride and it seems that he was in debt to someone, as Gregory was called out to assist the bailiffs whilst various goods were seized from the pub. According to Gregory, 'the door was not locked so we had free admission ... We were no sooner in than the house was filled with about 30 men who began taking the furniture down to carry it away as they had a waggon provided. One of the party immediately took a dragoon's broad sword and called out forcibly for Stride to get the pistols and load them with ball as "swords and pistols should end it". The sword was taken from the man, but the rest of Stride's party shut themselves inside, causing Williams, the sheriff's officer, to 'begin beating it open with a large hammer'. Eventually, the sheriff's men prevailed and the goods were seized.

The Crown & Sceptre in 1992

Stride seems to have overcome his financial problems, as he was still there in 1835 when the owner, George Trent, was made bankrupt – in fact, a report from the time describes him as having occupied the house for 30 years. A disaster was narrowly averted in 1838, when Stride sent a lad down to clean out one of the huge beer casks. He was overcome by the fumes and would have died had not Stride and another man pulled him out quickly.

The following year, James Steeds took over, but was only there until 1840, when he handed the reins over to a wheelwright named William Eastment, who ran things until about 1863. It was around the latter date, that the pub's name was changed to the Crown & Sceptre, although it also continued to be known as the Jolly Butcher for a time.

In 1889 the landlady, Sarah Wilcock, married Tom Phillips, landlord of the Swan in Broadway, which caused the magistrates some confusion as the rule was that a licensee should live on the premises, and married couples could not live in two pubs at the same time. The bench agreed to let the situation continue as Mrs Phillips had a competent manager who had been with her for nine years. The problem was solved within the year when the pub was sold to the Oakhill Brewery and the happy couple moved off to the Swan.

While the issue was being decided, it was pointed out that the late Henry Baily had at one point been licensee of both the Crown & Sceptre and the Bell immediately opposite without any problem. This is interesting, because it adds weight to the story that there was an underground passage, following a natural fissure in the rock, which ran under the road between the two pubs and enabled barrels of beer brewed at the Bell to be rolled down to the cellar of the Crown without having to be carried upstairs.

Oakhill Brewery, the new owners, were taken to court a couple of years later as some scaffolding they were using to build two extra bedrooms in the loft was blocking the road. The case was dismissed but the dormer windows of the new rooms can still be seen today.

In 1926 the local magistrates recommended the pub for closure as there were five other pubs nearby, it had few customers and, anyway, the Bell was a much better place. Landlord Henry Parker said his weekly takings were about £25 per week. It survived, passing through the hands of several more landlords and continuing even after a sponsored spaghetti eat-in to celebrate the royal wedding in 1981. Recent reports describe it as a very welcoming locals' pub with no real ale but some excellent proper cider.

Crown & Thistle, Market Place

On an island in the Market Place lay one of Frome's more obscure and now long-lost pubs, the Crown & Thistle. Until the 1811 Bath Street development, a building extended across the Market Place from where the HSBC Bank now stands, with only a small passageway between it and the Crown Hotel, and effectively splitting the Market Place in two. This building was the Crown & Thistle.

In a deed of 1681, the building is described as 'Phipps alias Phillips' House'. The deed conferred upon the occupant the right to a few feet of land in front of the house on which to set up stalls on market day. Originally, it was probably a private house, and the date it became an inn is not known. By the mid-1700s, however, it had become the Crown & Thistle, occupied by a victualler called Thomas Edgell. He was followed by Samuel Dowling, who leased it for 99 years from John Smith of Stoney Littleton and John Smith of Combe Hay. By 1762 Dowling had died and his widow held the licence. The inn at the time enjoyed the use of part of the neighbouring property, comprising a stairway and a room over the ground floor.

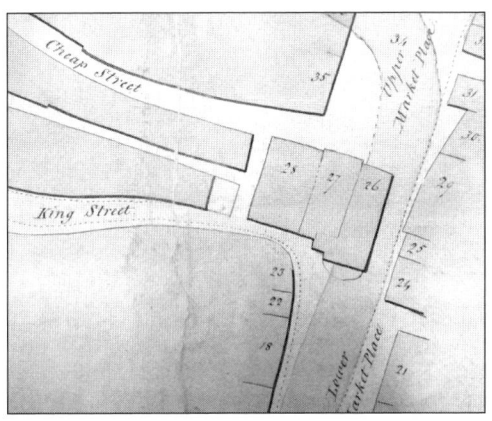

A map of 1808 demonstrating the awkward location of the Crown & Thistle, numbered 27

After Elizabeth Dowling died in 1765, the premises were occupied by Walter Long who married into the Dowling family in 1769. Then, in 1781, Thomas Beard, the man who leased the property next door, took it on. At the time, it was described as being 'located in Cheap Street against the Market Place', and had a stable, outhouses and a small portion of land. In 1785 Walter Long was back as publican, and, although the building was acquired by Frome grocer Charles Willoughby around 1795, Walter Long continued as innkeeper.

Prior to the construction of Bath Street, the only route leading out of Frome from the Bridge and Market Place in the direction of Keyford was less than satisfactory, being steep, narrow and precarious for man and beast. The 1810 Turnpike Act was an attempt to remedy this by linking the Market Place to the turnpike near the top of Rook Lane. Included in this scheme was a plan to clear the Market Place, and specifically to demolish the two properties immediately opposite the George – one of which was the Crown & Thistle. The 1810 Act included powers of compulsory purchase, so clearly the end of the inn was nigh. It was demolished soon afterwards, and in 1815 the trustees of the turnpike released 'all that parcel of ground, part of the site of the Crown & Thistle containing 170 sq ft'.

As you walk around the Market Place today, remember that beneath the broad pavement may well be the foundations of this ancient inn.

Dolphin, Market Place

The first mention of the Dolphin comes in the churchwardens' accounts for 1693, when the rates were paid by Henry Allen. He was still there in 1723 paying rates for 'the Dolphin Stables'. From that year until 1744 the inn was owned by Thomas Lacy, a blacksmith, and was sometimes referred to as 'the Old Dolphin'. Whether this means that there was a new one or just that it had been there a while is unclear.

From 1746 until 1770 the rates were paid by Thomas Pritchard, followed by William and Robert Parsons, and it is the 1770 entry which describes it as being in the Market Place – our only clue to its location. From 1778 Daniel Wayland appears paying rates on 'part of the Old Dolphin', initially with William Parsons but later by himself.

The *Royal Commission on Historic Monuments Report on the Trinity Area of Frome* by Roger Leech states that the Dolphin was at what is now 62-63 Naish's Street, but this is marked clearly on the 1774 map as the King of Prussia. Moreover, he does not give any source for this claim and we have found nothing to support it.

We have found no mention of it after 1791, so possibly it was one of those Market Place buildings cleared away to make way for Bath Street. Odd that there are not more references, given that it seems to have been there for over 100 years.

Dolphin / Farmer's Arms, Spring Gardens

The first definite mention of a pub at Spring Gardens comes from the census returns of 1841 when a beerhouse there was being run by George Francis and his wife Martha. There had been another pub with the same name in the town centre, but we have been unable to establish a connection between the two, and the other one is not mentioned after 1791. Francis was only 25 at the time of the census, but by 1848 he is described as 'the late George Francis', and the pub had been taken over by James Harvey, whose family remained there until at least the 1860s. During this time an application for a full licence was made, accompanied by the usual 'testimonial' or petition of support signed by local residents and the landlord's cronies. Magistrate Sheppard was rather robust in his judgement, declaring that 'the persons who signed the testimonial ... could not be aware of the number of drunken cases they have had from that house or they surely would not have signed ... There were plenty of licensed houses in Frome and they would not grant any more. Application refused.'

Its proximity to Sheppard's Cloth Mill and Leonard's Mill just down the road must have ensured a good stream of customers wending their weary and thirsty way back to their homes in the town.

In 1874 landlord Henry Rebbick was summonsed for having sold a half pint of beer before the permitted time of 12.30pm. His defence was that he believed his two customers were travellers, and, when questioned, one was able to prove that he had walked all the way from Radstock and had 'not tasted a morsel of anything on his way until he got to Spring Gardens. He had never been in the defendant's house before'. The bench believed him and dismissed the case.

By 1881 the Dolphin was being run by William Norvill and continued in the same family until 1932, but it was not until 1947 that it was finally granted a full licence enabling it to sell spirits along with wine, beer and cider.

When the Norvills left, the pub was demolished and rebuilt to the designs of Percy Rigg, a local architect, who chose a classic and attractive mock medieval farmhouse style for the new building.

With Sheppard's Mill long gone, the pub was rather isolated and making a living must have been hard, but by the mid-1980s it had changed its name to the Farmer's Arms and was being run, on behalf of Usher's Brewery, by Phil and Sue Henshaw, who slowly gained a reputation for good food, winning a number of awards. This reputation was enhanced when Bruno Bazzani took the helm in 1997. He was a trained chef who had held licences in Switzerland and Australia for over 20 years, and the place really took off, with Bazzani winning many awards for his food as well as encouraging and training young chefs and putting the pub firmly on the map. After he left in 2001, the pub never recovered. It struggled on for a while but, after a number of attempted sales, revamps and periods of closure, planning permission was finally granted in 2013 for conversion into a private dwelling.

The Farmer's Arms being converted to a private house in 2014

Dr Andrews, Milk Street

A very strange name for a pub and, in all probability, not a pub at all. It appears on the map of 1774 and is listed along with 40 or so other public houses but does not appear anywhere else – not in surveys, rates, deeds, or other maps or documents. Our guess is that it was placed in the wrong column when the index to the map was drawn up. There are numerous other buildings on the map that are not public houses, and it is likely that it was quite simply the abode of a doctor – named Andrews.

The map shows it as being across the road from what is now Vallis First School, and one of the victims of the clearances of the 1960s.

Was it a pub or wasn't it? The authors would love to know.

Was one of these an alehouse called 'Dr Andrews"?

Eagle, corner of Church Steps and Eagle Lane

The Eagle Inn gave its name to the street on which it stood. Originally known as Cokkestret in the 1300s, Cock Street in the 1500s, Cox Street in the 1600s and then Back Lane in the 1700s, it finally became Eagle Lane in the early 1800s. Before Bath Street was created in 1810, Eagle Lane was a great deal longer and the Eagle Inn was but one of four pubs in the vicinity.

William Hiscocks owned the Eagle from 1770 to the early 1800s and let it to various men who acted as landlords, including John Summers (1793) and Thomas Williams (1817). This was a busy inn in the early 1800s, and, when the lease was put up for sale in 1807, the stock comprised between 300 and 400 hogsheads of strong beer, spirits, casks, brewing utensils, household furniture, fixtures etc, and it had 'for many years past experienced a trade inferior to none in the populous town of Frome. It is well supplied with water, and for extent of cellar room, brewing-house, and every other convenient requisite, is scarcely to be equalled.'

The site of the Eagle in 2013

Running the Eagle was certainly not uneventful for Thomas Williams. In 1817, Constable Isaac Gregory recorded that he had been summoned to deal with a drunken and querulous customer, James Biggs of Mells, who had been abusing the landlord. Constable Gregory attempted to take Biggs to the guard-house and was violently assaulted in the process. Two days later, Biggs' tearful wife appeared and begged the Constable to drop all charges. The constable agreed – provided Biggs confessed his wrongdoings in a public statement, which ran thus:

> Caution to Drunkards – Whereas I James Biggs, Labourer, did on the night of the 10th instant, violently assault Mr Isaac Gregory one of the Chief Constables of Frome while in the execution of his duty, and did (being in a state of intoxication) give him a violent blow on the face, for which he has commenced an Action against me, that I may be punished with the utmost severity of the law, but in consequence of my publicly acknowledging my offence, and begging for mercy, and in compassion to my wife and child has withdrawn his prosecution against me. I hope it will be a caution to me and all drunkards not to interrupt the peace officers in the execution of their duty. Witness my hand in the presence of me, TS Champneys at Orchardleigh Dec. 12 1817.
>
> The X mark of James Biggs

In its later years, the inn probably operated as an 'off-licence' or wine & spirit stores. In 1856, when the owner, Joseph Oxley, died and the Eagle was put up for sale, it consisted of a 'commodious dwelling house, large and well arranged cellarage for bottled and draught wines, spirits etc ... large retail shop, back yard, and stabling, being well adapted for an extensive wholesale and retail trade'.

Following the auction, it was put to a new use – as a temporary police station – but once the new police station in Christchurch Street was completed the place was vacant again. The Mechanics' Institute was looking for a new location, and, although the Eagle was a perfect location, the building was unsuitable. It was demolished and in November 1858 the new Mechanics Institute was opened. In the 1930s the building became the Palace Theatre Cinema, subsequently destroyed by fire in 1961 and replaced with a modern yellow-brick building which must vie with the furniture shop opposite the Cornerhouse at the top of Bath Street as one of the most unsympathetic of Frome's buildings. During the 1990s the site was occupied by Brady's Plywood Store and is now Studio Prints.

Fleur De Luce (or Three Fleur de Luces), corner of Stony Street & Palmer Street

In 1749, Lionel Seaman, owner of a good deal of land in Frome sold 'all the messuage or tenement and inn called Flower de Luce Inn with all the outbuildings and buildings near Smiths barn in Frome' to Lord Cork. This is first reference to the inn, and it must have been more than a simple sale as Lionel's widow, referred to as 'Madam Seaman' in the church accounts books, is shown as paying the rates until 1780.

> To be Lett immediately,
> With the Stock and Furniture, or otherwise,
> An Old-accuftom'd I N N,
> Commonly called the Sign of the Three
> FLEUR-DE-LUCE's, near the
> Market-Place in FROME, Somerfet.
> The Houfe is fitting up to receive Gentlemen, &c. and any Perfon that is willing to take the faid Inn, fhall meet with good Encouragement.
> *** For further Particulars, enquire of the prefent Tenant.
> N. B. Good Stabling, &c. for 100 Horfes.

The lease of the Three Fleur de Luce's advertised in the *Bath Chronicle* on 28 April 1763

The lease was put up for auction in 1763 and it was probably then that James Hiscox became the licensee. During this time, the army sent parties of soldiers to various towns on recruitment drives and they were entitled to seven days' bed and board at a local inn while searching the area for suitable men. The billeting was arranged by the local constable who had the power to insist that the innkeeper provide for their needs at a rate of fourpence per day. Part of the soldiers' task was to spend a day or two at nearby fairs and markets looking for men who wanted to enlist. Their reading of the act was that they were then entitled to return to the town and receive another seven days' free board at a different house, and repeat this as often as they liked, thus making the innkeepers 'perpetually burdened'.

The notebooks of Thomas Horner, a local magistrate, for May and June 1770 record that 'James Hiscox, innholder was summonsed for refusing to receive two soldiers employed in recruiting, and to furnish them with victuals for seven days'. Hiscox felt that he had a good case and was granted an adjournment to seek counsel's opinion as the complainants acknowledged that they had been at other alehouses 'with diet etc' at fourpence per day for seven days or more. His point was that this was unfair as there were a number of recruiting parties in the town, and once they had had their seven days that should be that.

Learned counsel was in agreement with Hiscox, saying that, on that interpretation of the act, the constable might as well be expected to move the parties around continually from pub to pub for seven days at a time, whether they left town or not, and that it was an attempt to avoid the terms of the Act of Parliament.

The magistrate's account does not mention an inn by name, but in the late 1700s a James Hiscox ran or owned the Talbot in Trooper Street, as well as the Fleur de

Luce, so maybe he suffered more than most, which would explain why he refused to take them in and ended up in court. Presumably the bench accepted the counsel's advice as the matter is not mentioned again.

The pub is shown on the 1774 map on the corner of Stony Street and Palmer Street and in the photograph below part of it can be seen on the extreme right with a cart standing outside its door.

In November 1773, Thomas Horner, one of the Justices of the Peace, recorded that Henry Box, an alehouse keeper, had claimed that Abraham Saunders had entered his house at the head of a mob, assaulted him and tore his 'cloths'. He had also alleged that Saunders was 'wandering about the country exhibiting for gain, puppet shows, juggling etc' contrary to the Vagrancy Act. It seems that the case was contrived by Lord Cork, the bailiff and other principal inhabitants of Frome to have the performing troop removed from the streets, and that the assault was provoked 'by Box's kicking the man's drum to pieces as it was beating in the street'. The assault charge was dismissed, but Saunders was given seven days' for vagrancy.

There was a big auction of Seaman family property at the George Inn in June 1780 and the pub was bought by James Hiscox, although Henry Box remained licensee. Hiscox is shown as paying the rates until 1793, after which the property ceases to be mentioned as an inn. The Cruse map of the town from 1813 shows the premises in detail, with a forecourt for carriages and a yard or garden at the back. The last entry for the Talbot comes in the same year, so perhaps Hiscox died or retired from business and the Fleur was sold. It was demolished shortly after the photograph above was taken to build Dodge's furnishers, and rebuilt again in the 1950s for Kelsey's, the bedding and house furniture shop. The quaint old shop in the centre was also demolished.

The site of the Fleur de Luce in 2013

Foresters Arms, Locks Lane

On 1 January 1932, the *Somerset Standard* carried an article entitled 'Frome in the 1880's', which stated that, 'except for Percy Cottages, there were only two houses in Locks Lane, (not Hill): St Helens – originally the Foresters Arms – and Locks Lane House'.

This is the only mention of a pub called the Foresters Arms discovered so far and, were it not for the long building named 'Lock's Lane Malthouse' stretching down Adderwell Road on the Ordnance Survey map of 1886, it might easily be discounted as a mistake The plan shows a substantial building and it is very surprising that there are no records of it. It was no longer a pub by 1886 and in 1958 the villa known as St Helen's was converted into two houses. The malthouse became the local squash court until very recently when it was demolished for housing.

St Helen's

The remains of the malthouse on Adderwell Road

Fox, Blatchbridge Lane

The first reference for this obscure inn comes from the notebooks of Thomas Horner, a JP from Mells. An entry for 5 September 1771 simply states that 'the King of Prussia and the Fox both in Frome were refused licences'. No reason or further information was given.

Things were no better a year later, in March 1772, when Thomas Horner recorded that 'an application was made for a licence for the alehouse called the Fox in Frome but the same was rejected on account of the inconvenient situation of the house'.

The pub was not mentioned for the next 30 years, as far as we are aware, but in the church rates of 1803 the Rev William Ireland paid rates on a number of properties, amongst which was one occupied by 'J Guy' described as 'near Fox lands', and from 1807 to 1810 the property was described as being 'near Adderwell', certainly a way out in the country in those days. There is another mention, in the 1813 notes from the Cruse Survey, of a house and garden called the Fox with James Rossiter as owner, occupied by James Morgan and Thomas Parfitt. Its plot number is given as 1857 and the map shows a long thin house with a garden running along Blatchbridge Lane. In 1823, again in the church rates, the Marquis of Bath is shown as the owner and John Hoddinott the

The Fox, Blatchbridge Lane on the Cruse map of 1813

occupier of 'house and garden Fox'. The last reference comes from the tithe map of 1840 where plot 2110, leased and occupied by John Hoddinott Sr from Longleat Estate, is described as a 'house and gardens at Blatchbridge Lane'. None of these references describe the Fox as a pub, so it is possible it existed prior to 1771, and when its licence was refused it closed and lived on in name only.

Fox & Hounds, Tytherington.

A fine-looking building dating from around 1900 after the original pub was destroyed by fire. Records found so far go back to 1879 when an unnamed beerhouse was transferred from Mary Ann Cornish to George Dunning.

The 1881 census shows it occupied by Thomas Yeoman, and at that year's licensing sessions the magistrates were told that the house was 'better conducted than formerly'. It was later taken over by his brother, Simon Yeoman, who in 1889, was arrested for assaulting his wife there. The court was told that Yeoman went into the yard and, finding that one of his pigs was dead, swore at his wife and struck her on the forehead. This may seem harsh, but Maria was apparently in the habit of 'going to other people's houses', and he had found her 'sitting on another man's knee', so he gave her a black eye.

The Fox & Hounds in 2013

She wished to withdraw the complaint but the magistrate insisted on continuing and he was fined £1 plus costs which he refused to pay, receiving a month's hard labour instead.

Within a couple of months, Yeoman was out of the pub and off to grieve for his pig and sociable wife elsewhere. By 1893, William Davidge, after a short spell at the Crown & Sceptre in town, moved to the Fox & Hounds. In April 1898, a spark from a cottage chimney across the road set fire to the thatch and, despite 'pumping a supply of water through a quarter of a mile of hose', the place was gutted.

It seems that it was soon rebuilt, as Davidge was still there in January 1900, applying for an extension for a local supper club. The freehold was owned by the Marquis of Bath, so maybe that speeded things up a bit. Davidge had gone by 1909, but his son Private Ernest William Davidge, of the British Expeditionary Force, was killed in action on 26 August 1914 at the age of 18 having joined up a year before.

The pub continued as a beerhouse under various landlords until a full licence was granted to Alfred Barnes in 1953, and in 1976 the pub was proud to announce the arrival of draught Guinness. Tragedy struck in 1986 when Keith Witcombe, the son-in-law of the landlord, was killed while setting up disco lights. The pub is still going strong today.

THE FOX & HOUNDS INN
TYTHERINGTON, FROME, SOMERSET
Telephone: Frome 3048

Bed and Breakfast · Snacks.
Car and Caravan Park

Your pleasure is our business!
Lou and Bill Archer welcome you

An advert from the 1960s

Full Moon and Golden Lyon upon the Bridge

In a deed of 1857 relating to the new Bridge Inn, the Golden Lion was described as 'an inn or public house with cellars, outhouses and backsides with the river on the north and the town bridge on the east and was heretofore called the Golden Lion Inn but afterwards called or known by the sign of the Full Moon'. Tenants of the Golden Lion/Full Moon included John Rendall, followed by Thomas Gulliver, John Penny, John Chislett, William Taylor, and finally Harry, Mary and Sarah Edgell.

Documentation regarding the inn is scant. In 1724 Henry Lacy, a Frome bankrupt, was ordered by the court to surrender at the Golden Lyon, 'the house of John Rendall'. As for when it became the Full Moon, that is something of an enigma, but by the time of the 1785 census it had changed its name and was owned by Joseph Imber. The tenant at the time was Harry Edgell, it was occupied by two men and three women, and stood between a breeches maker's and a surgeon's.

A drawing from before the rebuilding of 1821 showing the Blue House from what is now the market car park. The rear of the Golden Lyon is to the right.

John Imber died in 1807, and by 1808 Mrs Sarah Edgell had taken over. The following year the Full Moon was sold by auction at the George Hotel, and in 1821 the bridge was rebuilt and the inn demolished. It was a prime site, however, located on the main river crossing in the town, and it was inevitable that somebody would put the land to good use. That man was Richard Strong, and the story continues as the Bridge Hotel.

George, Market Place

The centre of the social and business life of Frome for over three and a half centuries, the George is mentioned as far back as 1650 when it belonged to the Leversedge family, the lords of the manor. Two magistrates, Sir John Horner of Mells and Mr Bamfield of Hardington, are recorded in the churchwarden's accounts as having met there that year for a business lunch which cost sixteen shillings. This predates the reign of George I by over 60 years, indicating that the inn was named after St George rather than a member of the royal family.

From the Leversedge family, the inn passed to the Rev Edmund Seaman and, in 1751, to Lord Cork, who spent £426 4s 10d giving it what must have been a serious rebuild in 1754-55. It seems that there were arguments about the upkeep of four acres of pasture that came with the property and disputes over money between the tenant, John King, and his lordship, which resulted in King being thrown out and Henry Buckle taking over in 1755 at a hefty rental of £35 per annum. In 1757 the first meeting of the turnpike trustees was held there and, as well as hosting balls, dinners and other social events, the inn was used for a variety of official functions. Buckle was also host to at least one series of bankruptcy hearings before being made bankrupt himself in 1764. Described as an 'Innholder, Vintner and Chapman late of Frome Selwood', he even suffered the indignity of having his examination take place in his former inn, although he would have had the advantage of being familiar with the seating and catering arrangements.

The magistrates seem to have used the inn as an office and courtroom, with a number of people being 'bailed to return' there and matters of taxation and bastardy being decided within its walls – a sensible arrangement that would certainly cut down on court costs if reintroduced today. The clergy too made use of the place, with sums of ten or sixteen shillings appearing as a charge on the parish for entertaining church dignitaries during their 'visitations'. In 1770, it was also the venue for the first meeting of the Commissioners of Land and Window Tax.

The George was also a major coaching inn and many horses were stabled there for hire, along with a variety of carriages. The coaches kept to a strict timetable and quick changeovers were essential, which meant that horses had to be ready at all times, with the whole process seldom taking more than two minutes. Coaches also carried mail, so, as well as their many other functions, pubs acted as post offices.

By 1771 the landlord was John Wood, former butler to Sir William St Quintin, 4th Baronet and MP, whose family seat lay in Yorkshire, and who had died the previous year.

In the summer of 1788 the George had the good fortune to host a lecture by a Mr Warltire, an expert on 'substances that are, or may be, used in agriculture'. This learned chap, whose first name was not recorded, also hawked two cork models of Stonehenge around the south of England, giving lectures on them, as well as running courses on chemistry and experimental philosophy. It is a shame that we know so little about him.

John Hooper took on the lease in 1791, placing an advertisement in the *Bath Chronicle* to announce that he was moving to this 'well known and commodious inn' from the Lamb at Hindon. He stayed until 1814, when the lease was advertised once again, this time including a farm at Critchill – possibly the same plot of land that had caused the dispute with John King. Tom Harrington, from the Red Lion in Salisbury, took over and commenced 'alterations and extensive improvements in every department'.

A new landlord at the George, from the *Bath Chronicle* of 24 January 1771

Mr Warltire arrives in town, from the *Salisbury & Winchester Journal* of 16 June 1788

In 1813 plans were drawn up to remodel the front which, had they been carried out, would have produced a fine building of elegant proportions. The architect was John Pinch, who also sketched ideas for a magnificent range of stables worthy of any country house. Pinch was responsible for Babington House and various grand schemes in Bath including Cavendish Place and St Mary's church, Bathwick. Despite the backing and enthusiasm of Thomas Bunn, local landowner and worthy, and the Sheppard family of clothiers, the scheme came to nothing, but Pinch's drawings – reproduced below – survive in Frome Museum.

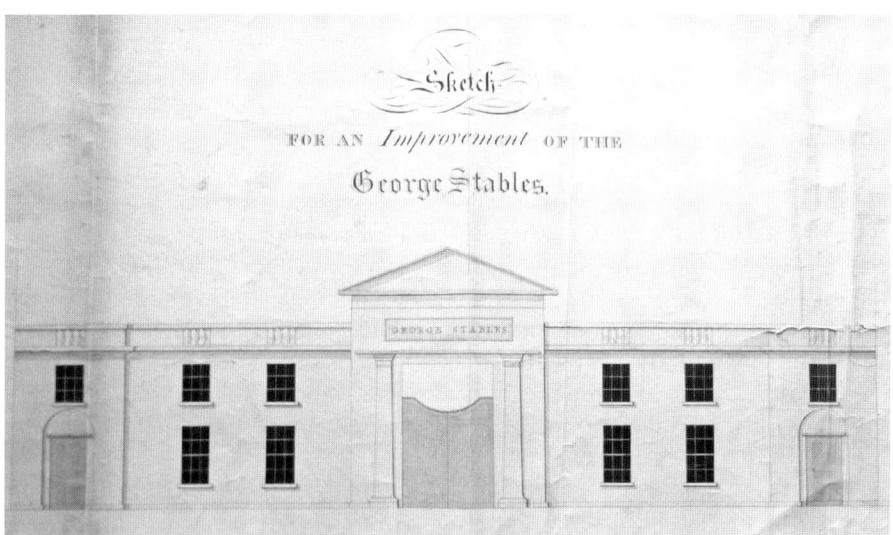

The inn's position in the centre of the Market Place made it ideal for issuing proclamations and making announcements such as election results which could lead to trouble. In August 1818, for example, there was a 'public dinner at the George on account of the re-election of the old members to serve in Parliament ... A great many people was lounging about all day, expecting there would be beer given away, but there was not, which made the rabble change their tune from praise to hissing.'

By 1817 Thomas Bunn, a great enthusiast of the classical style, who owned the land next door, had persuaded his good friend Lord Cork to build the assembly room first discussed in 1813. Bunn gave up part of his kitchen garden, and a fine new building was erected, which, although not as grand as the one originally planned, is a good example of the Greek Revival designed by GA Underwood. According to the local paper, the upper room, which was connected to the George, measured 48 feet by 24 feet and was an incredible 24 feet high. It opened on 14 August 1818 with a public dinner and was the venue for many concerts and society balls, including a banquet to celebrate the coronation of William IV. The lower floor was initially the meat market, but after 50 years or so became the market hall, before being sold off to become a branch of Stuckey's Bank, later the National Westminster.

All these developments enhanced the George's importance to the life of the town, and in 1819 the lease was taken by Henry Hilliar, who remained until 1838. His long tenancy was not without incident, however. In 1832, when Frome was given the right to elect an MP for the first time, he perhaps unwisely allowed the Tory candidate, Sir Thomas Champneys of Orchardleigh, to use the inn as his headquarters. A report in the *Bath & Cheltenham Gazette* tells us that Sir Thomas was addressing the assembled multitude from the hotel balcony when Tom Sheppard, the Liberal candidate, arrived, attended by 'at least one third of the constituency' and about 600 men from his factories. A Tory supporter attacked Sheppard as he was getting out of his carriage, 'tearing the coat from his back', and giving rise to a general free-for-all, which was eventually calmed down enough for speeches to be made – made but not heard as the noise was so great with jeering, insults and stones being thrown. According to the report, the Tory supporters 'attacked every person who wore the colours of Mr Sheppard, tore down his banners and broke the poles into bludgeons'.

Eventually Sir Thomas left to return to Orchardleigh with a large party of followers, and an upstairs room at the inn was taken over by local magistrates to swear in special constables. As they deliberated, some Tory supporters returned, and 'a body of ruffians armed with heavy staves rushed along the passage of the inn, forced their way upstairs and reached the magistrates' room destroying everything and knocking down everyone who came in their way'. They were eventually driven back to the street by a few spirited young men armed with fire-irons, candlesticks, fragments of chairs and even the railings from the stairs. Eventually, 'the arrival of a troop of 7th Dragoon Guards stayed other hostility for the night'.

Despite the military being 'judiciously stationed before the George Inn within an hour of the polling', jeering, murmurs and cries for blood continued, and

Sheppard's party was again attacked by the howling Tory mob, before they were beaten back by the magistrates and constables. The front door of the inn was barricaded leaving the 'fiends in human shape to gratify their malignity against the windows and freestone front of the inn'. Sheppard and his supporters made their way to the polling place through the Crown Inn next door, but, when this was discovered, a furious assault was made on the door by the rioters and the riot act was read.

One of the magistrates asked Sir Thomas to call off his mob and appeal for calm, but eventually 'the safety of the town urged that endurance should cease', and three carbines were discharged. The rioters instantly dispersed, but not before one man lost a leg and another had a ball enter his thigh. In the end, two people were killed, one of the rioters and one of Sheppard's men, attacked on his way home.

Despite all his efforts, Champneys lost the election to Sheppard by a majority of 63. Worse was to follow three years later when he went bankrupt and much of his furniture and personal effects were auctioned off on 31 July 1835 – at the George.

In 1838 the George had a new landlord. Edward Brunsdon, aged 47, formerly a house steward for the Marquis of Bath at Longleat, took over the lease and announced his arrival with a grand dinner. He was to remain for the next 36 years. Described

> GEORGE INN, FROME.
> EDWARD BRUNSDON begs to inform his Friends, that his OPENING DINNER is fixed for TUESDAY, the 12th of June next, at Four o'Clock precisely, on which occasion he respectfully solicits the favour of their attendance and support.
> Tickets, ONE SOVEREIGN each, to be had at the Bar of the George Inn. [6080

From the *Salisbury & Winchester Journal*, 11 June 1838

as 'tall, stately and dignified' he became a respected member of the town and a founder member of the Scientific & Literary Institute.

The inn continued to be the centre of Frome social life with its round of balls, dinners, lectures, concerts and social engagements – but you can't please everyone. In 1852, Jane Welsh Carlyle – the wife of Thomas Carlyle – visited and was not impressed:

> Frome is a dull dirty looking place full of plumbers ... I saw several inns and chose the George. I walked in and asked to have some cold meat and a pint bottle of Guinness's porter. They showed me to an ill-aired parlour and brought me some cold lamb that the flies had been buzzing around for a week ... I ate bread and drank all the porter and the charge for that refection was 2s 6d! The inn and town were so disagreeable that I went back to the station preferring to wait there.

In 1854 the George was subject to a second round of rioting when the Tory candidate, Lord Dungarvan, won an election over the popular Liberal, Mr Nicholl. The windows were broken, yeomanry called in and the riot act read, but this disturbance was nothing compared to that of two decades earlier. All was quiet by 8.00pm and there were no serious injuries.

It seems that Edward Brunsdon was not over-keen on spending money on repairs, as by 1872 Robert Porteous, steward to the Earl of Cork, remarked that 'the

The Market Place in the 1860s, with the George Hotel, before the front was remodelled, on the extreme left. The building next to it, with its windows protected by blinds – not yet part of the hotel – was at one time occupied by Prosser's organ builders. To the right of that is the Crown, while across the road, with a carriage outside its door, is the Blue Boar.

George Hotel is in a very ruinous state, but with the present old tenant, Mr Brunsdon, it is no use to try to do anything.' The old boy died at the age of 83 in March 1874 and Harding & Sons auctioned his property and effects in 407 lots over three days, with £877 14s 1d being realised.

It seems that the family couldn't wait to move on. In May, a Mr Hodder was summonsed for a breach of the bye-laws for 'not putting up a rail outside the hoarding' in front of the premises, which suggests that the inn was shut up immediately after the auction, and within weeks the hotel had moved at least some of its business to Argyle House in Bath Street.

The new proprietor was a William Turner from Coleford, who set about renovating the hotel, and in October 1874 the *Frome Times* reported that a 'roof-rearing supper' had been held for the workmen to celebrate the completion of the work. The George gained some attic rooms and a splendid iron balcony across the front, and

GEORGE HOTEL, FROME.

THE business of the above Hotel will be carried on during its re-building at ARGYLE HOUSE.

THE ENTRANCE TO THIS COMMODIOUS AND PLEASANTLY-SITUATED HOUSE WILL BE FOR THE FUTURE IN BATH-STREET.

A WELL-APPOINTED OMNIBUS WILL LEAVE THE HOTEL FOR EVERY TRAIN. WELL-HORSED LANDAUS, BROUGHAMS, FOUR-WHEELS, &c., ALWAYS ON HIRE.

W. TURNER (Late of the Hare & Hounds Hotel, Shepton Mallet),
PROPRIETOR.

From the *Frome Times*, 24 June 1874

Mr Porteus declared that 'the George Hotel has been almost rebuilt and tho' not very showy outside it is well done up inside and very convenient.'

The inn might have been nicely done up but the assembly room was in for a shock. In 1876 there was an election pending, for which a Mr Samuelson was the Liberal candidate. The assembly room was engaged for a meeting on 6 November, and on the previous day some members of the Liberal party went in to light the gas. There was a tremendous explosion, and the front windows of the room were blown out, the door was shattered and the ceiling seriously damaged. An election ballad soon appeared which ran:

> Come quickly, Mr Turner!
> I've been and turned the burner,
> And blown the George to glory
> And snuffed out Simple Sam.

The ballad was somewhat wide of the mark, however, for Sam – Mr Samuelson – went on to win the election.

William Turner died the following year, being found dead in his bed one morning, and the licence was transferred to his widow. She carried on until 1887, when one of her daughters married Frederick Kirbell, Lord Cork's agent at Marston, and the licence was transferred to him. Kirbell was a noted athlete who once astonished crowds at the Cheese Show by jumping a ditch and fence intended for horses for a guinea bet. He ran the George with his wife Georgina until 1899, when William Robert Bown, who had been at the Crown next door since 1884, took over.

In 1904 the new Earl of Cork & Orrery decided to sell all his lands and property in the area. Bown bought the freehold of the George for £4,350 and his name was soon displayed proudly over the door.

Bown's reign came to an end in 1911, to be followed for a couple of years by the delightfully named Miss Teek, about whom we know nothing except that her first name was Jane, which was better that than Anne, presumably.

On 23 October 1918, a lorry laden with over two tons of material going from the station to Singer & Sons took the porch off the front of the building, killing Wilfred Hassell, a farm bailiff from Lingmarsh Farm in Wanstrow, who was driving a small cart delivering apples. Edward Hull, the lorry driver, was going down Bath Street and, as he turned the corner, he saw the horse and cart by the hotel entrance. He braked, but, as the road was very greasy, he skidded into the lower pillar and knocked it down. The cart was crushed against the hotel wall, Hassell was thrown out and landed under the falling masonry. Dr Harris was quickly on the scene and found him unconscious and badly crushed. He was rushed to the Victoria Hospital

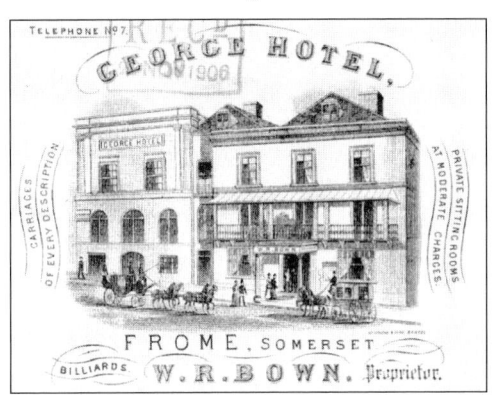

A billhead from 1906

Photographs taken shortly after the fatal crash on 23 October 1918

but he died shortly afterwards. The startling photographs opposite were taken within half an hour of the crash. A verdict of misadventure was brought in by the coroner with no blame attached to either party, and a little later Hasell's widow was awarded £300 in compensation.

In 1923 Sydney George Sewell took over the George. He had been educated at a public school in St Leonards on Sea, and started his career as an auctioneer, estate agent and stockbroker before settling into the George for 16 years. It was during his tenure that Sir William Bull, MP for Hammersmith and chairman of directors at JW Singer & Sons, collapsed and died whilst giving a speech at a dinner in the assembly room in January 1931. By the summer of 1937, Mrs Sewell's health had deteriorated and the hotel was put up for sale with local estate agents, Sewell eventually accepting an offer of £12,000.

The George seems to have lost some of its sparkle during the next few decades. There were still balls, dances and meetings, but the post-war years were grim and social life not what it once was. The flamboyant entrepreneurs and characters had gone, to be replaced by managers, as the pub was now owned by Simonds, who later merged with Courage. Early in 1971, the manager had to assure people through the local paper that 'there was absolutely no truth in the rumour' that they were closing, pointing out that the brewery had just spent £4,000 on a facelift. Despite this, the hotel rooms had not been used for over three years due to disputes over fire regulations, and in 1975 the brewery put it on the market.

The National Westminster Bank took over the top floor as office space, and the last function held there was a civic reception on 16 March 1974 to mark the end of Frome Urban District Council. There were applications to turn the George into a chemist's or a large retail outlet – the council would probably have fancied turning it into another car park – but it was decided that it should remain a hotel,

Soldiers line up outside the George during the First World War

and it was eventually rescued by Freddie Giles, a local restaurateur and property developer. His initial offer of £45,000 in the spring of 1975 was rejected, but it was obvious that the brewery could not make it pay, and a few months later he offered £35,000 and, as he puts it, 'they snatched my hand off'.

Having started as a chimney sweep and window cleaner, Freddie entered the catering business and built up a chain of five 'Farmer Giles' restaurants in the area. By the time the George reopened on 22 March 1977, he had transformed it. There was bedroom accommodation for 28 guests, central heating, and a manager's flat. The ground floor was gutted, with two of the bars on the first floor turned into one big 'Riot Bar' with large cut-out figures commemorating the events of 1832. He installed new kitchens and a 30-seat dining room with the promise of a full lunch for £1 under the direction of a Miss Mimi Rutt.

Finding it hard going with all his other businesses and staffing problems, Freddie eventually sold it on and a few years later it became a tied house once more when Wadworth's bought it. They still own it today, a quieter and more relaxed place that in its heyday.

The George in 2013

George in ye Woodlands, Marston Bigot

A bit out in the sticks, but a fine old building with a long history. The earliest reference found so far is from the church rates which records John Simes there in May 1705. A John Simes was still there in 1767, but he was probably his son.

By the time of the 1785 census, Mary Gifford, aged 44, was the owner of a 'messuage with garden, orchard and close, half an acre called The George Inn, Woodlands'. Samuel Wilkins was the licensee and the building was occupied by three men and three women.

In 1822 it was auctioned off as the property of the late John Stevens, and bought by James Hoddinott. He was still there in 1838 as owner-occupier when his poor wife Emma died of fright, as this report in the *Berkshire Chronicle* of 25 August records:

> On Monday night last a quarrel took place between some persons at the George Inn, Frome Woodlands; and on the landlord interfering to restore order, his wife (Mrs Hoddinott) became so exceedingly frightened that she expired in a fit. The deceased has left five children, the youngest being only five weeks old. An inquest has since been held and a verdict returned, 'Died from a shock given to the nervous system occasioned by fear'.

John Stevens was still there three years later, the 1841 census recording him as a widower, aged 40. The next recorded event is in 1855, when a James Randell sold the place at auction along with all stock in trade, household furniture, etc.

James Morgan is listed in the 1861 census as 'inn keeper, farmer and wood dealer', aged 41, with his wife Fanny, six children and three servants, which must have been quite a houseful. In 1880, he handed over to Francis Rendall, who was described in the 1881 census as a farmer of 104 acres and publican, aged 35, and was living there with his wife, Georgina, and two children. The last record of it as an inn comes in 1889, when Georgina Rendall was the licensee. It seems to have closed shortly afterwards and is now a private house.

The George today, now a private house

Globe, Back Lane (now Eagle Lane)

The only known reference to this pub comes from the Frome map of 1774, where it is shown on the corner of Anchor Barton and Back Lane (now Eagle Lane) The area was cleared around 1810 and has now largely disappeared under Bath Street. If the 1774 map is compared to Crocker's map of 1808 its location approximates to a plot numbered 49, described as a dwelling house owned by the trustees of the late John Stevens and occupied by Elizabeth Porch, wife of George Porch, upholsterer, and later landlord of the nearby Wheatsheaves.

Globe, 31 Vallis Way

Described in the Listed Buildings Record as a 'mid-nineteenth-century remodelling of a 1680s house'. The first record of this beerhouse comes from the *Bristol Mercury* of May 1847:

> FIRE – On Wednesday night a carter, in the employ of Mr Francis of the Globe Inn Frome, while attending to his horse in the stable, accidentally caught the straw on fire. The whole of the stabling was burnt to the ground but the horses were rescued.

Samuel Francis, who was from Beckington, survived the trauma. Quite possibly, he was the first landlord, which would fit in with the 'mid-nineteenth-century remodelling' of the building. He was still there at the time of the 1851 census, aged 52, with his sister Prudence Ashby, who later became matron at the Keyford Hospital for old men.

He had gone by the time of the 1861 census, replaced by Francis Forehead, aged 45, and his wife Eliza. In 1863, Forehead moved to the Rifleman's Arms at Murtrey, and by 1868 Robert Ames had taken over the Globe. He got into a spot of bother after ten women – some of them well-known prostitutes – were found drunk on the premises. Despite the police admitting that they had been sent for, he was fined forty shillings. In 1871, Charles Morgan, landlord and carpenter, received a special caution for selling outside of permitted hours, despite having been at the Globe for only a couple of months, but, apart from that the place seems to have slipped quietly through the next 100 years without little untoward to report: a man fell down drunk near it in 1891, resulting in fourteen days' imprisonment, and in 1908 two

The Old Globe in 2004

people started fighting and refused to leave. They became abusive to the landlord, but by the time the police arrived they had gone! Lack of news would indicate that it was a quiet and well-run house.

It eventually received a full licence, and in 1987 Usher's Brewery carried out major structural alterations and reopened the pub – now renamed the Trinity – with landlord Clive Thirwell. Next year they sold it to their rivals and fellow Wiltshire Brewers, Gibbs Mew. Another revamp took place in 1997, and, after unsuccessful attempts by the brewers to sell it, they spend £35,000 gutting the interior and refurbishing it once again – changing its name back to the Old Globe Inn. Despite some initial success, it was put up for sale again in 2003. After a period of repeatedly closing and reopening, it closed for good in 2010 and is now a private house.

Great Western Hotel / Live and Let Live, 42 Portway

Coach travel was the mainstay of many inns, but the arrival of the railways seriously dented this aspect of their trade. Railways gave rise to a new breed of public house, however. Wherever a railway line appeared, pubs and hotels sprang up in response. One of these was the Great Western. It did not begin life under that name, however, but as the Live and Let Live on what was then Coal Ash Walk.

The life of the Live and Let Live was brief. It began with Alfred Happerfield, who was granted the first licence in 1859 – but not without objections from Mr Williamson of the nearby Railway Inn. The bench readily appreciated the reasons behind Williamson's objections – the new venture was competition for the Railway Inn, being ideally situated as a watering hole for railway passengers. Nevertheless, they granted a license to Happerfield!

A view of the Portway in the 1960s with the former Great Western on the right

Alfred Happerfield suffered a good deal from other troublesome neighbours. He was also a farmer and in January 1860 sued Thomas Pope for letting cattle stray onto his land. The creatures destroyed and ate 'sundry wheat, potatoes, mangold murtzel [sic], cabbages, and brocoli [sic]'.

Happerfield also made problems for himself. In 1861 he was in trouble for possessing six pint-measures that were deficient in quantity and when he appeared in court his behaviour can hardly be described as respectful. As one newspaper reported, 'Mr Happerfield occasioned considerable merriment by the sensible defence he made. He said he was of the opinion that he might as well say nothing as summat.'

It seems likely that the Live and Let Live was not the most refined of public houses. In 1865 Albert Drew was charged with assaulting PC Keevill. Drew had been drinking there and afterwards caused a great disturbance in the street, along with some other 'roughs.' When Keevill ordered him home, he became abusive and kicked the constable violently in the knee. He was fined £2, or one month's hard labour in default. Wisely he chose to pay the fine.

By 1871, Alfred Happerfield was dead, his widow Lydia had moved up the road to manage the White Horse at Portway, and the Live and Let Live was in the hands of Charles Dyer – a wool dyer – and his wife Harriet, who was a laundress. The Dyers also had to contend with some rowdy clientele. In 1875, Charles Dyer was summoned to shed light upon a fight that had occurred at the pub. Not wishing to alienate any customers, he denied all useful knowledge of the dispute – much to the amusement of those in court. 'They got at it in the passages, and both of 'em were altogether,' was his description of the fracas. As to who threw the first punch, Dyer didn't know. Case dismissed.

Dyer left soon afterwards and the next landlord was Bristol-born Joseph Williams. He moved to Frome as a young man with his father, Henry, who opened a fruiterer's and fishmonger's in Cheap Street, but later went on to run the Victoria Inn, just up the road from the Live and Let Live. Joseph Williams changed the name of the pub to the Great Western, and in 1884 it was advertised to let as 'that well known roadside Inn, the Great Western, situate on Portway, Frome. Apply to Mr Joseph Williams, on the premises; or at the Lamb Brewery, Frome'.

The Great Western was transferred to Frank Gould, and Joseph Williams moved a few hundred yards up the road to the Railway Inn, where he was licensee for a number of years before moving to Marston Back Lane and working as a butcher. He died in 1928.

Frank Gould began his career in the licensing trade as an ostler in the tap room at the George, before taking over the Great Western in 1884, aged 29. Sadly, his time there was cut short, and he died in 1888, leaving his wife Elizabeth to run the inn. Her widowhood was equally brief for Elizabeth swiftly remarried. By 1890 her new husband, John H Lambert, was the licensee, and the couple were assisted by a young servant called Matilda Lintern. Elizabeth Lambert died in 1892, aged just 38, and, when John Lambert followed her to the grave two years later, it was Matilda who took over the Great Western.

Matilda herself was soon married, to George Henry Budden, an employee of the Great Western Railway, who had been born in Bridport in 1872 and started his working life as a railway guard. He married Matilda in 1895, took over the licence of the pub and rapidly became a dynamic force in Frome's economic and social life.

Amongst his many achievements, Budden founded the Frome and District Coursing Club – an attempt to deal with illegal sport and poaching. He also helped form the Great Western Quoit Club and an Angling Society. He was also secretary to the Great Western Benefit Society, vice-president and later president of the Frome and District Licensed Victuallers' Association, primo at the local lodge of Buffaloes and director of the Frome Aerated Water Company. The sudden and early death of a dynamic man like Budden was a tremendous loss to the town, and this was reflected in the great pomp surrounding his funeral in 1913. His coffin was conveyed on an open carriage, followed by three mourning coaches and 150 representatives from numerous organisations. Most of Frome's publicans attended, as did dozens of tradesmen and a contingent of uniformed railwaymen. The flag of the local Conservative Club hung at half-mast and hundreds of Frome's residents lined the streets. After George's death Matilda resumed her old role as licensee in her own right. In 1926 she retired to 30 Victoria Road where she died in 1941.

After Matilda retired, the Great Western was taken over by Edwin Say. A native of Rudge, Edwin had a sound track record in the pub trade in Frome. He had been licensee of the Somerset Arms for twelve years before moving to the Crown at Keyford for twelve and a half years. Edwin spent 18 years at the Great Western and died there in 1945. His funeral was also an impressive affair, with many of his fellow publicans in attendance, although his widow Mabel was too ill to attend. He left his entire estate to his niece, Alice Florence Ada Hillier. Mabel continued to run the place, although by 1951 Alice Hillier had taken over. Mabel died in 1953. The Great Western had two more licensees after this, during which period it has been described as very much a 'man's pub'. It closed by 1961, and during the 1980s was used as a Tax and Revenue Office, after which it became a private house, called appropriately Great Western House.

The former Great Western in 2012

Greyhound, 52-54 Milk Street

An inn called the Greyhound was first mentioned in 1739 in the will of Daniel Yerbury, but it is not certain that it was the one in Milk Street as no location is given. Entries in the churchwarden's accounts from 1781 to 1799 show that Joseph Mintrim, then Benjamin Carpenter, paid the rates the rates on the Greyhound. Mintrim also owned the Black Swan and possibly the Champneys Arms at some point, while Carpenter also owned part of the Pack Horse.

The first definite mention of the Greyhound in Milk Street comes in a newspaper report from January 1868, when William Norvill was fined forty shillings for selling 'at illegal hours'. He claimed that the imbibers were carol singers and that the beer was given to them, but the fact that the offence took place on 12 January probably didn't help his case.

A conveyance of 1887 mentions a couple of tenements owned by William Norville being converted into one house and run as the Greyhound. The property is covered in render, making it difficult to see its original construction, but quite possibly it was two cottages, similar to the one to the left, before being refronted.

There are various newspaper reports of drunken and unseemly behaviour at the house, and in 1869 Norvill was again warned about selling outside permitted hours. He

The former Greyhound in 2014

died in 1876 and the pub passed briefly through his widow and others to Frank Haddrill, who was described as a publican and joiner in the census of 1881. He was there just long enough to get nicked for allowing drunkenness and being drunk himself, after a policeman found two women drunk outside the house and bravely ventured inside. Haddrill was fined £10 and his pub was described as a disgrace to the town. He soon left and there were three more landlords in the space of a year.

Once a pub has a bad reputation, it is very hard to clear its name and this one was no exception. It closed around 1888 and never reopened, which was no great inconvenience as there were a number of others in the same short street. Today, as Conigar Cottage it is divided into flats.

Griffin, 25 Milk Street

The Griffin is another of Frome's very old pubs, going since at least 1717 when it was mentioned in the church rates as belonging to Robert Saxon. By the time of the 1785 census, it was owned by the Pobjoy family, who employed five men and four women, with Michael Ashman as licensee. The Pobjoys held it until about 1802 when a Mrs Brown took over.

In April 1818, Constable Gregory was hot on the trail of the evil doer as always:

> Sunday, found a man drinking at the Griffin, severely reprimanded the landlady and took the man some way in order to confine him in the stocks, but let him go as he was penitent and very civil.

That September, he 'found two men at the Griffin [presumably drinking after hours], they said they were lodgers.' Mrs Brown's ownership continued until about 1833, with William Stride as licensee for most of that time. A short note in the *Bath Chronicle* for 1838 reports the death of Mrs Stride of the Griffin Inn aged 82.

When Mrs Brown sold up or died around 1832-3, it seems that the new owners wanted to do the place up a bit. Frome Museum has a number of receipts from the period, covering items such as reroofing the brewhouse, repairing windows and doors, and giving the building a lick of paint. A man was employed for seven days at three shillings per day, and a painter for one day again at three shillings. A new kitchen grate with oven and boiler was also bought from the ironfounder, Edward Cockey, for £2 10s.

Mrs Ann Hobbs and her husband John took over in the 1830s. A report from the *Leicester Chronicle* of 15 March 1834 suggests she was not a lady to be trifled with. Mrs Hobbs was there until about 1840 when the premises passed to Henry Taylor and, by the time of the 1851 census, to John Collins, who was living there with his wife Elizabeth, four children, his mother-in-law, a servant, and Sam Cook, a wool stapler and presumably lodger.

In 1872 landlord Elijah Trollope was charged with assaulting Ellen Inglis. She said he beat her son for throwing stones and, when she went to see him, he called her a trollop – an odd choice of insult under the circumstances – and assaulted her, while he accused her of calling him names. The magistrates obviously thought it was six of one and half a dozen of the other and the case was dismissed. Thomas Norris was there in 1881 with his wife Mary-Ann, and they were both still there in 1891, now in their late sixties or early seventies.

By 1915 the landlord was Samuel Henry Henning, who was killed in action in France in August 1918, aged 25. He was hit in the head by 'a stray machine gun bullet' as he came out of the trenches and was buried with full military honours. His widow Evelyn carried on running the pub, with her three children, and later married Walter King. They ran the pub together until his death in 1932, when the licence reverted to her. After she retired, the Griffin was taken on by Fred Turk for a couple of years, before Joyce Moore, daughter of Samuel and Evelyn Henning, returned to run it with her husband

> ATTEMPT AT ROBBERY, AND FEMALE HEROISM.—Wednesday night two men called at the Griffin Inn, Frome, pretending to be just arrived and fatigued. They asked for a bed, when Mrs. Hobbs, the landlady, consented to their sleeping there, but could not immediately show them to their room, she being at the time engaged; when a third, who professed to have slept there before, offered to show them where to go. Mrs. Hobbs, on second thoughts suspecting all was not right, went up stairs, and discovered that the three men were in another room where a farmer was sleeping, to which room she proceeded alone, and detected the villains rifling the sleeping farmer's small-clothes. She closed the bed-room door, and would not allow them to leave until she had possession of the whole property, upwards of £30. Unfortunately, Mrs. Hobbs, in her alarm, let the villains escape with only a few blows to assist them down stairs. The farmer had been exposing his money during the day.

The Griffin Darts Team, 1924

Blocked entrance in the cellar.
A Frome tunnel or another room?

The Griffin in 2013

Charlie Moore. Charlie died in 1972, after which his widow followed the family tradition and carried on alone until retiring at the age of 68 in 1980. She has fond memories of her 65-year association with the place – her biggest fear being that a pint will become too expensive for ordinary people to enjoy!

There then followed a period of uncertainty, with the pub closing for a year and then going through a number of owners and landlords before being taken over by Nick Bramwell and Rick Lyall in 1999. They not only revamped the old place but reopened the brewery at the back, winning award after award for their home-brewed beers. The Griffin is now generally open only in the evenings, due to the demands of the brewery, but has become what every pub should be, independently run by people who love the trade and have a loyal customer base, a proper 'local' and an asset to the community. In 2010, it was awarded the coveted title of Pub of the Year by the Bath & Borders branch of the Campaign for Real Ale (CAMRA).

Half Moon, Castle Street (formerly Long Row)

Nothing much is known about the Half Moon before about 1870, although the building probably dates from the late seventeenth century. Deeds with Mendip Council refer to the conveyance of the property from Thomas Howell, a baker who moved to Canada, to ER Trotman, a brewer. In the census of 1871, Henry Wilkins, 'cellerman at brewery and beerhouse keeper', is shown as in residence, aged 27, with wife Ann. He got his name in the papers with an amusing case from 1879 (see right).

The pub was mentioned again in a fascinating and more serious case, reported in the *Frome Times* of 10 January 1883, under the heading,

POLICE NEWS.

PETTY SESSIONS, February 27th.—(Before P. Le Gros, and G. Walters, Esqs.)
CASE DISMISSED.
George Coleman was summoned for having on the 15th of February, unlawfully and wantonly disturbed Henry Wilkins, of the Half Moon beerhouse, Long-row, by knocking at his door and windows. Acting-Sergt. Milton, and P.C. Walter Parsons, proved hearing the disturbance, but as the landlord said it did not disturb him the case was dismissed.

'Tears of a Clown'. A man who had been staying at the Half Moon was found in the back yard with his throat cut. He survived this attempt at suicide, and it later emerged that he was Frederick Eugiene from Derbyshire, a well-known clown in the leading circuses of the day. However, he 'lost his engagements through intemperance' and was eventually induced to sign the pledge. Now known as 'the Converted Clown', he told his companions that they might call him 'Chump' and henceforth he was known by that nickname. He had toured the country as a temperance speaker holding 'thousands of persons almost spellbound by his eloquence', but recently, whilst 'earning an honest penny' selling umbrellas in Yeovil Market, he had mistaken a glass of brandy and aerated water for a glass of lemonade at a railway station, and was then 'unable to control his craving for more liquor'. 'It is expected,' concluded the report, 'that as soon as circumstances permit he will resume his profession as a temperance lecturer and many sympathising friends are willing to assist him in making a fresh start.'

A sad, but ultimately uplifting tale of a man fallen from grace but overcoming his failings and putting his past behind him, a tale beloved of Victorian moralists ... or was it? A short time later the same newspaper carried the following report:

THE ATTEMPTED SUICIDE BY A TEMPERANCE LECTURER

The 'Converted Clown', Frederick Eugiene, who attempted suicide in the Half Moon Yard three weeks ago, has made an interesting and somewhat startling statement respecting his life. When the news became known, intense surprise and regret was not only felt and expressed by temperance supporters generally, but another and unlooked-for effect was produced. It caused inquiries to be made respecting Eugiene, because someone in the east of England believed him to be a person by the name of George Fredrick Cook, and that belief resulted in investigations which established Eugiene's identity as Cook. It was found to be true that he had led a nomadic life, but the autobiographical account which he had given of himself in a teetotal print and in a lecture was at least in many if not absolutely untrue in all particulars [sic]. In fact he makes himself out to be a consummate hypocrite.

In 1898, Henry Wilkins was succeeded by a Mr Elton, who was in turn succeeded by Robert Cox in 1900. In 1909, Cox was 'engaged in fixing new cowls on the roof of the washing shed when he fell over the side of the roof owing to the ladder being dislodged by the high wind. The unfortunate man fell a distance of about 20 feet. No bones appear to have been broken but Mr Cox was terribly shaken.'

The house was owned by Frome United Breweries and Cox was still there in 1922 when the County Licensing Committee decided to close it down. He pleaded that he had been there for 22 years, averaged 300 customers a week, was making a living and was keen to stay. For reasons best known to themselves, the bench still refused to renew the licence and Cox was awarded £929 9s 4d compensation.

Much later the building fell on hard times, becoming a victim of planning blight in the early 1970s when the council thought they might put a road through it. Eventually they decided that they wouldn't, but not before the place was so bad that you could see the stars through the roof from the ground floor. It was rescued and restored by a local developer and is now a family home.

Half Moon Cottage in 2014

Half Way House, Clink Road

It is difficult to find out much about this one. Although the building is probably eighteenth century – with a datestone of 1723 above the window on the left-hand gable – it could not have opened as a beerhouse before the passing of the Beerhouse Act in 1830.

It seems to have been the residence of Jeremiah Singer, a 30-year-old farmer described in the 1861 census as having 32 acres and living with his wife Jane and young son 'at Clink', which we assume to be Clink Farmhouse. Although Singer was a farmer, it was common for an innkeeper to have two occupations. It was also common for a pub to be run by a woman, so his wife Jane may have run the place in the early days while Jeremiah was out farming.

John Lewis and his wife Maria from Upton Scudamore are recorded in the press as living at a beerhouse in Clink Road and having their application for a renewal of their licence declined in 1872, as the house was badly conducted and there were too many in the area already. We assume this to be the Half Way House, though there is no direct reference. Shortly after this, there is a reference to the 'beerhouse at Clink kept by Jeremiah Singer' having its licence refused 'in consequence of complaints'. Singer successfully appealed to the Quarter Sessions in January 1873, and there are no further references to the Lewis family.

In 1877 a 14-year lease began, and the house had a new landlord, William Bethell. Four years later, in 1881, when the freehold was put up for auction, it was occupied by Sydney Smith as under-tenant, while various bits of land attached to it were in the occupation of Jeremiah Singer. It seems that it failed to reach its reserve and was unsold. Sidney Smith – a 'cattle dealer and inn keeper' aged 38 from Westbury – was still there in 1882.

The former Halfway House in 2014

On 27 August 1887, the Somerset Standard reported an application to move the beerhouse from its present location in part of the farmhouse to a site nearer to the main road, as 'the present licensed house was about the most inconvenient place their worships could possibly conceive, and how people got there was a marvel ... Part farmhouse and part beerhouse, persons going there had to run the risk of getting immersed in a big pond and traverse 80 or 90 yards of dangerous road before they could get to it.'

JD Knight, brewer, of the Castle on Catherine Hill had entered into negotiations to purchase the proposed new property and was prepared to spend in the region of £50 on it if the application was successful. There were objections from nearby residents and their solicitor smelt a rat, pointing out that the current licence ran out in about four years and that this was no more than a ploy to get it renewed through the back door. The magistrates retired for a think and returned to decline the application.

The licensee throughout all this was James Garrett, who stayed on for a couple more years before moving to the Anchor in Catherine Street, where his family remained until about 1950. The last few months were seen out by Henry Hansford, and, when the tenancy ran out in August 1891, the doors closed for good.

As a sequel to all this, Freddie Giles, local restaurateur and owner of The George bought the farmhouse and lived in it for several years, at one point in 1976 applying to turn it into a pub and shops! Once again this was refused and the area is now heavily developed though the fine-looking building has survived.

Horse & Groom, Portway

This first appears on the map of 1774 and, in the 1785 census, Charles Greatwood is listed as the owner, with William Baker as publican. However, it may originally have been known as the Horse & Jockey, for in 1772 Thomas Horner recorded that Charles Greatwood, who kept the Horse & Jockey in Frome, had been accused of assaulting a couple after they complained of receiving short measures, and, when they refused to pay, of taking their hats and an apron as payment. The charge was dismissed, but he was convicted of selling unlawful measures, and ordered to return the couple's clothing.

When Charles Greatwood died in 1799, his will mentioning a 'dwellinghouse called the Horse & Jockey near Garston', and in 1812 this was referred to as 'all that tenement, brewhouse, backside and garden in or near Garston now occupied by William Hurle bounded on front or south by the highway from Frome to Warminster, formerly lands of John Smith and conveyed in January 1781 to Charles Greatwood'. Given the interchangeability of the names 'Horse & Groom' and 'Horse & Jockey' (see, for example, the following entries for the Horse & Groom and Horse & Jockey at East Woodlands), it seems likely that this was one and the same pub.

It is seems likely that, before Charles Greatwood was there, it had been a pub called the Wyredrawers Arms (see separate entry), but until further information turns up this must remain speculation. By the time of Greatwood's death, however, despite the later reference to a brewhouse, it seems to have been a 'dwelling house' rather than a pub. The plot and buildings appear on the 1813 Cruse map of the town and research by Derek Gill has identified No 17 Portway as the building in question. It is still there today, a substantial building of the sort which commonly would have had its own brewhouse until well into the nineteenth century.

Horse & Groom, East Woodlands

Another of the pubs once owned by the Marquis of Bath. There is mention in the church rates as early as 1770 of a piece of land being 'by the Horse & Groom', but the first proper reference comes in the census of 1785 when the lease was owned by Edward Pope and Joseph Hoddinott was the publican. The building and grounds was then occupied by 'two men, two women and four cows'.

The Hoddinott family was still running the pub in 1835 when the lease was sold at auction to William Peters, who is still shown as the owner on the tithe map of 1840. Now things get very confused, as just across the road was a pub called the Horse & Jockey, which was also owned by Mr Peters. The first census of 1841 lists James Hoddinott, a publican aged 45, living with his wife Emma and three children in Lower Woodlands so this we assume to be the Horse & Groom, but there is no pub name mentioned and they could have been across the road.

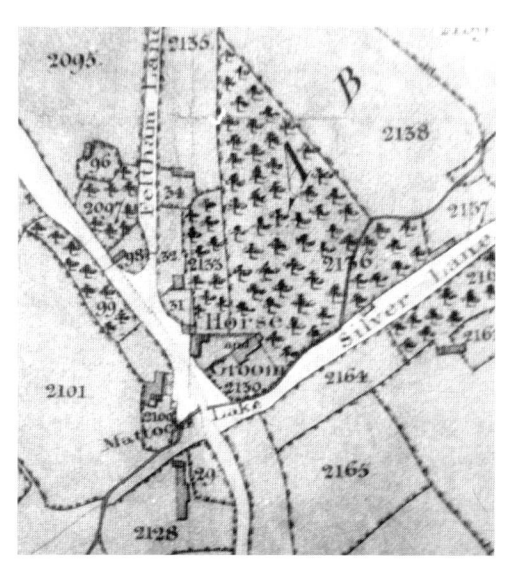

On the 1813 Jeremiah Cruse map, the Horse & Groom is clearly marked on the corner of Silver Lane and Feltham Lane

The Horse & Groom in 2013

In the 1851 census the Horse & Groom is being run and occupied by Henry Francis, an innkeeper and farmer of 32 acres, with his wife and three children. The family was still there in 1861, and six years later the leases of the Horse & Groom and the Horse & Jockey were put up for auction as separate lots at the Crown Hotel in the Market Place. The Horse & Groom was listed as

> all that valuable leasehold inn with the buildings, yard, garden and premises thereto belonging called the 'Horse & Groom' with [several] pieces of land, situate at the East Woodlands in the parish of Frome and occupied by Mr Henry Francis as tenant and held under the Marquis of Bath for the remainder of 99 years.

The lease was purchased by J Knight for £440.

The 1871 census listed Henry Francis as a publican and farmer, now living over the road at the Horse & Jockey, and it seems that Henry and his family stayed on as they are still listed in the *Directory* of 1875, by which time he would have been about 67. A couple of other licensees took over until 1880, when the pub was run by Job Hill from Dilton Marsh. He stayed there until 1901, when it seems that he moved across the road to the Horse & Jockey, passing the place on to Herbert Coleman of London. In 1916, it was taken over by Lewis Curtis, who was there until the 1930s.

The next few decades were pretty uneventful. A report in the *Somerset Standard* for August 1972 recorded the departure of Stanley Francis, local councillor and landlord for the previous 31 years, with a bit of a do attended by Lord Bath. Today the pub is still flourishing and appeared in a recent edition of the *Good Beer Guide*.

Horse & Jockey, Mattocks Lake, Silver Lane

Like the Horse & Groom directly opposite, this pub is first mentioned in the churchwarden's accounts in 1770 when the rates were paid by James Pope, Richard Whittington and John Guy. There was a Richard Whittington shown as owning a pub called the Cat in the same area in 1753, and Edward Pope is described as the owner in the Longleat Estate papers of 1780. Pope is described as 'Quartermaster Sergeant in the Portsmouth Division of the Marines, lessee of an alehouse known as the Horse & Jockey Feltham Marsh'. Other Longleat papers show that he was still the leaseholder in 1785.

Former tenants are said to have included John Boyce, Richard Pobjoy and William Pobjoy. The next mention is in 1800 when the rates are paid by James Hoddinott, probably from the family that ran the Horse & Groom. In fact, the two pubs seem so interlinked that it is possibly that they were owned and run together, at least in the early days.

The Cruse map of 1813 (reproduced on the previous page) shows the building at the crossroads (plot 2100), marked Mattocks Lake house and garden, but does not name the pub. By the time of the 1840 tithe map and 1841 census, both properties are leased by William Peters, with a John Peters and family in the Jockey and James Hoddinott with his family in the Groom.

In 1867 both houses were put up for auction at the Crown in Frome. Lot 6 was 'all those two leasehold tenements or dwelling houses formerly known as the Old Horse & Jockey ... situate at East Woodlands ... now occupied by Charles Trollop, William Coleman, and Henry Francis as tenants ... held under the Marquess of Bath. Bought by Mr Trollop for £150'. The wording suggests that it was no longer functioning as a pub, but the census of 1871 records Charles Trollope, a 48-year-old widower and beerhouse keeper, there with his four children. He was still there in the 1881 census and died in 1895.

In 1901 the Marquess of Bath granted a 21-year lease to Frome United Breweries, who undertook

The former Horse & Jockey in 2014

'at all times [to] keep [the] dwelling house to be kept and used as an Inn and to be managed in a proper and orderly manner using their best endeavours to provide and extend the trade thereof'. They appointed Job Hill as 'under tenant', and he moved across the road from the Groom to become the new landlord. The Horse & Jockey seems to have closed shortly afterwards.

King of Prussia, 62-63 Naishes Street

The King of Prussia is shown on the map of 1774, even though it had been refused a licence by the local magistrates three years earlier. In the 1785 Frome census it was owned was Mr Barnard, and by 1792 the rates refer to it as owned by 'Edward Barnard late Daniel Wayland'. It was named after Frederick II, King of Prussia from 1740 to 1786. He allied his armies with England against the French in 1756 and became a popular hero, with several pubs named after him around the country.

The Cruse map of 1813 shows it occupying two cottages, with a rear entrance to the yard in Brandy Lane (now Baker Street), although it had probably closed by then, as the last reference we have is from the church rates of 1799, when it was still owned by Edward Barnard. The Dixon & Maitland map of 1838 shows it divided in two.

Roger Leech, in *The Royal Commission on Historic Monuments Report on the Trinity Area of Frome*, states that it was formerly one building, later divided into two cottages, and estimates that it dates from around 1700. He goes on to say that it was 'probably the Dolphin' but gives no source for this statement. One indication is that both pubs were owned by Daniel Wayland, the Old Dolphin from around 1770 to 1791, and the King of Prussia sometime before 1793. It is possible that it changed its name from the Dolphin, but the church rates of 1770 place the Dolphin in the Market Place, so it is a confusing picture and more research needs to be done.

The former King of Prussia in 2013

King's Arms, Milk Street

One of a number of pubs in this short street, most of which were on the left-hand side as you walk towards the Griffin, and were demolished in the 1960s clearances.

The only record of it found so far comes in the census of 1785, when Edmund Hatson was the publican, Mr Sweetland the proprietor, and three men and two women occupied the building.

King's Head, The Butts

The church rates on this plot were paid by Thomas Brown in 1770, with the King's Head listed as 'void and uncollected'. In the census of 1785 James Hayes is listed as the owner and Ann Harris as the publican, while a 'cardmaker' called Samuel Allard, along with two other men and four other women, also lived there. Charles King was the ratepayer between 1781 and 1791, and from 1792 until 1824 it was Samuel Allard, with the last entry describing the property as 'King's Head orchard'.

The 1813 Cruse map and survey shows a sizeable plot numbered 887-890, including the house, gardens and meadows on the road to Marston and Shepton Mallet with plenty of room for coaches and travellers to pull in. The Reverend JM Rogers is shown as the owner with Samuel Allard in occupation.

In 1823 the rental entry reads: 'James Browning. John George Late the King's Head now a garden and house built thereon'. It seems that, although the inn had closed, the name continued to be used. In 1919 the plot was sold at auction by the Longleat estate as 'Lot 46: Close of pasture near the Butts known as King's Head Paddock'. It was sold to the tenant, Mr FW George for £280.

In 1947, the 'freehold land called the King's Head at The Butts opposite Rossiters Road' was sold again, 'to SMR Henley, 103 Nunney Road, Frome.

Nothing else is known.

King's Head, 1 Trinity Street (formerly Cross Street)

The building at what is now 1 Trinity Street is much altered since the photograph below was taken in the early twentieth century. A lovely little row of seventeenth-century buildings sandwiched between the overbearing Selwood Printing Works on the left and some drab brick-built tenements on the right, it is lucky to have survived the notorious clearances of the 1960s which destroyed so much of the area. Early on, this short stretch of road was known as Cross Street, and is sometimes referred to as Whatley Corner or Whatley Corner Market, though the derivation of this name is unclear.

The King's Head is first mentioned in the church rates of 1744 when it was owned by Richard Pobjay, and appears on the map of 1774. Rev Daniel, in his *Street Names of Frome*, states

In this early twentieth-century photograph, the King's Head, still with its original gables, can be seen in the distance on the right, with a group of people around the door

that 'the rights of toll were exercised by the owner of the King's Head Inn until they were extinguished when the Market Company bought the right of market from Lord Cork. Stalls were set up in Cross Street and a toll was payable through Whittocks Lane as far as St Catherine's Chantry.'

In the 1785 census James Cook is shown as the owner and William Jefferies as the publican, with the house occupied by two men and a woman. By 1818, when it was owned by Edmund Ashby and occupied by Charles Ashby, it was described as the 'King's Head and Market House Cross Street'. The Ashbys were there until 1840, being succeeded first by Henry Barber then by Henry Taylor.

Taylor retired in February 1860, having acquired considerable property whilst landlord. Newspaper reports claim that he had been in poor health for some time, 'caused by his fondness for drink', and in January 1861 he blew his brains out with a shotgun in an outside privy. He left a note blaming his brother-in-law James, whom he

The former King's Head in 2013

believed to be conspiring in some way with his wife Amelia. The census of that year shows Amelia Taylor as a 'retired inn keeper' living in Vallis Way with her children and a servant.

The next licensees were Charles and Louisa Miles. They had left by 1871, and in 1874 John Burgess was landlord. His wife Louisa was born in Umballa, India, and his family were at the King's Head until 1924. During his tenure the freehold was sold in 1889, under the will of James Knight, and purchased for £1,425 by the Frome Brewery Company. In 1919 he was fined 2s 6d for selling liquor to a child under 14 years of age in an unsealed container. John was succeeded by his son, Herbert Burgess, and Henry, the last of the line, died in 1924 and is buried in Vallis Road cemetery. There followed the usual line of brewery tenants without much incident until Watney's closed the place in 1970. Having been saved from demolition it has now been converted into flats.

Lamb / Cornerhouse, Gore Hedge and Christchurch Street East

The story of the Lamb is a tale of two halves since, midway through its history, the Lamb, like the chicken, crossed the road. It began on a site in Gore Hedge, the earliest reference dating back to 1693 when it was owned by the Whitchurch family, although it was almost certainly much older. In 1715 it was owned by Mrs Bull, passing to Betty Jenkins by 1753. Ownership then passed to Jane Bunn, sister of that great Frome man, Thomas Bunn. James Burt was landlord in 1785, succeeded in 1793 by George Markes.

By the 1800s it was an established commercial and market house, many market-goers preferring to put up at the top of the hill rather than descend to the Market Place. It was a good-sized inn with two bars and a smoking room on the ground floor. Upstairs was a sitting room set aside for the use of farmers' wives on market days. Located as it was on the main route to Warminster and beyond, it had obvious advantages for trade. Later, with the coming of the railway, it was the nearest 'inn of consequence' to the station.

A photograph from around 1880, with the Lamb Brewery on the right and the original Lamb Inn beyond it

Richard Baily was running the Lamb in the 1820s, after which his sons John and Thomas took over. John was a keen racehorse breeder but still found time to run the inn, and in 1853 the brothers founded the Lamb Brewery in premises adjoining the pub in the Gorehedge Triangle. The new brewery consumed the output of at least four local malthouses, including the brewery's own malthouse in Gentle Street, and the *Frome Times* of 24 April 1861 was moved to highlight the contrast between its immensity and the modest size of the old inn:

> Despite the paradox, the Lamb is undoubtedly one of the lions of Frome. For a two-fold reason it enjoys a celebrity peculiarly its own. In the first place the Lamb was a hostelry long before the very oldest inhabitant was even thought of; and,

in the next as a specimen of the architectural capabilities of our forefathers, the Lamb commands prominent attention. In the days when the Lamb was built people believed not in piling bricks steeple high. They could not have been so pressed for room then as we are now. Our forefathers had a liking for the substantial. Their aspirations did not reach to a fourth or fifth storey ... Even in this speculative age there are few who do not prefer a house on terra firma to a castle in the air ... An inn of the conservative kind is the Lamb; building reform has left it unscathed. Its roof of many pointed gables still attracts the attention of the visitor; and the dust of many years is preserved with religious care on its venerable walls ... and there are few old-fashioned towns which can boast of so old-fashioned an inn as the Lamb at Frome ... In the courtyard-like premises of the Lamb has recently arisen a new building which frowns down upon the Lamb as a giant would upon a pygmy. The builder of the old Lamb would not ascend above a storey – but see how high his descendant has ascended – four floors – under the guidance of host John Baily we are on the floor of the Lamb NEW Brewery.

The character of the inn in the mid-1800s was not always as spotless as the Bailys would have wished. In 1861, local customer James White quarrelled with his wife there and smashed her nose and one of her eyes. Such occurrences perhaps made hands-on public-house management quite unappealing to the Bailys. If John Baily had any spare time, he preferred to spend it on his prized thoroughbred horse, Rector. In 1858 he even offered a prize cup for the best colt sired by Rector. Mr Parker of Mells won the cup, with Mr Fussell of Chantry taking second place.

After they founded the brewery, the Baily brothers delegated the day-to-day running of the pub to tenants. William Perrett was licensee when the inn was robbed in 1873, and later that year his beautiful black-and-tan terrier was poisoned. It was widely held that the culprit was an embittered supporter of the defeated party in the recent elections. Personal politics were far more public in those days and the political persuasion of Mr Perrett would have been common knowledge. Prominent residents often found themselves mentioned in the various propaganda songs which circulated before elections and the Bailys, owners of the Lamb, were no exception – as a ballad from 1876, quoted on page 49, reveals.

The Lamb Inn at Gore Hedge disappeared in 1887 with an application from the Bailys to relocate the licence to alternative premises on Christchurch Street East. The old inn, which lacked adequate stabling and had no pavement outside, was demolished to expand the brewery. A new, more spacious Lamb Hotel soon opened just metres away in premises previously occupied by Frederick Snook's China and Glass Warehouse.

The first landlord of the new premises was John Jacob, followed by RA Wright, and two years later by Walter Edwin Yerbury. Yerbury was an enterprising chap, and wisely made the decision to marry Lily Bryant, the daughter of the landlord of the Angel in King Street.

Yerbury also ran into strife during election time. In August 1895, the *Somerset & Wiltshire Journal* published lurid accounts of the drunken shenanigans in Frome after the elections. 'Deplorable scenes of drunkenness and demoralization' and 'wholesale debauchery' prevailed. The shouts of drunken men were only drowned out by the screams of equally inebriated women. 'Youths and maidens of 13 and 16 were to be met staggering drunk, while the language they indulged in was profane and filthy.' The scenes were repeated the following day, with men fighting in the gutter and children reeling about drunk.

And where was the epicentre of this Bacchanalian debauch? The Lamb Hotel. Living opposite was Anna Burgess, who described scenes worse than anything seen during all her years in India! 'I am grieved to add that the drunkenness was not wholly confined to the so-called lower order,' she concluded in her letter to the *Journal*.

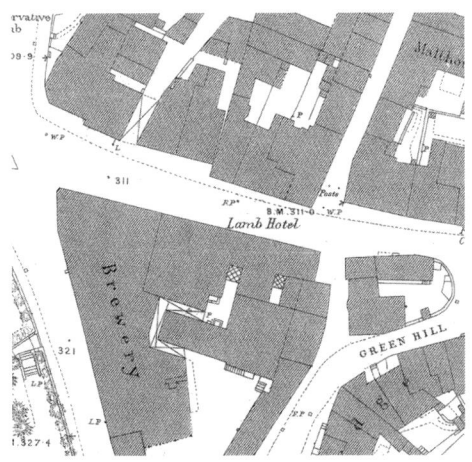

Above: An OS map of 1886 showing the Lamb before it moved to the corner of Christchurch Street East

Right: An invoice from 1898, shortly after Walter Yerbury took over the Lamb

Below: The Lamb Brewery

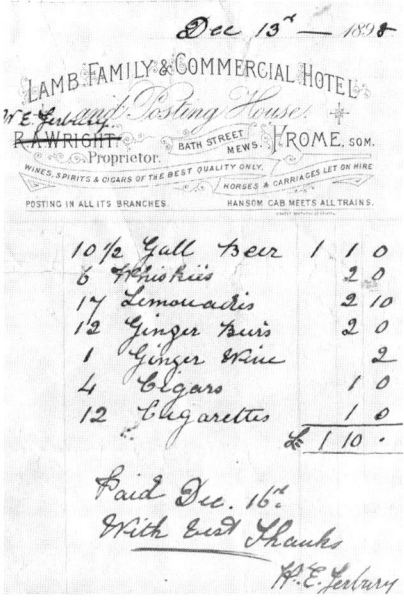

The newspaper's rival publication, the *Somerset Standard*, gleefully responded with alternative testimony, including an epistle from Mr Yerbury himself:

> I have been landlord of the Lamb Hotel for over five years. During those five years there has not been a single police complaint regarding my mode of conducting my business ... I was born and brought up here, and my fellow townsfolk know me and all belonging to me. Mrs Burgess is, I am told, the wife of a clergyman, and, therefore, should be acquainted with the scriptural injunction, 'Thou shalt not bear false witness against thy neightbour' ... No one who bears evidence of drunkeness is permitted to be served in my house.

The drunkenness Mrs Burgess claimed to have witnessed existed 'only in her excited and, I fear, hysterical imagination', insisted Yerbury, since the festivities at the Lamb consisted solely of two old ladies 'dancing with great vigour, and much hand-shaking and hearty congratulation'. Debauchery or genteel celebration? No doubt the truth lay somewhere in between. Interestingly, Walter Yerbury had only just buried his 27-year-old wife Lily a couple of weeks before the election. Within months, however, he had married the Lamb's barmaid. Walter, his new wife and their daughter Norah left in 1899, moving down to the Market Place to run first the Crown and then the Bull. Life, alas, did not go quite as he had planned at those establishments. But that's another story.

Meanwhile, Arthur Wall had taken over the Lamb, where in 1904 he had the misfortune to experience the curious case of the customer who liked driving over policemen. In November that year Edward Creed of Bruton was apprehended for being drunk in charge of a pony and trap. PC Keedwell had noticed Creed staggering up the road before disappearing into the Lamb. He emerged 20 minutes later, swaying wildly, and climbed into his trap. Keedwell, who was leaning on a lamp post at the corner of the street, was then almost run down by Creed. The constable called out, receiving the drunken response, 'I do like to drive over a policeman'. Incredibly, the pub's ostler testified that his customer was not drunk but simply burdened with a feisty pony. A case of the customer always being right? The magistrates emphatically ignored the ostler and convicted Creed.

The Lamb in 1905 ...

During World War One the Lamb was run by Frederick Webb and his wife. Like many others in Frome, they had a son in the forces and in October 1918 Philip Henry Webb was promoted to the rank of lieutenant in the Durham Light Infantry.

Both before and during World War Two, Frome (Pigeon) Fanciers Association held their meetings at the Lamb and during the post-war period it was a popular venue for Frome's numerous sports clubs, many of whom held their dinners and

... in 1992 ...

... and undergoing conversion to the Cornerhouse in 2007

AGMs there. In 1947, licensees Mr and Mrs Crew played host to the Home Guard Reunion Dinner when over 50 ex-Home Guards and guests sat down to a grand meal.

The Lamb closed in 2006, after years of decline had left much of the building ruinous. Few expected it to reopen, but Paul Edney and Lloyd Chamberlain of Blindmans Brewery, based at Leighton, to the west of Frome, took on the challenge of refurbishing it, and it reopened in January 2008. Renamed the Cornerhouse, it was not only the tap for Blindmans Brewery, but had as a restaurant and conference suite on the first floor, and seven ensuite rooms. In 2011, Paul and Lloyd sold the Cornerhouse to the Penguin Dining Company in order to devote more time to the brewery, but it continues to offer the same high standard of food, drink and accommodation.

Lamb & Fountain, 57 Castle Street (13 Fountain Lane)

The Lamb & Fountain is surely one of the oldest and least spoilt of the town's pubs. Originally recorded in the church rates for 1753 as 'The Fountain' in Fountain Lane, the first known owner was a Mrs Usher who paid the rates until 1783. The lack of 'Lamb' in the original description may have been the churchwarden's shorthand but from 1781 until 1799 it is referred to as the 'Old Fountain'. Mrs Usher's executors took over and the Frome census of 1785 shows John Moon as proprietor and publican with the place occupied by two men and seven women. Mrs Usher's executors continued to pay rates until 1792 when John Moon started paying them. There are indications that the building may be older still, as in 2005 a brick-built chamber was found beneath the building – probably an ice-house predating the existing structure.

By 1800 the pub is referred to in the church rates as the Lamb & Fountain, with brewhouse and cellar attached, owned by John Moon Sr with J Moon Jr manning the pumps. Maybe the new name celebrated a partial rebuild or renovation. When John Moon Sr died in 1829, the *Salisbury & Wiltshire Journal* described him as 'deservedly respected by all classes as a truly honest and honourable character and by his family as the best of husbands and fathers'. He left his estate to his five children and the inn was taken over by Samuel Moon. He was still there, aged 50, with his wife Elizabeth,

Above: The Lamb & Fountain, with the malthouse to the left, in 1979
Below: The Lamb & Fountain on the 1886 OS Map
Bottom: One of the cellars running under the pub

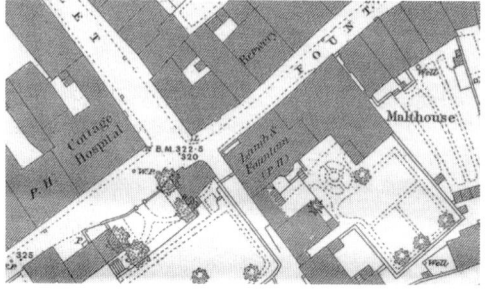

at the time of the 1841 census, but left in 1848 when Richard Bailey leased it from the Moon family. The Baileys remained until at least until the census of 1861, when Richard is described as a 'maltster and inn keeper', aged 65, from Batcombe, with wife Elizabeth and five employees.

The Moon estate was auctioned off in 1877, when Francis Wilkins was innkeeper. He had been there since before the census of 1871, in which he was described as 'innkeeper, farmer and brewer', which must have kept him busy. By 1881 he had four sons – one a solicitor's clerk – and was at the pub until 1891, when Alfred Austin Rossiter from the Queen's Head in Whittox Lane bought it, with his brother, for a sum in excess of £2,000.

Rossiter's advertisement in the *Somerset Standard* for February

1890 is impressive. Not only was 'Good Old Fashioned Beer' available at the pub, but he could 'supply families with beer in casks of any size', along with 'Champagnes, Whiskies, Ports, Sherries and Clarets' and promised to 'give customers the benefit of increased value as the concern was "absolutely free"'. Rossiter died in 1904 and the property was advertised to let by the Wilkins Brothers, brewers of Bradford on Avon. Their advertisement described it as a 'home-brewed house together with a three quarter brewery, in-going by valuation. No goodwill. Possession early in January'. This firm became a major brewery in Bradford and the surrounding area during the nineteenth century, before being taken over and closed down by Ushers of Trowbridge in 1914. When they purchased the Lamb & Fountain is not known, but the indications are that it was shortly after 1904.

After being one of the most settled pubs in Frome, it now went through a number of landlords including Thomas Relf, a former soldier who once had a pub in Wincanton, Charles Abbott, who was made bankrupt and become a caretaker at the Working Man's Club in Radstock, John Muir, a former travelling draper, and William Burnard from Gloucester, whose wife's parents were French.

Early in 1916, Fussell's of Rode bought the house, and Percy Fussell himself became licensee until a suitable manager could be found. They thought they had found one in William Burt, but Percy had to get back behind the bar himself, as Burt was about to be called up for military service. They placed adverts in the local paper to promote the pub along with their other Frome pub, the Crown at Keyford.

Yet more changes occurred as various other prospective licensees left for military service. After the war, Ernest Griffin took the helm and was there until around 1948. Fussell's were still the owners in 1946, when the council surveyor received a complaint about the condition of steps outside and informed Percy Fussell that the council were prepared to carry out repairs for a nominal charge of 2s 6d, which seems remarkably reasonable.

In 1968, Harry and Freda Searle took over the tenancy from the new owners of Fussell's, Bass Charringtons. Harry continued to work at Wallington & Weston's, leaving Freda to run the pub for much of the time. This may not have been as much of a challenge as it might seem, for she had been in the trade since the age of 14, when she started washing glasses at the Red Lion in Somerton. What was a problem, however, at least initially, was the lack of customers. In an interview for *This Is Bristol* in 2008, she recalled that 'the first Sunday we had one customer, and I cried and said we have lost our money. But then it got so busy I could not cope.' After Harry died, aged 56, in 1975, Freda was determined to carry on after other former pub landladies said it would help stave off loneliness. For a time, she continued to provide

The Lamb & Fountain in 2014

cooked meals, such as faggots and sausages and mash, but, although the pub no longer serves hot food, she still pickles the eggs which stand in a jar on the bar.

'Mother', as Freda is known to one and all, has seen many changes, and some memorable events. 'We nearly had a birth in the passage once,' she recalled in 2008, 'and another time we had funeral party in this bar, all crying, and then a wedding party arrived without warning in the other bar and all started singing.' Reflecting on how she had made the pub one of the best-loved in Frome, she explained that, 'you have to be a psychiatrist, a doctor and a bouncer, listen to other people's woes and always have a smile on your face.' Despite this, changing times and new legislation have brought new challenges. 'I have lost nine out of ten customers with the ban on smoking,' she admitted. 'It has ruined pub games too. People go out for a fag when they are playing darts and they lose concentration.' Nevertheless, 'Mothers', as it is universally known, remains very much a locals' pub and pretty much untouched since the late 'sixties, with a large former malthouse adjoining and the lower levels honeycombed with disused cellars and passages.*

Lamb & Lark, Woodlands

Despite its delightful name, very little is known about this beerhouse. The first we hear of it is in 1841, when, on 12 April, the *Salisbury & Winchester Journal* reported that James Pope, aged 48, had died of consumption at the Lamb & Lark, Frome Woodlands, on 28 March, leaving a wife and seven children. Two days earlier, however, the *Bristol Mercury* of 10 April 1841, had reported that James Pope of the Lamb & Lark had died 'lately, at Frome from the effects of a fall whilst out hunting'. While the manner of his death is unclear, it was followed, a couple of days later, by a further tragedy, for on 15 April the *Bath Chronicle* reported that on 'March 30, at the Lamb & Lark Inn, Frome, West Woodlands, the wife of Mr J Pope,' had been delivered of 'a dau[ghter] and a still-born son'.

Despite all this, the Lamb & Lark remained in the Pope family, possibly being run by Mr Pope's widow before being taken over by his son, also called James, who was listed as a 'farmer of 30 acres and retailer of beer' in the 1841 census. One of his brothers and two of his sisters – one of whom, Harriet, was his housekeeper – were also living with him. On the 1851 enumerators' returns, the farm-cum-beerhouse is shown as close to the Abbotts Moor and Gillenbury areas of Woodlands, and in the 1861 census James Pope, now married with three children, is described as a farmer living at Abbotts Moor Farm. Although it is possible that he moved to a

---

* The 2015 issue of The Frome Society Yearbook (No 18) has an article on the malthouse by Amber Patrick, with some interesting photos and interpretations. It is obtainable from Alastair MacLeay, Prospect House, Trudoxhill, BA11 5DP or Frome Museum.

new property, the likelihood is that, having decided to give up the beerhouse to concentrate on farming, he had renamed it accordingly, for there are no further references to the Lamb & Lark.

Masons Arms, Marston Gate

The Masons Arms was established by Samuel Hurd around 1862 'at great expense' to cater for both travellers and local workers. The name comes from Samuel's profession, for he was a mason who simply converted his home into a beerhouse, as was common at the time. In 1863, he applied for a full wine & spirit licence, claiming 'he was often asked for spirits and a licence would be an advantage to the neighbourhood as where there was prohibition there would be sure to be smuggled spirits'. Despite his well-worded argument, the application failed, as did another application the following year.

Hurd barely had time to settle into his new role before he died in 1866 and the inn was taken over by young Walter Francis and his wife Laura. Walter was well-suited, having grown up at the Horse & Groom in Woodlands where his father Henry was landlord. Nevertheless, Mrs and Mrs Francis did not remain long. Two doors down were farm worker Charles Austin and his family, including sons James, a copper and tin worker, and Joseph, a carpenter. From the early 1870s, various Austin family members ran the Masons Arms.

The Masons Arms, 2014 – a pub created from a row of cottages

First to try his hand was youngest son, Joseph. Unfortunately, by 1873 the respectability of the house under Joseph Austin was being called into question. In April that year, he was up before the magistrates for illegally serving beer on Sunday. A local policeman had found two men at the inn – and spotted a third man sprinting out of the back door. In court, Joseph Austin explained that he had not actually broken the law, for his pub was not open and he had simply provided refreshment for a man who had delivered some parsnip seeds. Not entirely convinced, the bench dismissed the case with the bizarre warning, 'don't deal in seed again on Sunday'. I think we know what they meant, but Joseph hardly heeded their words.

A decision was made to keep a close eye on the place. It was around this time that Joseph Austin handed over the reins to his older brother James, and moved to Easton in Gordano where he resumed his work as a carpenter. Joseph's wife had died young and presumably he wished to make a fresh start. In January 1876 James Austin was summonsed for keeping his house open during prohibited hours. PC Maidment had been sent to watch the house and had found Austin's father there, along with two customers, after closing time. He was not only fined but had his

Draymen outside the Masons Arms when Albert Yeates was licensee

licence endorsed – the first step on the road to losing it. It was not the last instance of such trouble. On a later occasion, PC Valentine found nine men and a half-gallon can of ale in the skittle alley after closing time. There had already been complaints to the police about the way the pub was run. Austin's solicitor knew there was no point denying what had happened, so he simply asked the bench to deal with the case leniently because 'a little licence was usually allowed publicans at Christmas time, in respect of the closing of their houses'. Bah, humbug. The magistrates levied a heavy fine and ordered Austin's licence to be endorsed. Likewise, the skittling men were dealt with harshly, each receiving a fine. Nevertheless, later that year James Austin had his licence renewed – with a dire warning from the magistrates. He was known to the police for after-hours drinking and his card was marked!

It was proving difficult to turn a profit, so by 1881 James Austin was also working away. He was in Radford in Nottinghamshire, leaving his wife Sarah to manage the Masons Arms single-handed – whilst raising eight-year-old Florence and one-year-old Henry! Hopefully, her in-laws, Charles and Sarah Austin, who lived two doors away, were of some help – although they were now in their seventies. Despite continued complaints about out-of-hours drinking, the Austin family were still in residence in 1886 when the Lamb Brewery put the lease up for sale.

In the late 1890s, another local man, Robert Wolsey Williams, took over. He was barely in his twenties and, when the Boer War broke out, his sense of adventure led him to enlist. Initially, his sister Rose took over on an ad-hoc basis before finally applying for the licence in her own name in early March 1900. Rose Williams only remained for another seven months and it is tempting to think that perhaps some prejudice against female licensees explains why. In reality, there were plenty of women running inns and beerhouses in Frome. The most likely explanation is Rose's age, for she was barely 21 when she took over and few people – male or female – ran such large houses alone at such a tender age. In October 1900, she handed the business over to Albert Yeates, a seasoned publican well suited to running a labourers' beerhouse.

Quite how Robert Wolsey Williams felt about the whole matter when he returned home wounded from the Boer War a few months later is impossible to know. Nevertheless, Albert Yeates was a good replacement, for he had successfully run a beerhouse in the Butts for a number of years. Former landlord Robert Williams seems to have simply licked his wounds, returned to the family home and married the girl next door. His wife was the daughter of James Austin, who had been landlord of the Masons just a few years earlier.

During World War One, James Jeffery took over. An ex-sergeant in the Royal Marines with 21 years' service, when he was not busy with the Masons Arms, Jeffery worked as a recruiting officer. Not that this meant he was immune to trouble with the authorities.

DORA – the word every landlord hated during World War One. Otherwise known as the Defence of the Realm Act, its effects were far-reaching and no doubt entirely pointless in the opinion of many. In August 1916, James Jeffery was summonsed for breaching the act. He had allegedly permitted customer Austin Smith to take a quart of beer from the premises after closing time. PC Underhill spotted Smith sneaking out of the pub's rear entrance with his illicit tipple, a bottle, tucked into his pocket. The PC dragged Smith back into the pub. 'I know nothing about it,' Jeffery declared, 'as I have been away and only got back five minutes before nine. I have served him nothing. Perhaps the missus has.' Indeed she had. Mrs Jeffery said that she had sold the bottle to Smith early in the evening, after which Smith had left. Unfortunately, Smith later bumped into a sailor friend and returned to the pub, with both his friend and the bottle. That was their story and they were sticking to it. The court was having none of it, and whilst they believed Mr Jeffery to be personally innocent, he was still fined as the proprietor in overall control.

In 1922, the local magistrates considered closing six Frome pubs, including the Masons Arms. After some consideration they decided that they would renew the licence if the owners closed up certain exits, a seemingly bizarre request which was nevertheless agreed to and trade was allowed to continue. Jeffery remained landlord for 27 years. He died in March 1950 aged 84, having spent his retirement at The Bungalow, Marston Gate. His genial disposition had earned him a wide circle of friends and on the day of his funeral the flag of the Conservative Club flew at half-mast.

In 1947 the *Masons Arms* was finally granted a full 'on-licence' for wines and spirits. Two decades later, the pub was freed from brewery control. It became a free house under the ownership of Nancy Moore, who extended it into two adjoining cottages and opened a lounge bar and restaurant. In 1979 the pub was acquired by Trowbridge property developer Kenneth Evans who gutted and modernised the adjoining cottages. The interior was revamped and parking added on both sides of the road to attract passing motorists. New managers were installed – Clare and Ralph Williams, experienced licensees from Bristol. In 1993 the pub returned to brewery control as part of the Ushers chain. It closed in mid-2009 when the landlords moved to the Cross Keys at Blatchbridge, but reopened a few months later, with a new landlord from the Bladud's Head in Bath.

Masons Arms / Queen's Head, Whittox Lane

This appears on the map of 1774 on Whittox Lane, just along from the corner with Catherine's Hill. In the census of 1785, when Robert Moon is publican and proprietor, it is described as being on the 'east side of Whittox Lane', and is occupied by three men and four women. The Moon family owned it for a long time, being recorded in the church rates from 1800 until 1837, with various publicans running the pub for them.

John Moon was also the owner of the Lamb & Fountain in what is now Castle Street, his ownership of that house traceable back to 1770. He died in 1829, aged 86, leaving his estate to his five children. One of his tenants was John Gregory, a baker formerly of the Anchor in Stony Street, who, when he drew up his will in 1824, described himself as 'victualler of the Masons Arms'.

Robert Moon was still listed as the owner in 1837, with William Densham as occupier. In October 1838 an advertisement appeared in the *Salisbury & Wiltshire Journal* for a

> FREE PUBLIC HOUSE FROME SOMERSET
>
> TO BE LET and entered on immediately, or at Christmas next – a FREE PUBLIC-HOUSE, situated in a central part of the Manufacturing Town of Frome. Rent moderate, and coming in easy. – For particulars apply (if by letter post paid) to Mr Densham, Masons Arms, Frome.

The last records for the Masons Arms come in Pigot's *Directories* for 1842 and 1844, which contain entries for 'James Candy, Masons Arms and stone mason Whittox Lane'. This is probably the same James Candy recorded in the 1841 census as a mason, aged 45, living in Milk Street with his wife Sarah and son William. We have found no references to the Masons Arms after 1844.

However, the Ordnance Survey map of 1886 shows an extensive building called the Queen's Head on the same site as the Masons Arms on the 1774 map, and it seems likely that it changed names in the mid-1840s in homage to the young queen crowned a few years earlier and possibly coinciding with a change in ownership. Although this is supposition, the only Queen's Head mentioned before 1841 is one at Badcox, which is not recorded after 1778, and the only other Masons Arm's is the one out at Marston, first recorded in the 1860s. More detailed research may shed more light on this, but for present purposes we will treat the Masons Arms and the Queen's Head on Whittox Lane as one and the same.

The 1841 census has a brewer named Edward Haines living in Whittox Lane, possibly involved with the pub, which is certainly recorded as brewing its own beer later in the century. The next census of 1851 has Thomas Frankland as an innkeeper with some younger members of the Haines family boarding there although their occupations are not given.

John Ashman, described as a wine & spirit merchant, is there in 1871 with his family, and eight years later the freehold was put up for sale with Mansford & Baily of the Wheatsheaves in Bath Street named as tenants. The pub comprised a serving bar with double entrance, large cellars, brewhouse, carpenter's shop, small yard, two sitting rooms, five bedrooms and various other rooms. It was bought for £750 by Thomas Parsons from Mells, who took over the licence from John Ashman. He

Above: The Queen's Arms on the 1886 OS Map

Right: The building today

died around 1887 and, when his executors put the pub up for auction, it was sold to Alfred Austin Rossiter, previously at the Castle in Bradford on Avon. Four years later, he and his brother acquired the Lamb & Fountain, and the Queen's was taken over by Albert Simister and his wife Francis, with brother William brewing the beer. They had moved on by 1898 and, over the next ten years, ten licensees are named in local papers and directories, a sure sign that all was not well. At the annual Brewster Session of 1910, it was 'referred to the Council Licensing Committee for non renewal' and closed its doors for the last time.

Mechanics Arms (aka the Roebuck or the Antelope), Water Lane

The extravagantly named Alfred Marquis Showering was born in 1835 into a family of part-time victuallers in Shepton Mallet. His father Francis combined innkeeping with shoemaking, but Alfred set out to break the mould, moving to Frome, where in 1861 he worked as a pattern maker at an iron foundry. He lodged with his sister and brother-in-law John and Frances Edwards, who ran the Rose & Crown in the Butts. The apple rarely falls far from the tree, however, and before long Alfred had moved a few doors down from his sister and set up his own beerhouse, the Mechanics Arms in Thorne's Rank, with his new wife Mary. By 1867 Alfred was sufficiently confident to begin work on a new skittle alley at the back of the pub – the only problem being that he had neglected to get planning permission. Construction stopped midway until the Frome Board approved the idea. Alfred liked to bend the rules in other ways too – in 1870 he was convicted for illegally selling beer on a Sunday, his ever-helpful spouse Mary confirming to the authorities that he often did so. Mrs Showering at this time was running a grocery business out of the pub.

In April 1872 Francis handed over the reins to Frederick Howell. Within a year Howell had renamed it – and the Antelope Inn was born. That same year Howell was charged with using improper measuring cups. He insisted the drinks had been poured into imperial measures and then tipped into unmarked 'illegal' cups for drinking. The court accepted Howell had not intended to break the law – but ignorance was no defence. His cups were forfeited and a fine imposed.

Unable to stay away from the pub he had created, in May 1876 Alfred Showering took over from Howell. Later that year, in November, he allowed the premises to be used by Frome Liberal Association for Mr Samuelson's election campaign. Showering was even included in a political ballad, 'Blue Rocket No 3', circulated in Frome at the time, and reproduced on page 35.

Showering seems not to have remained at the Antelope long and quickly moved on to the Somerset Arms, which he left in 1878 when a new tenant, Mrs Emma Clacee, took over. Within a year, however, Mrs Clacee was running the Antelope! Meanwhile, Alfred Showering had moved back to his native Shepton Mallet and taken over his father's pub, the Ship Inn, which was taken over in turn by Alfred's son Albert. It was at the Ship in 1912 that Alfred Marquis Showering welcomed the birth of his grandson, Francis Edwin Showering, better known at the inventor of the iconic 1960s tipple, Babycham. Alfred Marquis Showering died a wealthy man in 1915.

Returning to the Antelope in Frome, in 1880 we find that it had been renamed again, this time as the Roebuck, most probably by Emma Clacee's successor, John Perkins. In April 1880 Frederick Barry took over – for a month. The licence was then transferred to John Starr, under whose tenancy the pub and the attached shop were sold in June 1881. Freeholder William Knight was unable to pay his debts to the bank, and his three pubs – the Clothier's Arms, the Red Lion and the Antelope – were put up for auction. In the sale details, the Antelope was described as 'newly built, [in] good repair [and] occupied by John Starr'. We also know it had two underground cellars, one tap bar, a parlour bar, a small bar, four bedrooms on the first floor, two bedrooms on the second and a club room. Altogether a fairly substantial property, far larger than many of Frome's other nineteenth-century beerhouses. It was sold for £295 to William Shore Baily of the great brewing family, who acquired the slightly more expensive Rose & Crown and the Clothier's Arms in the same auction.

The former Mechanics Arms in 2014

When Baily died eight years later, the Roebuck was auctioned off once more. Landlord John Starr was long gone, the tenancy having been taken over by William Hawkins in 1882. In 1881 he had been landlord of the Rose & Crown, which suggests that Mr Baily was in the habit of shifting his tenants from one beerhouse to another. At the annual licensing sessions that year the magistrates had described the Roebuck as a 'badly conducted house', so perhaps Hawkins was installed as some sort of troubleshooter. He died not long after taking over the pub and his widow Elizabeth took his place,

Alley leading to separate shop entrance

running it successfully for many years. Richard Tickner acquired the tenancy in 1897 but also died soon afterwards, leaving his widow to run the beerhouse. After a run of successful landladies the Roebuck came into the hands of Luther Ashman from 1909 to 1921.

He ran into trouble almost as soon as he took over. Until 1960, gaming or gambling in pubs was strictly prohibited, yet these activities were very much a part of the public-house scene in the early 1900s. In 1909, Luther Ashman was summonsed for unlawfully permitting card playing on his premises. A local policeman happened to pop into the pub the very moment some 15 youths were happily gambling in the tap room. Ashman pointed out that a notice prohibiting gambling was displayed in the tap room and the youths were simply playing an innocent game – not gambling at all! The court disagreed and fined Ashman £2.

In 1922 several pubs in Frome were considered for closure by the licensing authorities. The White Swan and the Masons Arms were considered but spared, but the threat continued for others, including the Selwood Inn, the Half Moon – and the Roebuck.

Clearly there were problems afoot at the Roebuck. In September 1922, the landlord applied for permission to sell cooked meats from the shop on the first floor of the building. The shop was well-established, already sold groceries, and had a separate entrance from the road. The application was nevertheless declined because it was held that the shop also stored barrels of liquor and selling cooked meat would attract more children to the shop. Thus the pub was denied a much-needed opportunity to augment its income. The repercussions were entirely predictable.

By March 1924 the Roebuck had had three different licensees in just four years, the current licensee David Walter Phillips having been there only since the previous September. Competition for business was intense, with three fully-licensed houses and a beerhouse within 506 yards. Trade was so poor that Phillips was unable to make a living and was actually in receipt of unemployment pay whilst technically still running the pub. Other public houses in the neighbourhood had better accommodation and did better trade. Phillips had had enough, and the Roebuck closed.

Murtrey Inn, Orchardleigh

According to Crocker's 1803 survey of Buckland, the Murtrey Inn, garden and orchard was leased to William Singer for the lives of John Carpenter, 17, James Marchant, 12, and Samuel Ferris, 42. It is named as plot 283, which consisted of 0.2 of an acre and was owned jointly by Sir Henry Strachey and Sir Charles Warwick Bampfylde. No other reference has been found to it. It stood to the right of the site of the Murtrey Lodge entrance to the Orchardleigh Estate, and Castle Lodge stands on roughly the same site today.

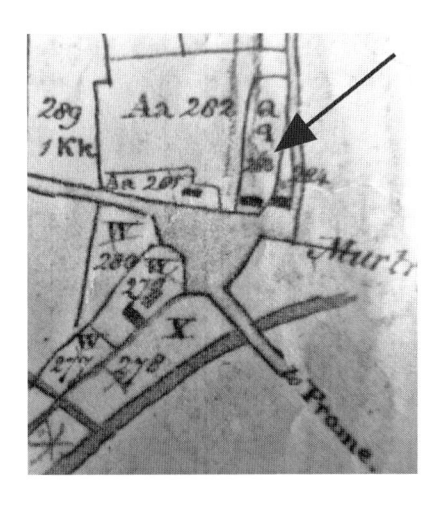

Nag's Head, King Street

Little known and short lived, the Nag's Head was next door but one to the Three Swans on the same side towards Iron Gates. It was first mentioned in 1770 when the rates were paid by William Horler and was once part of the large Smith family estate which included several other Frome pubs before it went bankrupt in 1776. In the Act of Parliament required to sort out the bankruptcy, a John Cayford is named as leaseholder and it seems that he then purchased the property and paid rates on it until 1791 when Michael Griffin took over. Griffin was also involved with the Three Swans at around the same time.

There is no mention of the pub after 1799. The building still stands next door to the enlarged Three Swans, but has been substantially rebuilt, losing the gable and top floor shown in the painting of King Street on page 147.

The former Nag's Head in 2014

New Inn / Weaver, 6 The Butts

In September 1829 an auction was held, at the Wheatsheaves, of 36 houses in the Newington Butts area, including 'retail beer premises and large gateway in front together with a well arranged brewery, malt house, cooperage, extensive yard stable and outhouses late in the occupation of Mr Thorne'. The premises are unnamed, but the adjoining building was a large bakehouse, and – as this fits in with what is known of its later history – this is possibly an early reference to what became the New Inn.

The tithe map and census of 1840/41 show the site as occupied by Francis Harman or Herman, a 69-year-old baker, with no mention of beer being brewed or sold on the premises. The first positive reference to the New Inn comes in 1857 when George Jelly, beerhouse keeper at the Butts, was fined ten shillings for selling out of hours. A sad entry in the burial record of the Vallis Road Cemetery from March 1859 is for a stillborn son of George Jelly, described as an 'innkeeper'. The family appear in the 1861 census, when George is described as a 'general dealer' in the Butts, but there is no mention of a pub. Jelly was, however, granted a full wine and spirit licence in August 1868 'despite there being a licensed house within 200 yards' – presumably the Mechanics Arms (later the Roebuck) across the road on Water Lane. The Jellys were there until 1886, by which time George had died and been replaced by his widow Ann, who in turn gave way to his son Edward.

In the 1871 census Edward is described as a 'solicitor's clerk' but ten years later he had embarked on a proper career and become a cattle dealer. After taking possession of the New Inn, he put it up for auction, describing it as that 'substantially built, well known old established Free and Full licensed FREEHOLD PUBLIC HOUSE with the stable, coach house, cow house and small garden in the rear thereof known as the New Inn having a frontage of 42'9" by 35'6" and for many years in the occupation of the owners during which period a most profitable business has been carried on'.

The freehold was bought by local brewers J&T Baily of the Lamb Brewery, but, just before the sale went through, Edward was nicked for diluting his whiskey. This was not illegal at the time, provided that you put a sign up saying that it had been done. When the police sergeant who bought a pint of whiskey had it analysed, it was found to be 37.9% under proof – 12.9% below the regulated strength. Now Edward's previous occupation came in handy. He defended himself, stating that the whiskey he had supplied to the sergeant had not been diluted as much as it ought to have been, and produced a witness to say that a notice regarding the dilution of whiskey had been hanging in the bar for the past four years. The case was dismissed.

In 1887, when the licence was transferred from James Doherty to Francis Haines, the fixtures and fittings were, as was customary, valued by an independent party. The record of this valuation survives in Frome museum and makes interesting reading. The bar, for example, contained a deal table with turned legs, two Windsor chairs, fixed seating with backing and framework around the room, India matting including four supports with elbows, a painted settle with elbows and supports, a painted bar screen with supports, an iron rod with curtain, a gas bracket with glass shade, four ornaments (one broken), a cupboard and some shelving. There was also a serving counter with a lead top, till drawer and shelf under, and a four-motion mahogany-frame beer engine with a lead drip-tray attached, with 118 feet of piping.

For serving drinks there were four two-handled quart cups (one broken and two cracked), nine one-handled pint cups, along with various assorted glassware and measures in pewter. Similarly comprehensive lists were drawn up for the other rooms, which included a parlour, back kitchen, dressing room, sitting room, club room, cellar, and three bedrooms.

The New Inn darts team in 1928

The Weaver in 1992

Between 1886, when Edward Jelly sold the New Inn to the Lamb Brewery, and 1891, there were eight transfers of licence, a fair indication that all was not well at the house. The brewery prospectus of 1893 described it as having a dwelling house adjoining and being fully licensed. In 1916 Charles

Arthur White was asked by the brewery to move from one of its other pubs, the Red Lion, and sort the place out. This he seems to have done extremely well, for he remained there until he died in 1944, to be succeeded by his wife until she retired in 1946.

Colin White, the grandson of Charles White, who still lives in Frome, recalls an incident from the Second World War:

> One morning on the way to school I called in at the pub to see my grandmother but my uncle came out and stopped me going in and told me just to go to school. Apparently the night before, US soldiers had come into town. The black soldiers were staying in the 'tan yard' [Keyford] and the white soldiers were in billets around the town and at Marston. The soldiers had come into town and had brought their own drink with them. They came up to the New Inn and when my uncle decided they couldn't drink their own liquor in his pub … they smashed up the place – tables, glasses, anything to do with the pub was all smashed up. His uncle went to the phone box at the end of the road and rang up Marston camp. The military police came down in force and arrested the soldiers. My grandparents were left in a state of chaos. The next day the commandant came down and asked them to value it. He then wrote out a cheque and paid for it. It was quite a substantial amount. They paid up and everything was put right. This was in around 1944 when I was about ten.

In the early 1970s it was renamed the Weaver, but continued as a traditional local's pub with darts, skittles charity events and quiz sessions before closing in 2009. It was bought as a development project by Frome Reclamation who had a planning application for six flats refused in 2010 and again in 2012. In February 2013 the building was demolished and in 2015 the site was sold to a property company.

THE NEW INN
Trevor Byfield

A pleasant house at which to call and sample Ushers Ales, providing snacks and quiet refreshment.

THE BUTTS, FROME

An advert from the late 1960s

The end, February 2013

Pack Horse, 13 Christchurch Street West

First mentioned in the church rates of 1770, the Pack Horse is likely to have been well established by then, with a possible building date of 1730-50 according to local architect and historian Rodney Goodall. It was on the main route from Radstock and Mells, which had been made a turnpike road in 1757. William Singer is the first landlord that we can trace. The *Bath Chronicle* for 24 March 1774 reported that a cooper named James Moss was committed to Shepton Mallet prison for 'having taken out of the bedchamber of Mr William Singer, at the Pack-horse inn in Frome Selwood, Somerset, a large oaken box containing upwards of £45 with the book and articles belonging to a friendly society which used to meet there in order to make provision against sickness or death. The said Moss was a member of the society, and had acted as steward.'

The Singer family had an interest in the pub until 1826 and are shown as paying the rates until that date, sometimes along with others such as a Benjamin Carpenter who seems to have had part-ownership of the Greyhound in Milk Street during the 1790s.

At the back of the building was a coal merchant supplied by ponies which brought coal from Radstock and Mells. Once the coal was unloaded, they were set to graze in the field across the road, named on the 1774 map as Baily's or Pack Horse ground. In 1817 Christ Church was built on the site. Understandably, the colliers were a thirsty and lively lot and kept the local constable Isaac Gregory busy as his diaries for 1817-18 record:

> 17 November1817: Was sent for to the Packhorse to quell a furious row, it appeared there had been some hard blows passed by the marks of their faces which were much swollen and black – the quarrel was occasioned by four colliers who called for a quart of beer, three of them went away but the landlord insisted him that called for it should pay for the whole which he refused and so the row began. It was desired he should pay for the beer or go to the guardhouse. Alter much altercation I brought him to.

> 23 July 1818: Sent for twice to the Packhorse in the course of this day to quell disturbances, they appear to have colliers at their house drinking and quarrelling almost constantly.

> 30 July 1818: Called at 9 & 10 to suppress a row, the house was much pestered with lewd women singing to the colliers.

From 1827, the lease was held by William Crumbleholme and his wife Charlotte. William was in the building trade but in ill health; in 1828 he put his business up for sale and died in February 1828, aged 40, prompting the following advertisement in the *Salisbury & Winchester Journal* on 5 May 1828:

FREE PUBLIC HOUSE

> To be Let with immediate possession, All that well established inn or Public House with ample stabling, Coach House &c &c called the Pack Horse Inn, most eligibly situated in the principal thoroughfare of the town of Frome. The whole of the stock of beer is of superior quality; coming in moderate. Further details may be known on application to Mrs Crumbleholme, the present tenant,

who is leaving in consequence of ill health or to Mr Porch, auctioneer, Frome. The above concern is well deserving the notice of any person inclined to embark in such a business.

Instead of finding someone to buy the pub, Charlotte found a new husband – Frederick Watts – and the two of them ran the place until her death in 1833, after which Frederick carried on alone until around 1837. There is an excellent memorial to them in Horningsham parish church.

The *Frome Times* for 23 November 1859 reports what should have been one of the most self-defeating demonstrations of sobriety for some time, when 'William Smith landlord of the Pack Horse Inn was charged with being drunk and allowing disorderly conduct in his house.' The police were called to the disturbance and found a number of men in the house. Some were fighting, some were trying to prevent them, several had black eyes, others were covered in blood, and two men were trying to make another man drink out of a jug. The landlord insisted that no one was drunk and refused to clear the pub. Following the constable outside in his shirt sleeves, he offered to fight any of the bystanders and, as further proof that he was sober, 'he went out into the middle of the road dancing and flinging his arms about. He was shortly afterwards persuaded to go indoors.' The local magistrates were seemingly convinced that this was proof enough and, despite two previous convictions, the charge was dismissed, with Mr Smith being warned to be 'very circumspect in the future'. You don't seem to get landlords that entertaining, or magistrates that understanding, these days.

The Pack Horse in 1992

Things were pretty quiet until another interesting case reported in the *Frome Times* in 1875. James Clacee, a farmer of Wanstrow, was summonsed by the Inspector of Nuisances for 'having in his possession a carcass of meat, the same being dressed for the purpose of sale, [which was] unfit for the food of man'. The meat was on a cart in the Pack Horse yard and, by all accounts sodden and in a very bad state, the heifer being diseased before death and then drowned. In his defence, Mr Clacee stated that it was not intended for human consumption, but for Mr Baily's dogs, and, when asked why it was so well dressed, he replied that it had been sawn up by a carpenter. The bench decided that there was no evidence he was intending to sell it and dismissed the case, but, when Clacee asked for reimbursement as the meat had been destroyed, he was advised not to push his luck.

The rest of the nineteenth century seems to have passed without incident or reportage in the local press, but in 1914 the government brought in the Defence of the Realm Act, part of which enforced the closing of pubs during the afternoon, a bizarre inconvenience that was to last for over 70 years. An even more bizarre clause was the 'no treating' rule. Designed primarily to prevent gangs of soldiers buying huge rounds of drinks for their mates and rendering themselves incapable, it was to have some unfortunate consequences.

In November 1918, Elsie Rogers, a factory worker, met her friend Emily Russell in the Pack Horse for a drink. The landlord, John Brown, supplied them with a glass of beer each, for which Emily paid. All three were arrested and taken to court, the girls being fined five shillings each and the landlord ten shillings. Their crime was not to have gone up to the bar and paid for their drinks separately. Emily's defence that Elsie had given her the threepence for her drink was no defence at all, and nor was that of the landlord, who claimed rather lamely that he thought the treating order had 'gone dead', and had not put the notices back up as he had just had the place decorated.

They were lucky, as the maximum penalty was £100 or six months inside, and, although customers were largely incredulous when the law first came in, and tried all manner of ruses to get round it, publicans failed to see the funny side after a while and vigorously enforced it, compliance being preferable to risking livelihood and liberty. On the plus side, of course, a man could not buy a drink for his wife or girlfriend – they had to go to the bar and buy their own. Liberation of a sort, perhaps.

John Brown, who was landlord throughout most of World War One, was also responsible for introducing motor vehicles to the pub in an effort to modernise his postal business, and sold off his horses and harnesses at the same time. He was originally from Radstock and a former coachman to Jonathan Knight of Innox Hill House. In the 1920s he moved to the Victoria in Christchurch Street, but in 1935, after his retirement, he took his own life at his home in Fromefield, aged 59.

Harry Clements was behind the bar briefly in the 1920s, but died after a couple of years. His widow applied to take over but police superintendent Stewart stated that, although 'he was very reluctant to do anything that would turn a widow into the streets ... at the Pack Horse it was essential that the house should have a man to manage it – and a good man'. Edith Clements was only granted a temporary licence and the following year, 1927, Fred Dallimore became licensee.

These unusual twin door surrounds, which date from the 1600s, were sinking into the cellar before restoration was carried out in the 1980s. This photograph was taken before the work was done.

By 1967 the pub was the property of Courage Brewery, and in the 1970s David and Lal Mills took over. They embarked on a programme of cultural and charitable activities including plays, history courses, pub games tournaments and training schemes for those wishing to enter the pub trade, and stayed at the pub for 30 years before selling up in 2009.

In 2010 there was a report in the local press of a ghost photographed by a customer 'who did not want to be named'. He took the photo on his mobile and it shows a soldier from the American civil war in full uniform with musket and tobacco pouch. Landlords Jason Rowlson and Alison Johnson said that they often experienced strange goings-on at the pub but had not come across this before. The photo brings to mind eighteenth-century polymath and philosopher Jeremy Bentham's remark that he did not believe in ghosts because he didn't see how there could be ghostly clothes – and he had never heard of anyone seeing a naked one. Perhaps Photoshop has solved this problem. In 2014 the inn was sold once more and is ready for the next stage of its long career of public service.

The inn sign in 1969

Packsaddle, Broadway

First shown on the 1774 map, the Packsaddle was situated in Broadway on the left hand side facing Badcox, between the White Swan and the Red Lion. The first mention of it comes in the church rates of 1781 when Henry Austin is the owner of the 'Pack Saddle and nine tenements', along with other properties.

In the census of 1785, Austin is still the owner, with John Neal as publican, and the place is occupied by six men and three women. The last reference to it, again from the church rates, comes in 1791, and it seems likely that it closed around this time. There is a record of a John Neale at the Swan from 1793, possibly the same man although we can't be sure.

The site has since been developed for housing.

Plume of Feathers, 26 Keyford Street

The Plume of Feathers at Keyford was long known colloquially as the Drum and Monkey, a strange but not unheard of pub soubriquet which often has naval associations. This maritime link may indeed be pertinent, for this nineteenth-century beerhouse was run by navy pensioner Joseph Staples and his wife Betsey from 1872. Joseph ran into the sort of problems that beset most beerhouse proprietors, and in 1883 was summonsed for keeping the house open after hours. When Joseph died in 1887, Betsey took over and stayed until 1895. The Plume of Feathers at this point was owned by Frome United Breweries.

George Harper Greenland took over and ran the pub whilst also working as a coachman, which he did right up until the outbreak of World War One. His time there was relatively unmarred by the sort of bad behaviour that plagued other beerhouses. He was succeeded by George Harper who ran the pub during World

Two views of the Plume of Feathers. On the postcard above, it can be seen just right of centre with a young lady in the doorway

War One, followed by Redvers George Brown, a former railway worker. Brown began his career in 1919 working on the railways both as an engineman and a fireman but a burst appendix in January 1921 seems to have hampered his prospects and he failed his subsequent medical. In September 1921 he was examined by the company doctor who concluded, 'Brown is never likely to reach a standard sufficient to withstand the exposure and heavy work of the footplate.' He was offered work as a carriage cleaner in Wales and, although he travelled to take up the post, he changed his mind and returned to Frome. There he was dismissed and went into the licensed trade.

After Redvers Brown left, G F Bond and Dennis Edward Garvin took over in quick succession. At one point between the wars, the Plume of Feathers was considered for closure, even though it was both well-conducted and in a fair state of repair. There were at that time 'two fully-licensed houses and one "on" beerhouse within 298 yards'. Over the preceding two years there had been a noticeable decline in beer sales at the Plume, although an increase in cider sales compensated for this and kept the pub afloat.

In 1950, the licence was transferred from Garvin to Francis Joseph Johnson, recipient of a Distinguished Conduct Medal in World War One, and during his time plans were approved for structural alterations. Despite this, the pub closed in 1957, and Frank and his wife Winifred moved down the road to become licensees at the Beehive.

It has proved difficult to find decent photographs of the Plume of Feathers as a pub. Part of it can be glimpsed on the right-hand side of the photograph of the Crown on page 47, but, apart from the two oblique and partial views above, that is all we have to go on. Fortunately, the building survives as a private house, and a photograph of it today appears on the right.

Portway Hotel, 20 Portway

Though strictly speaking not a pub, the short-lived Portway Hotel – originally opened around 1934 as the Portway House Hotel – had a licensed bar and, for many Frome inhabitants, played a role akin to a public house. It is a late-eighteenth/early nineteenth-century listed building but has a modern extension to the side.

By far the most interesting chapter in the Portway's history occurred in secrecy during World War Two. In the immediate aftermath of Dunkirk, the Portway was used as the headquarters of Field-Marshal Viscount Montgomery when he was reforming the 3rd British Division. In May 1947 a bronze tablet was unveiled by General Sir John T Crocker on a wall at the Portway to commemorate the event. The plaque was designed by H E Stanton, former headmaster of the Frome School of Art & Science and made by the Frome Art Metal Workers Guild. At the unveiling there was a parade of the British Legion, the British Legion Women's Section, the Air Training Corps, the Girls' Life Brigade, the Boy Scouts, the Girl Guides, the St John's Ambulance Brigade and the Red Cross.

A postcard produced shortly after the hotel opened

The Portway has since closed and been converted into retirement flats.

Prince of Wales, 30 Vicarage Street

The Prince of Wales beerhouse opened sometime in the mid-nineteenth century, and for much of its brief history was run by a series of short-term licensees, which suggests it was not the most profitable of establishments.

During the 1860s, it was run by William George, a cordwainer, who handed over the reins in 1872 to Samuel Bough, formerly a butcher in Milk Street. Bough was evidently quite a character and a man not averse to a flutter on the ponies. Unfortunately, in May 1875, whilst returning from the races in Bath, he discovered to his cost the drawback of lighting a cigar whilst riding a horse. He was pitched to the ground, landing on his head with such force that he was rushed with all due haste to the Royal United Hospital. Rendered insensible for several days, he was not expected to recover. Yet he did. However, his luck had run out.

The former Prince of Wales in 2012

He remained at the Prince of Wales for just four more years before moving to Bath where his life spiralled downwards. His son Walter died in 1881, followed by his wife in 1884. By 1891, he was a workhouse pauper and he died, still impoverished, eight years later.

In 1879, 27-year-old cloth weaver Luther Dew became landlord of the Prince of Wales. His life proved just as tragic as his predecessor's, and both he and his wife Sarah died in early 1886. Their son Herbert went into service in Wales, whilst his little sister Florence ended up in a Bristol orphanage.

The next few years were very unsettled ones for the Prince of Wales with a host of landlords coming and going. Henry William Moody was there for just over a year before Samuel Pickford took over in 1889. His stay was similarly short-lived, for Henry Trimby took over later that year. Joseph Press became landlord early in 1891, but in September 1891 passed the licence to John Handle who remained until 1893. His successor, John Miles, was there for a grand total of four years. Frank Butcher was next, lasting just a year.

There next followed a licensee of comparative longevity: Emma Minty, a widow, who was there from 1898 to 1905, when she left to run a boarding house on Portway. Her successor was Archibald Dray, who ran the Prince of Wales for just one year. The aptly named Alfred Henry Prince became landlord in 1908, but in July that year the Somerset Compensation Authority met at the Shire Hall in Taunton to decide which public houses should close. The first house to be considered was the Prince of Wales, described as an 'ante-1869 beerhouse', meaning that it opened sometime before 1869. Neither Archibald Dray nor any other representative from the Prince of Wales attended the meeting to oppose the extinction of the licence, and, after it closed, the building was taken over by a shoemaker called Mr Lee. It is now a private house.

Queen's Head, Badcox

Little is known about this one apart from three references from the 1770s. It was contemporary with the Swan but existed before the Woolpack on Badcox, so one possibility is that it was an earlier name for that pub.

The first record comes in the church rates for 1770, with 'Widow Glover' at 'a howse Queen's Head late Freestones Badcox'. The church rates for 1778, however, show Widow Glover at 'two houses Queen's Head late Freestones'. The only other record is the transcript of a conveyance from 1773, when William Hussey of Frome Selwood, glazier, sold to Richard Stradling of Chedzoy, gent, 'all that messuage with backside stable outhouse etc. Formerly called Freestones but now and for many years The Queen's Head at Badcox bounded on south with highway leading to Egford now occupied by William Hussey'. Stradling paid £100 for the freehold, and the original lease survives in the Somerset Record Office.

The name 'Freestones' can be traced back to at least 1723 in the church records, when rates were paid by George Lock for 'part of freestones'. They continued to be paid by Mrs Lock until 1767, after which Mrs Glover took over in the next rating year of 1770. The Locks also paid rates on other properties at Badcox: George Lock paid rates on 'part of the Angel' in 1742, followed by Mrs Lock until 1767, and Mrs Lock paid rates at the White Hart from 1753-1763.

Railway / First & Last, Wallbridge

Frome station opened in 1850 and the Railway Tavern opened a short distance away soon afterwards. Thomas Williamson was granted a beerhouse licence in 1855, and was described as a coal & timber merchant, as well as an inn keeper, in the census of 1861. He was convicted of an assault in the Angel in 1861, during which a man's coat was torn, and fined fifteen shillings, and in the same year was fined £1 for using 'false measures'. It was also noted that, when the police called to check his measures, he had 'used very abusive language to the constables'. Williamson was himself severely beaten up by Samuel Joyce of the Wheelwright's Arms in 1862.

The present building is not the original, which seems to have been somewhat unprepossessing. A writer reminiscing in the *Somerset Standard* on 1 January 1932 recalled that 'the Railway Hotel, then called Tavern, was a ramshackle old place, with a rank of lanky looking cottages on its eastern side.' Sadly, we have not found a photograph of the original building.

Williamson had gone by 1865, which was probably no bad thing, and the new landlord was Samuel Cuzner, aged 39 in the 1871 census, with his wife Mary and son George. Lodging with them was Stan Humphrey from Hampstead, a railway worker on the GWR, and Oliver Chandler, a railway fireman from Salisbury. Joseph Williams took over in 1884, moving the short distance down the road from the Great Western, but seems to have made rather a mess of things as he was bankrupt by 1890.

Henry Fear, a former coachman to Mr Horner of Mells and Sir Richard Paget of Cranmore Hall, had taken over by 1891, but had little more luck than his predecessor. In 1894 he was arrested for 'interfering' with two little girls in his greenhouse, one of whom was the daughter of William Davies of the White Horse on Portway. He lost the pub whilst on bail, but towards the end of the year was acquitted of all charges.

His place was taken by Isaac Bray who was there until 1895. In 1926 Bray was murdered, along with his landlady, at his lodgings on The Mount. The murderer then slit his own throat and his motives were never explained.

The Lamb Brewery had taken over the Railway by 1893 and in a prospectus described it as 'fully licensed with four dwelling houses attached'. They applied to have it rebuilt to the design of architect William George Brown,

The Railway Hotel in the 1950s

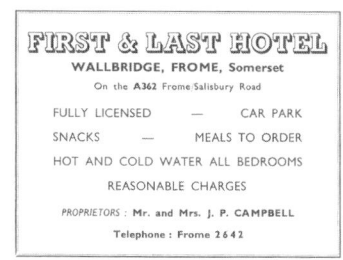

FIRST & LAST HOTEL
WALLBRIDGE, FROME, Somerset
On the A362 Frome/Salisbury Road

FULLY LICENSED — CAR PARK
SNACKS — MEALS TO ORDER
HOT AND COLD WATER ALL BEDROOMS
REASONABLE CHARGES

PROPRIETORS : Mr. and Mrs. J. P. CAMPBELL
Telephone : Frome 2642

An advert from the 1960s

The First & Last in 1992

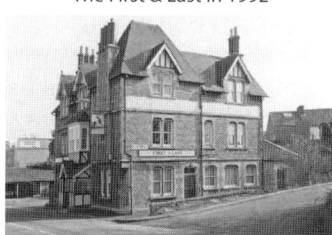

and the building was completed in time for their AGM in May 1900.

Robert Winsor, originally from Hastings, was landlord from 1926 to 1937. He had been in the Royal Flying Corps from 1915 until 1920 and flown some the earliest machines in Belgium and France before taking part in bombing raids over Germany. He attained the rank of Flying Officer before one of his planes crashed, injuring him so that he had to have a silver plate in his face. After leaving Frome he was at the Horse & Jockey, followed by the Pulteney Arms, in Bath. He died suddenly aged 54 in 1947.

There followed a number of landlords, seemingly without much incident, and in 1960 the Railway was renamed the First & Last. It thrived for a while under Martin Talon, who took over in 1975, but its glory days ended with the gradual closure of the Wallbridge Mills. Without their custom, the house was too far out of town and separated from the drinking community by a bend on a murderously busy road.

Ushers, the successor to the Lamb Brewery, sold it to Gibbs Mew in 1988, and it struggled on, catering for local road crews and a dedicated band of regulars, with Martin Talon still behind the bar, before closing around 2005 to reopen as the Tong Dynasty Chinese restaurant.

Red Lion, Broadway

The Red Lion at Broadway appears on the 1774 map and is known to have been run by William Budget around this time. He applied for a licence from Justice Horner on 3 September 1773, by which point the inn had been disused for some years. Clearly it was not an especially popular tavern. A decade later, Thomas Harvey is recorded as the proprietor. Subsequently the Red Lion passes into obscurity. It may well be that this public house was later transformed into the Wheelwright's Arms, later known as the Lion, although this is mere speculation at this point.

Red Lion, 37 The Butts

The Butts in the 1800s was an area inhabited by labourers and small-scale artisans, and was where the great art-metal entrepreneur John Webb Singer, son of a builder, grew up. It was also characterised by numerous beerhouses, a consequence of the loosening of licensing laws during the first half of the nineteenth century. Beerhouses also offered a tempting sideline for men – and women – from a variety of backgrounds. The ranks of workers and craftsmen provided a reservoir of recruits, and dual occupations were common.

When Henry Noble ran the Red Lion during the late 1840s and early 1850s, he combined the role of landlord with his day job as a carpenter. His father, who lived with him and assisted in running the Red Lion, worked as a thatcher, and during the day his sister Fanny pulled the pints. They were fairly typical inhabitants of the Butts and their beerhouse was just as representative.

At some point, Henry Noble decided life would be far simpler if he just concentrated on carpentry, and mason James Singer stepped in. He was landlord from the late 1850s through most of the 1860s before moving to a house in Nunney Lane to concentrate on his trade as mason. Such was the pattern of innkeepers at the Red Lion – short tenancies and dual occupations.

Not that James Singer's time at the Red Lion was uneventful. In July 1861, there was a serious disturbance there. When local man Henry Hillier came in for a drink, another customer, William Davis, was already there with a friend. On seeing Hillier, William Davis offered up a toast: 'Any man who has ever done a foul deed, may be found out before he dies'. This was quite clearly a heavily-loaded comment and, when the toast-master left the tavern, he found himself verbally set upon by Henry Hillier. The true meaning of the troublesome 'toast' became clear when Davis proclaimed, 'if thee didst kill the man at Nunney, I hope thee wilt never kill me.'

'Take care,' replied Hillier, 'for thee dost not know.'

The reason for this spat was that, some years earlier, Hillier had stood accused of murdering a man at Nunney. The case had gone to trial and he had been acquitted. Davis was just stirring up trouble and, when he had Hillier summonsed for using threatening language, the case was swiftly dismissed. Nevertheless, it added some excitement to the Red Lion for one evening at least.

Nineteenth-century licensing laws were in many ways more complex than those of today. There were exceptions to the legal opening hours, whereby a landlord might sell drink to somebody who lived beyond a certain distance from the inn and was thus classified as a 'traveller'. Landlords would frequently invoke this rule, but risked prosecution. Thus in 1864 we find James Singer prosecuted on the grounds that he 'suffered beer to be drunk on his premises, by persons other than travellers between the hours of two and five o'clock'. Singer failed to prove they were travellers and incurred a sizeable fine.

His successor, John Hughes, kept up the tradition of combining beer-selling with another trade, in his case working as a wool stapler. He was at the Red Lion from the late 1860s until 1874 when he moved to Aston in Warwickshire to take over the Fountain Inn there. Meanwhile Alfred Youdle moved into the Red Lion, which he ran without much incident for six years. He left in 1882, and died relatively young five years later. Following a spell under the management of Ernest Turner, the pub was taken over by John Cocksedge in 1887.

The former Red Lion in 2014

A popular route into the licensed trade was from occupations with limited life-spans, such as the military. John Cocksedge was a former soldier from Essex and whilst in Frome he no doubt continued to practice the farrier's skills he had picked up in the army. Often when a publican pursued another occupation, his wife looked after the day-to-day running of the pub. In this case it was not Cocksedge's wife but his 15-year-old niece Margaret Barry who did the work. Though using such a young barmaid may seem outrageous today, Cocksedge was certainly not the only Frome publican to do so at the time.

In 1895, the Cocksedges moved to Stratton on the Fosse and John Whately, an ex-Navy man, held the fort at the Red Lion until 1899, when wood carver Arthur White took over with his wife, Annie, daughter of the landlord of the Anchor in Catherine Street. Marrying a woman with experience in the licensed trade was always a good move. Sadly, Annie died in 1900, aged just 25. White continued running the Red Lion with the help of his housekeeper Emma Youle, before marrying her daughter Ruth.

Midway through World War One, the Red Lion was taken by H Watts, followed by Albert Heydon in 1922. During his time the Red Lion darts team achieved a high profile locally and his son Bill Heydon was the only darts player from Frome ever to reach a national final. Ill health, in the form of paralysis, had prevented Bill taking part in outdoor sports as a boy but he was a keen darts player and honed his talent at the Red Lion. In 1948 he entered a national contest for the first time but ill health forced him to withdraw. The following year, aged 34, Bill Heydon won the North Somerset area championship and the Western Counties divisional championship and reached the News of the World Darts Championship Final at Wembley. During their time at the Red Lion, in 1949, the Heydons secured a full licence, allowing them to sell wine and spirits. When his father died, Bill and his mother moved to Bridge Street, and, although busy working as a sheet metal worker and plagued by infirmity, Bill still found time to play for the Castle Inn darts team, winning countless medals and trophies. Following Albert Heydon's death, the Red Lion was run by a succession of different landlords until 1982, when the owners, Ushers Brewery, applied for change of use and it became a private house.

Red Lion, Feltham Lane

The Red Lion in Feltham Lane is all but lost to us, consisting merely of a few meagre references in parish records. It existed in 1747, and in 1753 the proprietor was James Pope, remaining so until 1790 when Thomas Harvey's name appears in the church rates. Twenty-three years later the site was owned by James Harvey, but was shown on a map as just an empty field, indicating that at some point between 1790 and 1813 the inn was demolished.

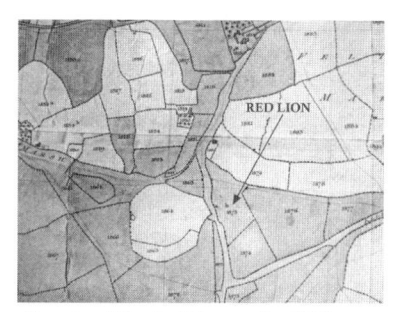

The site of the Red Lion on the 1813 map

Rifleman's Arms, Murtrey

'Here is a house, of the largest and best dimensions, already licensed for the sale of spirits, the applicant is of unblemished character, there is not and has never been any complaint against the house, and yet the licence is mysteriously withheld.'

Such was the state of affairs as expressed by counsel representing the prospective landlord of the Rifleman's Arms at the Wells Quarter Sessions in October 1863. But what had led to this unlikely impasse?

Just three years earlier, Henry Harris of Frome, sometime innkeeper at the Blue Boar and the Angel, had bought a piece of land at Murtrey. On it he built a house which he called the Rifleman's Arms, at a total cost of £1,300. It was a handsome building, constructed in first-class style. Situated on the high road between Frome and Radstock, at the junction with the main road from Frome to Elm, Mells and Kilmersdon, the inn was in a key spot. On both these roads there was a constant and ever-increasing flow of traffic, such that the tolls taken at the tollhouse adjacent to the inn far exceeded those at any other toll house in Frome. Nearby was the Spring Gardens factory, where 300-400 people were employed in cloth making,

The former Rifleman's Arms in 2012

and the grounds of the Frome Volunteers, some 150 strong, were also close by. Clearly, with no other licensed house for one and a quarter miles in any direction, it was a profitable place to set up an inn.

Henry Harris first applied for a licence in 1861, but was unsuccessful. When he applied the following year a licence was granted but with one peculiar condition attached:

> In the event of an application for the transfer of the licence, the application for renewal of the licence at the next annual licensing meeting shall be considered as an application for a new licence.

In other words it was really Henry Harris who was to be licensed, not his house. If he left or died the whole licensing process would begin anew – a unique set-up. When Francis Forehead applied for a licence for the Rifleman's in September 1863 he discovered this to his cost.

With no complaints against the house, a respectable and experienced prospective landlord, no other inn nearby and a large volume of traffic requiring refreshment, it should have been simple to transfer the licence from Henry Harris to Francis Forehead. Francis was a former coal haulier and licensee of the Globe in Vallis Way. He had lost an arm and fractured one leg, leaving him permanently lame and compelling him to give up his job as a coal haulier. His disposition, however, eminently suited the licensed trade. Nevertheless, when he applied for a licence at the licensing sessions in 1862, the bench declined his application.

Forehead's solicitor exercised his prerogative of appealing to the sessions in Wells and in October 1863 the case of Francis Forehead v the Justices of the Frome Division was heard. The question was why the licence for a peaceful, well-built inn had been declined, especially when there were no other licensed houses nearby. The problem was that the inn lay within 300 yards of the entrance to Orchardleigh Park, whose owner William Duckworth Esq, was a magistrate of the Frome Division, as was his son Russell.

One of the spurious arguments levelled against the inn was that it was used mainly by coal hauliers, who generally did not drink anything but beer, and thus it had no need of a spirit licence! It was also suggested that the Rifleman's Arms was a source of 'temptation to the young people of Frome who might possibly resort thither, as freer from observation than the public houses in town'.

Fortunately for Francis Forehead, the justices in Wells were freer from the observation of Orchardleigh than those in Frome, and voted unanimously in favour of renewing the licence. Forehead remained at the Rifleman's Arms until around 1881 when owner Henry Harris returned as landlord. Perhaps the opposition from Orchardleigh proved too much for him, and by 1887 the inn had closed. It is now a private house.

Ring O'Bells, 75 Broadway

In an interview with the authors in 2013, one Frome resident recalled how, during the 1950s, when he was a young lad, there was a separate area at the Ring O'Bells where the older women used to come and drink 'out of sight'. Being a mischievous chap, he made a point of always 'accidentally opening the wrong door to name and shame the old dears inside!' This notion of the Ring O'Bells as a more or less genteel establishment where the older folk could drink in peace – except for irksome lads and their tiresome pranks – was quite different to the tavern that existed a century earlier.

Although the main bar is the oldest part, this may simply be because the rest has not always been part of the licensed premises. Currently used as a snooker/pool room, the skittle alley still has fixtures and fittings inside relating to its use as an alley. Externally, to the rear, where the stonework is exposed, it is possibly to discern the ghostly traces of former windows and doorways. These architectural shadows reveal that the skittle alley was once – probably in the eighteenth century – a row of two or three cottages later incorporated into the public house.

There are other interesting clues at the back of the pub. Now a garden storage space, the old outside privy still retains its tell-tale tiling around the doorway, dating from the days when inside toilets were a luxury. It was in fact the ladies' toilet. For the men, there was the garden wall!

The back of the Ring O'Bells in 2012

The first recorded mention of the Ring O'Bells is in 1721, when Nicholas Payne was maltster there, although the building in all probability dates from a century earlier. In the eighteenth century, it was owned variously by the Balls, then the Humphries, Giffords, Abrahams and Drews – more often than not members of one family intermarrying with another.

In 1836 Daniel Morgan was landlord, followed by James Baily from 1840. George Hill took over in 1852 and was evidently successful enough to send his son Joseph away to boarding school, something his wife would live to regret – although most of his family would not! At Christmastime 1858, a distressing series of events was set in motion at the Ring O'Bells. On 14 December, Joseph arrived home from school in Weston-super-Mare with a note saying he had been ill, but not specifying with what illness. On 20 December, his six-year-old sister Emily also became ill. Three days later, she was diagnosed with typhus fever, and she died on the 29th, as did her 17-year-old sister Grace. Next to fall ill was 16-year-old Sarah Hill, although she recovered. Finally, in early January, landlord George Hill himself succumbed to typhus. Widow Elizabeth Hill was left to deal with the aftermath and run had become a rather disorderly house.

The Ring O'Bells in 1992 ...

... and in 2014

Pubs never cease to provide us with an insight into the goings-on in a community in times gone by. In 1859, James Gregory attacked Caroline Coombs in the Ring O'Bells. It was the finale to a quarrel that had begun earlier in the day. Caroline had been walking along Broadway when she spotted her son Edward in a field with James Gregory. They were behaving 'indecently' with some girls and Caroline intervened to put a stop to it. Evidently, James was still annoyed later that day when he saw her in the inn. After being knocked down by him, Caroline attempted to stand up, only to receive a second punch of such velocity that it knocked her head clean through the window. Unable to pay his £1 fine, James Gregory was committed for six weeks' imprisonment.

In August 1859, William Newport was charged with assaulting his wife Mercy at the Ring O'Bells. She explained that, 'I was with my husband at the Ring O'Bells. We had a quarrel, and he frequently ill-used me. He struck me several times in the face.' William Newport had been committed many times before and was sentenced to six months' hard labour. This was the nature of the inn which newly-widowed Elizabeth Hill was left to contend with. She gave up soon afterwards and Henry Lewis took over briefly.

What the Ring O'Bells needed was a firm hand. That is what Alfred Stevens was determined to supply. Did he take it too far though? In 1866, he was summonsed for assaulting one of his own customers, Alfred Keyford. The bench, however, dismissed the case since 'it appeared that the plaintiff deserved all the punishment he received'. Before long, ex-soldier George Watson had taken over, but he was not to have an easy time either.

In September 1873, the authorities in Frome decided to clamp down on the use of illegal measures in public houses. Countless pubs were caught up in the sweep – the Lion, the Half Moon, the Crown & Sceptre and the Ring O'Bells. It must have been quite some pub crawl for the constables that night. All the landlords were fined sixpence each, even though the bench was convinced none of them had had any dishonest intentions! It was simply a matter of law that only certain measurements were allowed to be used. Many landlords had been in the habit of serving beer in a so-called halfpenny-cup – about three-fifths of a pint – because that was what their customers preferred. George Watson soon opted to live on his army pension rather than continue to navigate ill-conceived licensing laws.

William Quartley, who took over next, was clearly a man to be reckoned with. In June 1876, customer James Whimpey was charged with assaulting Quartley and refusing to leave when ordered to do so. Quartley had ordered Whimpey to leave but instead Whimpey struck him and pulled out chunks from his whiskers, making his chin bleed. He also punched Richard Quartley, the landlord's brother. In court, Whimpey also looked like he had been badly beaten, a fact which did not escape the attention of the magistrates, who decided that he had been on the receiving end of 'very considerable punishment at the landlord's hands'. In the opinion of the bench they were 'quits'.

Quartley remained at the Ring O'Bells before retiring to live in the Butts with his wife, grandsons and adopted child, earning a living as a jobbing gardener. The Ring O'Bells was then run by Arthur Francis, followed by Arthur Adams, the latter establishing a friendly society before he left in 1904. In July that year, the licence was transferred to Henry Wells who was landlord until the outbreak of World War One.

Wells' tenure at the Ring O'Bells was marked by a singular act of bravery in 1909, when he forced his way into a neighbouring cottage that was on fire to extinguish what was rapidly turning into a veritable inferno. Anybody familiar with the geography of Victorian Frome will no doubt be aware that the fire station was a mere 300 yards from the Ring O'Bells. So why did Wells not summons the professionals? The reason was simple – there was a call-out charge and nobody wanted to incur the not insubstantial fee!

Wells left in September 1914 and was replaced by ex-soldier William Allibone from Northampton. Frome was by now filling up with soldiers and they needed somewhere to eat. Naturally, Allibone was only too glad to provide mess facilities for the 22 soldiers billeted next door. Occasionally, however, the presence of soldiers caused him a few problems. In March 1915, he was summonsed for serving ale to three members of the Royal Field Artillery – Sergeant Joseph Potts, Bombardier Matthew Conway and Bombardier William Cummings – on a Sunday morning. It was a borderline case at best and seemed to hinge on whether one of the parties involved had a watch that was running a few minutes fast. Fortunately, the sitting magistrate, Lord Bath, took a pragmatic approach. Although the police had been correct in bringing the case, as there was no evidence of guilty knowledge it was dismissed.

In March 1916, William Allibone, along with two Frome horse-dealers, Oliver and Alfred Drew, was summonsed for 'causing unnecessary suffering to a pony by omitting to supply it with sufficient food'. The pony belonged to the Drews, and Allibone had allowed them to keep it in his field for a short while. When they did not collect the pony, Allibone fed it on occasion, but it was dangerously emaciated by the time the matter reached the attention of the police. In court, Allibone explained that he had fed the pony 'out of sympathy. I could not see the pony starving in the field.' He was not responsible for the pony and was surprised to have received a summons for acting as a Good Samaritan. His daughter, Ellen, corroborated his story. The court concluded that Alfred Drew was legally responsible for the pony and fined him – but added that the landlord of the Ring O'Bells was also morally responsible!

Later that year Allibone left the inn and Robert Hugh Carr took over – at least until he joined the Royal Garrison Artillery in June 1917. The links between the Ring O'Bells and World War One servicemen lingered long. In 1943, ex-soldiers with the 1/4th Somerset Light Infantry from Frome and Midsomer Norton who had sailed on the Braemar Castle on 14 October 1914 were reunited in a meeting at the Ring O'Bells.

In 1992 Ushers Brewery sold the Ring O'Bells to Inntrepreneur Estates. It then passed on to Inspired Pubs in 2005 and finally to Punch Taverns. This fine old pub has suffered from serious lack of investment, despite the efforts of Liam Moore, the landlord for 20 years. After closing in 2014, the freehold was advertised for sale, and it was under offer at the time of going to print.

Rose & Crown, 20 The Butts

The Rose & Crown was a classic Victorian beerhouse, first run by John Edwards, part-time iron moulder and part-time innkeeper. His wife Frances was a member of the Shepton Mallet-based Showering family, who ran inns and went on to develop the famous Babycham brand in the twentieth century. John and Frances began running the Rose & Crown around 1860. With John Edwards working at the foundry, it would have been Frances, with her licensing-trade background, who managed the house during the day. In the evenings, John ran the house, assisted by Frances's brother, Alfred Marquis Showering, who went on to run the nearby Mechanics Arms and Somerset Arms. John's young cousin, Sarah Mills, also lived with the family and no doubt helped in the business.

Beerhouses first came into being under the 1830 Beer Act, designed to introduce free trade in beer by removing the requirements of a justices' licence, although opening hours were slightly more restricted than those of fully-licensed houses. Within the first three months alone, 26,291 licences were issued. Men like John Edwards saw running a beerhouse, often in tandem with a day job, as a handy means of turning their homes into money-making enterprises.

That the Rose & Crown was a rough and ready sort of place in the 1860s is evidenced by the countless scraps that took place there. For example, in 1860 customer Joshua Sainsbury was charged with assaulting John Davies, who was drinking quietly with some friends when Sainsbury came in and nearly upset the table. Davies was about to sing a song and the landlord told Sainsbury that he would not permit dancing there and asked him to be quiet and allow Davies to sing. But Sainsbury became noisier and, when Davies quietly spoke to him, he took hold of him and threw him back with such force that his head went through the window, breaking four panes in the process. It took three policemen to quell the disturbance.

In May 1862, Ann Jelly was summonsed for being drunk and riotous and 'cursing fearfully' outside the pub. John Burgess of New Buildings, along with Mary Ann Harvey and Martha Daniels, were summonsed for similar behaviour at the same time. Martha was so drunk that two passers-by had to carry her home. All were fined. This gives us some inkling of the type of establishment the Rose & Crown was when the Edwards family ran it.

In March 1863, John Edwards was summonsed for opening his house on a Sunday for the sale of beer. It seemed that at 12.30pm a woman went to the door of the beerhouse and Frances Edwards handed her out a half-gallon jar of beer. In his defence, John Edwards claimed he was unwell that night, otherwise he would have prevented his wife from selling the beer. He was still fined, however. Just possibly the magistrates did not believe his tale of ill health.

In June 1864, Harriet Barry was summonsed for unlawfully assaulting Eliza Jelly, who had gone to the inn to have a drink with a young man. Harriet Barry cursed her incessantly, threatened her life and tried to push her over. The case was dismissed as both parties were held to be at fault.

Interestingly when their children were born – Leonora in 1861 and John in 1863 – landlord John Edwards was described as a 'moulder' in the parish records, suggesting that his wife was running the inn. By 1865, the Edwards had left and were living in King Street. The beerhouse business was still in his veins, however, and he was soon running a house in Catherine Street, although ultimately he ended up as an unemployed moulder in Keyford.

Meanwhile, Thomas and Charlotte Coleman had taken over the Rose & Crown, moving from Tytherington Lane where Thomas had worked as a labourer. Thomas, like his predecessor, had two occupations, being both beerhouse-keeper and a labourer on the highways. So no doubt as before, the day-to-day running of the Rose & Crown was the responsibility of the landlord's wife, who had to balance this work with raising a large family.

In April 1872, the licence was transferred from William Coleman to Henry Yerbury, yet just how amicable an arrangement this was is open to question. Matters came to a head in 1874, by which point Charlotte Coleman was running another beerhouse in Frome. Henry Yerbury, while still landlord of the Rose & Crown, was summonsed by Charlotte Coleman for assaulting her and refusing to leave the beerhouse she was running. Under pressure from her family, Charlotte was compelled to drop the case.

In 1874 Julia Ransome, a 'loose character' with a string of convictions to her name, was summonsed for refusing to leave when landlord Yerbury asked her to and he was compelled to throw her out himself. The case, however, was not as clear cut as Yerbury first made out. Julia had been drinking there from ten in the morning to eleven at night. Clearly, the Yerburys had no reservations in taking every last penny she had. Eventually, Julia even exchanged her clothes and possessions with the landlady for fresh beer. As the night drew on, Julia's mother came to take her home, and she started to finish up her beer. Yerbury, however, ordered her to leave straight away. Julia insisted on drinking up every last drop, whereupon Yerbury threw her violently into the road. Julia produced two witnesses to back up her story, but, since they had both been in trouble themselves in the past, the bench did not listen to them. She was sentenced to 14 days in prison, with no option of a fine. Yerbury subsequently barred not just Julia but all of her relatives from the Rose & Crown. It is hard to see any real justice in this case.

Henry Yerbury did not remain long after this and was succeeded by Samuel Lusty, who went on to run the Albion in Cheap Street. By 1881, James S Stevens was running things, although he left within a year and was succeeded by John Philip. Like his predecessors, Philip did not remain long and was succeeded by equally short-lived tenants, Frederick Ghode and William Chambers.

In the late nineteenth century, the Rose & Crown joined the ranks of Frome's long lost pubs. The building was later demolished and the site redeveloped.

Royal Oak, Broadway

The Royal Oak at Broadway, or Cottles Oak, occupies a building dating from the early 1700s which was originally a short row of cottages, although the surplus doors have long since been obscured. It has been much altered since, losing the mullioned windows on the first floor during the twentieth century, although an ogee three-light mullion window survives on the ground floor. It has also been extended, with a modern addition to the rear, and, as is to be expected, the interior reflects little of its eighteenth-century past.

It opened in the early 1830s and in 1836 was targeted by burglars. They broke into the cellars, broached the casks and carried off two hogsheads of strong beer. The identity of the culprits was well-known – or at least strongly suspected – but insufficient evidence precluded conviction. The landlord at the time was 67-year-old Nathaniel Flower, previously a slubber – somebody who prepared wool for spinning into cloth. He had recently married 49-year-old widow Hannah Biss.

When Nathaniel died in 1846, Hannah ran the Royal Oak until the late 1850s, when her son, Charles Biss, became landlord. He passed on the business to his son, Charles Biss Jr, who died in 1882. Subsequently, the inn passed in quick succession from Joseph Picard Clifford to carpenter Herbert Jelly. Jelly's parents, George and Anne, were also in the licensing trade, running the New Inn in the Butts, so the Royal Oak should have been in safe hands. Jelly, however, was less than steady and his tenure at the Royal Oak was brief and somewhat eventful. Within a week, there was trouble. Inebriated customer William Coleman refused to leave even when the police were summoned, and was ably assisted in his obstinacy by fellow drinkers, Thomas Coleman and Albert Sparey. William Coleman was fined ten shillings, Thomas Coleman five shillings, but poor Albert Sparey had to endure 14 days' hard labour because he could not afford his 7s 6d fine.

It was a bad start for Jelly and things scarcely improved, as in July 1887 he was fined £1 for keeping unlicensed hounds. A bad reputation was forming and, at the licensing sessions in August 1887, Superintendent Joseph Williams told the magistrates that

> this house has, it appears, been kept open till eleven o'clock at night; but as it is not, so far as I can ascertain, within the limits of the town of Frome ... it should, I believe, if this be so, close at 10 o'clock at night.

Jelly had drawn unwelcome attention to the Royal Oak. Time was called on his tenancy and the next month he was ousted. There followed over the next decade a series of landlords who had very little success. Walter Mattock went bankrupt and Herbert Barter got into trouble for selling beer to intoxicated men. Henry 'George' Lapham could only afford to take the place on in 1909 if he continued working as a mason whilst his wife Emily ran the pub. Not that he was complaining, having begun his working life as an agricultural labourer in his early teens.

Emily Lapham outside the Royal Oak before the First World War

At the outbreak of war, James Wilkins was landlord. When he was called up, his wife Clara was granted a temporary licence to manage the house for him. She was a popular landlady, as is evidenced from her accommodating approach to her customers – which frequently landed her in trouble. In January 1917, she was summonsed for breaching 'DORA' (the Defence of the Realm Act) by 'knowingly allowing soldiers to be on her premises at 9.35pm' – the closing time under DORA being 9pm. In her defence, Clara pleaded that she had asked the soldiers to leave three times, had never had trouble with soldiers before and that her husband had been called up and she was 'trying to do her best for him'. The bench was unmoved, fining her and issuing a sharp warning.

Even after hostilities ceased in Europe, trouble still brewed at the Royal Oak. In January 1919, William Horler, a Frome miner who had received head injuries during the war and was suffering from shell shock, was summonsed for stealing a half-pint glass from the Royal Oak. The prosecution was not brought by the landlady but by the police who had seemingly been keeping the house under surveillance. With a soldier for a husband and a brother who had spent four years in a prisoner of war camp, Clara would have been unlikely to testify against an injured veteran. Horler, she claimed, had only drunk ginger beer all evening and had put the glass in his pocket absent-mindedly whilst chatting to a man he had served with in France. In her opinion, he was an honest, sober and reliable man. Clara's fierce defence of her customer won the day and Horler was given the well-deserved benefit of the doubt. Nevertheless, the police did manage to convict Clara of breaching DORA a few months later – this time for selling beer after hours.

The Royal Oak in 1992 ...   ... and in 2012

Clara Wilkins and her husband left in 1921 and the pub settled down. Following World War Two, another ex-serviceman took over. James Henry Singer had served in the Navy for 22 years before entering the licensing trade. After a spell at the Sun Inn, he took over the Royal Oak and was both successful and popular. In 1948 he was granted a full licence, allowing him to sell wines and spirits as well as beer. Sadly, he died the following year and was much lamented in Frome.

In more recent years the Royal Oak's claim to fame has been as the watering hole of one-time Frome resident and former Bond Girl, Lois Maxwell, and it survives as an excellent local with friendly staff, well-kept beer and good food.

Royal Standard, 12 Horton Street

In January 1831, the *Salisbury and Wiltshire Journal* contained the following marriage notice:

> Married, a few days since, Mr James Poolman, of the Royal Standard, Frome, to Miss Hannah Cooke of the same place.

Despite this, no inn or beerhouse by the name of the Royal Standard is recorded in any directory of Frome during this period. What is more, within a decade James and Hannah Poolman were living in the Market Place, not Horton Street, and James was working as a carpenter. He was still so employed a decade later when he was living in Catherine Street. There was still no beerhouse or inn in Horton Street by the mid-1800s. So the question remains, where was the original Royal Standard and what happened to it? All of which leads us to the subject of the Royal Standard in Horton Street itself.

Its first recorded landlord was Thomas Rouse, a wheelwright, who was there from 1872 to 1886. He had been landlord of the Sun on Catherine Hill for a brief period in the 1860s, but continued to work as a wheelwright throughout. Did he perhaps open the beerhouse on Horton Street, taking its name from the pub once run by James Poolman? Possibly, although he had bought the Horton Street premises as far back as 1859 from the Barber family, who had been unable to keep up their payments on the house. It failed to reach its reserve at auction, so Thomas Rouse shrewdly swooped in after the auction had finished and made them an offer they could not refuse. Rouse paid the Barbers £140, of which £103 was used to pay off their debts. The sale included a patch of 'garden ground and weaving shops built thereupon'. On 1 September 1886, Rouse sold the long lease (950 years from 1755) to William Baily for £505. The Royal Standard was intriguingly described as a freehold property comprising

> that substantially-built, well known, old established, long leasehold free beerhouse, situate in Horton Street, Frome, known as the Royal Standard, with outbuildings and three storied brewery at the back thereof, now and for many years in the occupation of the owner, during which period a profitable business has been carried out.

Naturally, 'old established' is not a precise term and it could simply refer to the 15 years Thomas Rouse had been running it; it is impossible to say.

Thomas Rouse

William Smith took over as landlord, but his time there was not always happy. In 1889 tragedy struck. Mrs Mary Ann Smith raised the alarm when she could not find her four-year-old daughter Alice. After a frantic search, William Smith and neighbour George Humphries decided to climb down into the well to look. At the bottom they found the poor child dead under the well cover. The inquest was held the following day at the inn, and the jury and coroner gave their fees to Humphries in recognition of his brave attempt to save the child.

In February 1893, Edward Cosh, Walter Cosh and Samuel Smith were all summonsed for being drunk at the Royal Standard. When the police arrived, they had found Samuel Smith slouched by the fire, Edward Cosh sitting on a table and Walter Cosh propping up a wall in the passageway. They were all inebriated but Mrs Smith claimed they had only had a couple of pints, and she had not noticed they were drunk until after she had served them. So how had they come to be so drunk? The answer was simple – they all worked for Frome United Breweries and had been helping themselves to the stock all day! They were all fined, and, rather unfairly, poor William Smith also found himself charged with permitting drunkenness! The bench considered there had been negligence on the part of the landlord and his wife but concluded that justice would best be met by issuing them with a caution rather than a fine.

William Smith stayed at the Royal Standard until 1911, when William Henry White took over for two years, followed by Charles Plume who held the licence for only one year.

Thomas Curtis became licensee at the start of the war, but a decade later, in 1924, the Royal Standard, now owned by Frome United Breweries, faced the threat of closure. This was despite the building being in a good state of repair with trade increasing. However, there were two fully-licensed houses and two other beerhouses within 520 yards. A petition, signed by 99 regulars, helped to win a reprieve, and Thomas Curtis remained landlord until 1935, when Alfred Curtis took over. The Curtis family still held the licence in 1961 when the Royal Standard closed.

During the 1950s, local man Trevor Biggs lived opposite. His recollections provide an invaluable picture of the pub and its landlord in those days:

> When I was tall enough to reach the Jug & Bottle window, I would go to get mum's Woodbines. Alf Curtis was the landlord. His wife lost both her legs late in life. Charlie Adams, the council plumber, and Ken Whatley would go in each night and carry her upstairs on a kitchen chair. Alf made his own darts boards. The saw mills at Spring Gardens would cut him slices off the trunk of a tree, about two inches thick. He would mark them up, and fit wires using bicycle spokes, with pipe for the bull. He sometimes used hacksaw blades instead of spokes. The only setback was they had to be soaked in the rainwater butt every couple of days or they would dry out and split. He made me one, but I forgot to soak it. Alf hated the introduction of the trebles board. He would mark his both sides, trebles one side and doubles the other for the REAL darts players to use … What he would think of today's darts players not having to start on a double, I cannot imagine.

Another local resident, Trevor Weston, also recalls visits to the Royal Standard in the 1950s:

> When I was a boy my friends and I used to crawl out the back and get the empty bottles and then take them to the pub to collect the money back for them!

Colin White of Frome also recalls the landlady being carried up to bed each night on a kitchen chair, and tells another story which illustrates her resourcefulness:

> She found a novel way of cooking dinner. She had a large biscuit tin in which she would put the meat and the vegetables and roast it on the fire.

He also recalls how well-kept the beer was:

> Alf Curtis was a meticulous barman. The beer he served had to be perfect. He kept a lighted candle in the window by the bar and would hold the glass of

In this view of Horton Street in the 1950s, the Royal Standard can be seen in the distance on the left

beer behind it to make sure it was the right colour before he would sell it. Once a month a friend, Mrs Clark, would cook a tray of faggots. These would be served in the evening free of charge to regulars. Some mornings Alf would open at 6.00am for the quarrymen to go in!

In the early 1960s many public houses in Somerset were being closed down. At this time, the owners of Royal Standard also held the licence for the Eagle at Great Elm and the White House Hotel in Frome. When they applied to take over the licence of the Woolpack in Lower Keyford, this was granted on condition they relinquished the licences of the Eagle and the Royal Standard. They agreed and the pub was no more.

The former Royal Standard in 2014

Selwood Foresters Arms / Selwood Gardens Inn / Selwood Inn, Clink Road

The tithe map of 1840 shows a small house and a garden on plot 651 but gives no indication that it was selling beer. Phillip Crocker was the owner and John Young the occupier. In 1847, when it was up for auction at the Crown Inn, it was described as a small cottage situated at Clink Cross Ways with over an acre of land and gardens lately in the occupation of John Hamlett, nurseryman, recently deceased. It had substantial high walls, a 'hot house warmed by a heating apparatus upon the newest and most approved principle', a seed-house, cucumber and melon frames, peach trees, 'vines of the best sort which are vigorous in growth', etc, etc. A thriving nursery in fact – all it needed was a pub to complete the enterprise.

In 1868, a wine & spirit licence was granted to Jeremiah Singer of the Selwood Foresters Arms, Clink Cross Roads, on the grounds that the two nearest fully-licensed houses were the Black Swan and the Ship at Oldford, an indication that the Vine Tree had yet to be built. Little is known about this house which is a shame as it must have been quite a novelty, part pub and part nursery.

By 1875 it was being run by Edmund Parfitt, described as a brewer and spirit merchant. By 1879 it had become the Selwood Gardens Inn, and was in the hands of Isaac Elton, listed in the 1881 census as a widower, gardener and innkeeper. The OS map of 1886 (reproduced on the right) shows a range of low buildings with lots of outdoor seating and what look like greenhouses and extensive grounds.

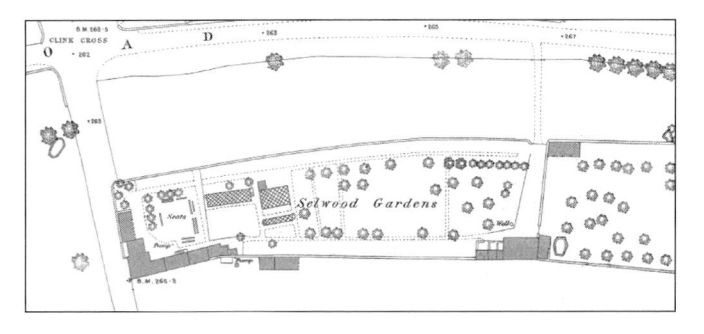

John Wilcox and his wife Fanny outside the Selwood Inn around 1910. The two people on the left are probably their son Herbert, who worked as a gardener, and their daughter Winifred.

A somewhat better conducted gathering than the notorious rabbit-coursing meeting, with John Wilcox carrying a beer out to one of his customers.

130

Isaac Elton moved to the Albion in Cheap Street in 1881 and was replaced by John Wilcox, another professional gardener, who decorated the pub with plants from his greenhouses for the annual pub supper in 1901. He changed the name of the beerhouse once again, shortening it to the Selwood Inn.

Gardening and pulling pints were not Wilcox's only interests however. In 1906 he was the promoter of a rabbit-coursing meeting near the pub which resulted in a fight, during which his head was pushed through a glass door and three men were arrested. The bench was not particularly sympathetic, telling him that, if he was going to hold such meetings, he 'could not be surprised if the house became the resort of disorderly characters and disturbances took place'.

In this photograph, the name of John Wilcox can just be made out above the entrance to the Selwood Inn

The site of the Selwood Inn in 2013

They asked the superintendent of police to make further enquiries as to the general conduct of the house and, if necessary, bring them up at the annual licensing session. This took place a couple of weeks later, with Wilcox's licence being renewed on condition that he did not promote any more rabbit coursing and that those terms be endorsed on the licence.

He must have stayed well away from rabbits, as he continued at the pub until 1922, a total of 43 years. In that year, the licensing committee decided to close the pub despite his pleas that he had between 200 and 300 customers per week, and could accommodate over 150 cars on Cheese Show day. The inn was described as a very pleasant place with lawns and flower beds – the sort of place that the magistrates might like to encourage – nonetheless they closed it and he was paid £942 11s 4d in compensation.

In May 1923 the Licensed Victuallers' Association presented him with an 'easy chair in which he might sit and reflect upon his past good work for the association'. He was one of its founding members and had served on the committee for 20 years. John Wilcox retired to Rose Cottage at Clink where he died in 1938, aged 85.

Ship / Olive Tree / Artisan, 6 Christchurch Street West

Along with the Three Swans, the Crown and the Sun, the Ship at Badcox is one of Frome's oldest watering holes. It is unclear when it opened, the first record for it dating from 1633 when an unfortunate local by the name of Robert Jesser died there after a bout of heavy drinking. The landlord at the time was William Chapman. The building dates from the late 1500s or early 1600s, and thus predates the main Trinity development, which began in 1665. This was a time when public houses had their own private wells and one still exists within the property, covered with reinforced glass. In the shaft are two entrances, believed by some to lead into Frome's infamous and largely unexplained tunnel system. Despite countless alterations, one other indication of the building's great age survives – an unaltered window from the 1600s on the first floor looking out onto Christchurch Street.

The 1774 map of Frome shows the Ship as a square building facing out across an area called Seven Dials, which is now known as Badcox. By 1813, when a survey of Frome was conducted, the inn had been enlarged on the east side with the addition of an adjoining house, the front of which was aligned towards what is now Christchurch Street West.

As for the early ownership of the Ship, it was probably in the hands of the Leversedge family, Lords of the Manor of Frome for many generations. They never occupied the premises, which explains why in 1727 Thomas Edgill was paying the church rates 'for ye ship 8d'. In 1738, Rev Dr Lionel Seaman inherited the manor of Frome Branch from his Leversedge kin, and in 1742 became vicar of Frome. The Ship was not the only pub the vicar owned; he also had the nearby Pack Horse Inn. Rev Dr Seaman was a remarkable man, possessed of a unique talent for inspiring passionate loathing. In 1750, some Frome residents even took the time to drop him a line to express their thoughts:

> Seaman, or Sea Devil, we send this to let thee know what the people of this parish say by thee. They say that thou art a damnable wicked villain to use the parish as thou dost and that thou art no more fit to go up in the pulpit than the Devil himself, for he is far honester than thou and that thou lookst when thou art at church like a ... son of a whore full of malice against most of the good people there and everyone at Frome that knows thee hates thee and wish the devil had come to Frome before thou hadst ... We do assure thee, that God and man is full resolved to take thee off very soon and ... for thou being such a damnable wicked dog we have ordered thou shalt have no Christian burial. We have already looked out a place to put thy cursed carcase in at Marston Cross Ways and we have got long stakes to drive through thy cursed body. We would have thee prepare very soon for thy departure for Charon the Ferryman of hell was ... with his boat to carry thee over the river Styx and on thy corpse this epitaph shall be fixed: Here lyeth the body of Lionel Sea Devil aged 47 years taken off by God's appointment on 25th November 1750 born in the parish of Scudamore Upton near Warminster in the County of Wilts, a Swine Herd.

Aside from the near-comical vehemence expressed in the letter, what must immediately strike us is the writer's relative erudition. These were not the words of a labouring man. But why was it written? The answer lies at least in part in Seaman's attitude towards the town's victuallers. Despite happily accepting their rent, Rev Seaman was no friend to the publican. In 1744, for example, William Dew, Richard Singer and Johan Hinton were prosecuted by Seaman's churchwardens for 'prophaning the Sabbath by entertaining Tiplers in Time of Divine Service'.

Was it perhaps the enmity of Frome's innkeepers that inspired the great diatribe? A subsequent letter of 1758/9 suggests this may have been the case:

> Mr Seamen this is to let you know we will soon put an end to you if you do ever offer to stop the Rafling or Bull Baiting as you talk of making every house pay ten pounds you heratick we will when we do catch you in any by road we will dig a grave and bury you a live as shure as you are now living there is no one in the Town of Frome but what hates you and we who are going to write our names will surely do it
>
> From your humble servant. R.W., I.L., R.O., J.W., O.R., L.L., A.H., O.M., L.H., A.R., J.T., R.B., A.T., F.W., H.J., W.T.

Activities like bull-baiting were closely linked to public houses and banning them would have been perceived as a threat by licensed victuallers. As a result of the second letter, the churchwardens were ordered to be even more vigilant in their prosecution of victuallers guilty of gaming or 'rafling'. How ironic, then, that some publicans were paying rent to the very man attempting to crush their livelihoods. In 1751, Rev Seaman sold most of his estate to the Earl of Cork, but for whatever reason kept the Ship. Finally, in June 1780 the remaining estate of the by-now deceased Rev Lionel Seaman was auctioned. Lot 1 was 'a messuage or tenement called the Ship Inn with the stables, outhouses, gardens and timber yard to the same belonging, in the possession of William Butler or his undertenants'.

William Butler is recorded as occupying the inn as early as 1766 and it seems likely that he actually bought it himself at the 1780 auction. He later sold it to William Stokes, by which time a somewhat insalubrious reputation was fast attaching itself to the inn. In 1817, when Constable Gregory was summoned to deal with a disturbance there, he found that money had been stolen and the occupants were fighting. By 1829, when ownership had passed into the hands of William Hiscocks and his wife Martha, William Stokes was languishing in a debtors gaol in London. Hiscocks died childless in 1855 and the inn passed to his four siblings, before eventually ending up in the hands of his nephew, ER Trotman, who, over a period of several decades leading up to 1881, purchased his family's shares in the Ship.

A young Joshua Rendall took over as landlord in 1850, and, after his death in 1862, the licence passed to his widow Elizabeth. That the Ship was a rough and tumble sort of pub in the 1870s is beyond dispute, but few would have guessed quite how explosive things would get. In early May 1871, gas pipes had been laid in Christchurch Street West. Shortly after eight o'clock on the evening of 14 May there was a huge explosion in the vicinity of the Ship. Paving stones were torn up for a 20-yard stretch, many being left six inches above their beds, and at the Ship an entire water closet exploded. Two boys walking past were thrown up into the air and out into the road. The blast was heard and felt some distance away and people living close to the exploding toilet reported being knocked to the ground. Mercifully, there were no serious injuries. It was supposed that the gas had somehow found its way into the town drain and had been accidentally ignited.

Combustible lavatories were the least of landlady Elizabeth Rendall's worries. Located as it was in a neighbourhood notorious for loose-living and immorality, the Ship was inevitably a magnet for dubious characters. Fortunately Mrs Rendall could always rely on the ready assistance of her daughters Georgina, Alice, Arethusa and Sarah. And what assistance it was! In May 1873 customer Charles Dix got into a fight in the tap room, resulting in considerable damage to Mrs Rendall's furniture. Another man, Sidney Dunford, guarded the door to prevent anybody interfering with the fight. Poor widow Rendall and her helpless daughters, their business being smashed to pieces in front of them! Helpless? Not a bit of it. The young Rendall ladies, broomsticks in hand, battered the pugilists into submission. Dix later complained of a deep cut to his head, but was nevertheless fined for fighting.

Not everything could be solved with a swift swipe of a broom. Breaches of licensing legislation were a far trickier matter – particularly the 1872 Licensing Act. This act codified the offences which a licence holder might commit. Repeated convictions led to the loss of a licence and it was deemed particularly reprehensible to permit prostitutes to linger on the premises. For the Ship, located near a rendezvous for such women, the new legislation was especially inconvenient. In December 1873, Mrs Rendall was summonsed for 'knowingly allowing immoral characters to remain in her house for longer than necessary for the purpose of taking reasonable refreshment'. At the hearing it was revealed that the police had repeatedly cautioned Mrs Rendall as to the 'disorderly' state of her house. As a consequence, the policemen of Frome had been ordered to visit the house frequently! The Ship, claimed Superintendent Deggan, was known as 'an habitual resort' for prostitutes. Mrs Rendall put up the only defence possible – that she had not knowingly done it. It worked and the case was dismissed. This lenient treatment did not pass without comment, and one irate resident sent his thoughts to the *Frome Times*:

> Dear Sir,
> I am at a loss to understand the decision given by the bench on Thursday last in reference to the summons against the landlady of the Ship Inn. It appears to me ... that the police know little about their work ...

Mrs Rendall weathered the storm and remained at the helm until 1879. In May that year she complained that a new drain was defective and causing problems with sewage, and requested compensation for lost business as a consequence of her yard and stables being closed. The application was declined and in August the licence was transferred to James Peacock.

The seedy reputation of the pub persisted, and in June 1882 a rather curious incident occurred. Three men – Walter Long, Henry Benger and James Wilcox – were drinking together when Walter broke a glass and the ostler asked him to pay for it. Long refused and opted to strike the ostler instead. Wilcox joined in while Benger kept watch, occasionally hitting the landlord, James Peacock, for good measure. Not surprisingly, the three maladroits were duly summonsed to appear in court a few days later. In the meantime, something happened. For reasons which never became evident, James Peacock changed his story – Benger had not attacked him after all. In fact Peacock dropped the charges against all three men. The magistrates were unimpressed and concluded, no doubt correctly, that Peacock was now lying. Had pressure been brought to bear on him? It seems likely, but it could never be proven.

A labour demonstration marches past the Ship in 1917

Renovation underway in 1992
The Olive Tree in 2013

In early 1916, the pub was in the papers once more, this time on account of the animosity between the landlord, Thomas Henry Courts, and his wife Annie, who were going through a publicly acrimonious separation. Annie wanted shares in Frome United Breweries and certain other money and took her husband to court to obtain them. They had married in 1895, and in 1896 her husband had gone to South Africa, remaining there until the outbreak of the Boer War. During his absence she had worked as a dressmaker and deposited her earnings in a savings bank. Fortunately, the feuding pair reached an agreement out of court.

After they left, there was a string of landlords, all of whom seemed to manage to keep the Ship in good shape. It closed in 1989 and remained empty for the next four years until it was bought by local businessman Paul McGuinness. He sold it on to Scottish and Newcastle Enterprises in 2003 and, after a £250,000 refurbishment, Adrian Moore and Nikos Andriakopoulos reopened it as the Olive Tree pub and restaurant They left in 2007, but the Olive Tree remained open, specialising in Thai cuisine, before closing early in 2015. It was subsequently acquired by Anna Brady and Siobhan Cook, and reopened in June 2015 after a major redecoration and refit as the Artisan Pub & Kitchen.

Ship, Oldford

Little seems to have been recorded about the early days of this pub, but a large L-shaped building appears on a 1799 map of Lullington drawn by A Crocker, the surveyor for Viscount Weymouth, and there is a reference on the 1813 Cruse map to a meadow 'behind the Shiphouse at Old Ford' (identified as plot 528), which was owned by the Rook Lane Meeting House with Steven Goddard as tenant. The church rates of 1823 and 1826 also refer to a plot owned by the Earl of Cork and occupied by Stephen Goddard, which is described as 'Ship Oldford'.

Apart from these rather sparse references, the first substantive reference to it as a pub comes in the 1861 census, where the bizarrely named Forehead Eames is listed as a beer seller, aged 26, living with his wife Fanny and two sons at Oldford.

On 7 September 1864, the *Frome Times* reported that a spirit licence had been applied for: 'Mr Messiter (solicitor) put in a memorial which had been signed by a large number of the inhabitants of the district. He dwelt on the distance at which the house was situated from any licensed house. The premises were commodious and had recently been greatly improved and Mr Eames bore a very high character. After a brief deliberation the bench granted the application.'

An indenture of 1864 records the transfer of the freehold, which included some tenanted cottages, from Alfred John Taylor, a hairdresser, to Edmund Baily for £555. It also refers to a James Pickford running the place before Mr Eames.

The inn sign in 1969 ...

... and in the 1990s

By the census of 1871, Eames had added three more to his brood, and by 1875 he had moved on, popping up at the Eagle Inn at Elm in Somerset in the 1881 census. His place was taken by William Bennett, followed by Henry Kitley, a shoemaker.

In 1889, a licence was granted to John Broadribb, and in 1905 magistrates approved plans by Frome United Breweries to rebuild the pub further back, so that the lane could be widened. They added that 'the company would probably ask the bench for permission to carry on business in one of the adjoining cottages whilst work was in progress'. The present building dates from this time.

By 1911, Fred Nicholas, who was married to John Broadribb's daughter, had taken over. In 1946, his son, also called Fred Nicholas, who had been born in the pub, succeeded him. When he retired in 1963, the pub had been in the Broadribb and Nicholas families for 74 years.

The Ship became an Ushers' house, followed by a spell with Scottish & Newcastle, and remained a lively local, serving food and raising various sums for charities, but its quiet out-of-town location and the smoking and drink-drive laws proved its undoing and it closed in 2008. Since that time it has been completely refurbished, and reopened as the Bay Leaf Indian restaurant in 2012.

The Ship in 2014 ... as the Bay Leaf restaurant

Somerset Arms, 90 The Butts

There is one respect in which the Somerset Arms is unusual – we know exactly when it opened and when it closed. It was opened as a beerhouse in 1861 by Francis Franks. A year later, when he applied for a full licence, his solicitor argued that he had built fabulous premises at great expense and there was no other fully-licensed house within half a mile. The population of the Butts, numbering at that time over a thousand, seemed to justify a fully-licensed house. Francis Franks, though not a native of Frome, had lived there for eleven years and was clearly committed to establishing a place in the community. A petition in favour of granting the licence was signed by a large number of respectable residents and, more importantly perhaps, the police had no objections.

Unfortunately, WJ Harvey, reporter for the *Somerset and Wiltshire Journal*, happened to be in court when the application came up, and raised an objection. He lived a few doors away from the Somerset Arms, and claimed that, since it had opened, he had witnessed a large amount of drunkenness and rioting in the neighbourhood. When questioned, Harvey admitted that he was a teetotaller and that, although he claimed that such disturbances were frequent, he had never called the police.

Superintendent Deggan had no issue with the way Franks conducted his house, since no complaint had been made against him. Whilst there was indeed a good deal of drunkenness in The Butts, it had not increased in the year since Franks had opened his house. Nevertheless, whilst Lord Bath had no objections to the spirit licence being granted, the other two magistrates had, and Franks' plans were foiled. The following year, he tried again, armed not only with another year's experience, but also a memorial signed by Rev de Gex of Christ Church, Mr Brice, the churchwarden, and a large number of the leading inhabitants of the town. All testified to the eligibility of the house, the respectability of Mr Franks and the requirements of the neighbourhood.

He was successful, and to celebrate produced a series of tokens for the pub, featuring his likeness on one side! It was not all plain sailing, however. Right from the outset he had trouble, and was assaulted by a drunken, bellicose customer who both smashed up the pub and bit Mr Franks. He left in 1872, and for the remainder of that decade there followed a series of short-lived landlords, beginning with Robert Green, from the White Hart in Wells.

In 1873, Franks, who had moved to Floral Cottage, next door, put the Somerset Arms up for auction, describing it as a 'freehold public house fronting the turnpike road from Frome to Bruton'.

The next landlord was former soldier Alfred Brown, newly returned from spells in Ireland and Gibraltar. In November 1878, the licence was transferred from Alfred Showering to Emma Clacee. Both these individuals had previously been licensees of the nearby Antelope Inn, which like the Somerset Arms, was now owned by the Lamb Brewery. By 1890, however, the Somerset Arms had been taken over by Frome United Breweries.

In December 1885, James Knight took over what was becoming an increasingly troubled public house. One customer, Annie Jelly, was particularly troublesome. In 1887 she was fined five shillings for disorderly conduct and refusing to leave, and two years later she stabbed her husband in the face at

The former Somerset Arms in 2013

the pub. The trials and tribulations were endless for poor James Knight, who in 1890 was summonsed for unlawfully supplying customer Richard White with drink when he was already intoxicated. It was his second offence, but the magistrate decided not to endorse his licence. Nevertheless, he left the following month, perhaps persuaded to do so by the brewery or perhaps because he had had enough.

James Rogers, former landlord of the Angel, took over. He was soon in trouble too, summonsed for allowing drunkenness on the premises and for keeping his house open after hours. Both cases were dropped, not least because the alleged illegal drinking had occurred only three minutes after closing time!

During World War One, the pub was run by Edwin Say, a well-known face on the Frome scene, who had previously run the Crown at Keyford. But this was war, and even busy publicans were expected to do their bit. Edwin Say was 40 when conscription was introduced, and classified C1, meaning he was not fit for active service but suitable for carrying out war work at home. For Edwin this meant spending an exhausting day making munitions at Messrs Singers, followed by an equally tiring night running his pub. Still, there was room for other activities. Almost a month to the day before the Armistice, Edwin dug up a large May Queen in his vegetable patch – this, of course, was a potato and it weighed in at a staggering 21 lbs 12 oz.

The licence was revoked in 1926, as there were two other pubs nearby and the takings only amounted to £24 per week. The property was acquired by the Smith family who lived there for a number of years, and it survives today as an imposing private house.

Spread Eagle, 25 Castle Street (formerly Long Row)

First mentioned as being run by Elizabeth Cooke in 1753, the Spread Eagle seems to have remained in her family until around 1778, when the rates started to be paid by Thomas Morgan. In the census of 1785 it is owned and run by William Hiscox, but from 1792 to 1807 the Cook family name appears once more in the churchwarden's accounts, so possibly there is some marriage link here and the Cooks never really left. The entry for 1800 has the owner as Mrs Cook with Ann Cook as the occupier. The Cook family also owned the Unicorn and the Cross Keys at this time.

It passed to Charles Tibbuts around 1814, but by the time of the 1841 census it was occupied by Henry Harrold and his family. On 1 January 1859, the *Somerset & Wilts Journal* reported that landlord Benjamin Sheppard had dared to sell beer outside of permitted hours:

> Sergeant Banting saw a woman come out of the house at a quarter to twelve on the night of Christmas Day, with a jug concealed under her apron. The defendant pleaded that the beer was being sent to his daughter but the magistrates did not recognise this excuse and on the superintendent stating that the house was one that gave them much trouble he was fined 20s.

Mr Sheppard must have been an interesting chap. The 1861 census describes him as a 'Chelsea Pensioner and innkeeper' from Taunton, aged 62, which implies that he had served in the army for 20 years or been injured in service. Whatever his story, he seems to have had scant regard for the law as he was cautioned several times for serving out of hours and disorderly conduct. On one memorable occasion, two men were arrested in his house for 'behaving indecently' in front of three women. What actually happened is unclear: the report only stated that 'the evidence, which is totally unfit for publication, disclosed proceedings of the most disgraceful character'. It must have been bad, as they were both fined the huge sum of £5 plus costs!

Benjamin's fun came to an end in 1863 when Joseph Plank, shoemaker and former landlord of the Boot, took over. He began advertising carriages

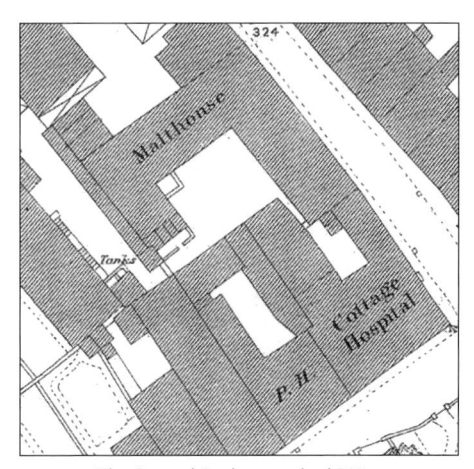

The Spread Eagle – marked P.H. – on the 1886 OS map

for hire which he could not have done at his previous place, as it was very small and there was no space for horses or carriages. He was only there for a few years and by 1873 the pub had passed to William Coleman.

The licensing laws at the time specified that beer could only be sold in certain quantities. 'Frome strong beer' was sold at two and a half pence per pint, but many landlords sold two-fifths or three-fifths of a pint for a penny or a penny-halfpenny respectively. They claimed this was done because customers requested it, and, although the charge of 'selling illegal measures' makes it sound as though the customer was being sold short, this was not the case at all. The practice was very common and convenient for all – apart from the law. Coleman and many other landlords in the district were fined 2s 6d in a great purge during 1873.

By the census of 1881, William Coleman, licensed victualler, age 37, was at the Spread Eagle with his wife Eliza, and his brother and sister Robert and Sarah. A report in the *Western Gazette* for 30 November 1883 tells of a fight involving Eliza Chambers, William Coleman's former housekeeper. It seems that Eliza was estranged from her husband John and had been having a relationship with her employer of the past four years, resulting in the birth of a son, Edward, during 1883.

William Coleman left the pub soon afterwards, possibly because of this incident – and worse was to follow. Early in 1887, Eliza was arrested in Birmingham, having left Frome and taking with her two £5 notes, £5 10s in gold, two silver watches and a quantity of bed linen, 'the property of William Coleman now of Dyers Close Lane'. She appeared in court with a baby in her arms, alongside a young man named Walter Long, who was charged with receiving the money and watches. They pleaded guilty and each received two months with hard labour. The grandson of young Edward Coleman still lives in Frome and we are grateful to him for this information.

A few years later, in 1887, the then landlord Albert Stone was summonsed for allowing 'skittling for beer' on his premises. Stone and his wife had asked a youth to play skittles with them for a pint or so of beer, which he did, but this apparently harmless bit of fun was classified as gambling and therefore illegal. The landlord pleaded total ignorance of this law, but was nonetheless convicted and fined forty shillings, with the report stating that 'this has lately been a growing practice and has attracted the attention of the police'.

For whatever reason, the Spread Eagle's days were numbered and in 1891 the owners, Frome United Breweries, sold it to Mr J Tanner of Butler & Tanner, the printers, and it closed. Between then and 1925 the building was partly demolished and appears on photographs of the time pretty much as it does today. We have been unable to find any pictures of it before its demolition.

All that is left –
the Spread Eagle in 2014

Star & Garter, Coward's Batch, Milk Street

The invaluable Frome map of 1774 shows that this pub stood on the corner of Castle Street and Milk Street on a small patch of land known as Coward's Batch, named after a previous owner, 'Widow Coward', who is shown as paying land tax on the site in 1766. There is a portrait in Frome Museum of a James Biggs which states that he was landlord of the pub around 1760 but we have found no confirmation of this, and it is not mentioned in the list of his other holdings in the church rates for that period.

The first positive mention comes in the church rates for 1763 which mention 'Josh Cooke at ye Star & Garter'. Edward Barnard is shown as ratepayer from 1783 with Charles Sweetland taking over in 1790. Sweetland owned a number of buildings in the road although Barnard is still shown as paying rates on 9 Coward's Batch in 1792. Barnard, who died in 1819, owned a good deal of property in Frome, including the King of Prussia. The Star & Garter last appeared in the church rates in 1799. This side of Milk Street was demolished in the 1960s, but the site still retains the shape shown on the map of 1774 with Trinity Walk cutting off the corner.

Site of the Star & Garter in 2014

Coward's Batch, Milk Street, the site of the Star & Garter, on the 1813 Cruse map

Nothing else known.

Sun, 6 Catherine Street

Without doubt one of Frome's oldest establishments, the Sun was originally a coaching inn dating from the 1600s. It has been repeatedly altered over the centuries. At the end of the 1600s, the inn and its land was purchased from John Yerbury by William Whitchurch, passing into the hands of his daughter Mary Hellier in 1691. Her husband, John, mortgaged part of the land in 1701 and the first Badcox Lane Chapel was built there in 1711. He sold the rest of the land, including the Sun, in 1716 to Thomas Cornwall. In due course the Baily family acquired ownership, so that in 1755 we find innkeeper Joseph Brown leasing the inn from John Baily. In the 1760s the inn fell vacant for a spell, but by 1785 the innkeeper was William Golledge, although John Baily still owned it. William Golledge stayed at the Sun until his death in 1791, when his son Richard took over.

In 1812, Zachary Baily Sr sold part of the inn to the neighbouring Badcox Lane Chapel, who demolished it to make way for the construction of a new chapel which opened in 1814. The inn may well have shifted next door for a few years until it re-acquired the remaining portion of the old inn and rebuilt it, although just how much was incorporated into the nineteenth-century rebuild is unclear. Publican Richard Golledge died in 1822 and James Tanner took over as landlord. We know little of Tanner, except for one thing – he had bad eyes, as this endorsement which appeared in a local newspaper reveals:

> Having suffered for the last eighteen months from frequent and severe inflammation in my eyes [I] was induced to try [Bruton's] Eye Salve; and have the satisfaction to inform you, that I found it the best remedy by far I had used. I therefore recommend it to the public as very efficacious in inflammatory cases.

No doubt a nice little earner for the Frome publican.

In May 1832, when the Sun was let with immediate possession, it was described as 'that well-established inn, or public house, called the Sun Inn, together with a seven-quarter malt-house, good walled garden, stables, skittle-ground, and other premises, situated in the centre of the town of Frome'. Thus departed Mr Tanner, and Charles Wilcox arrived, followed three years later by Mr Goodwin.

By 1839, William Harding had taken over. Unlike his predecessors, he managed to make a living at the inn, supporting numerous children from two marriages. There were, of course, the usual incidents of petty theft: in May 1862 the lyrically-named Harry Barry stole a jacket belonging to the inn's tap-boy, Oliver Parfitt. The only witness refused to attend court and the magistrates were compelled to dismiss Harry Barry with a reprimand, knowing full well he was 'morally guilty'. Whilst newspapers often feature the names of innkeepers, it is generally only when reporting such incidents that they reveal the identities of their employees. Another example is that of James Brimson, a waiter employed by William Harding. Poor James died of heart disease at the Sun in 1850, aged just 23, and the inquest was held at the inn.

Landlord William Harding's own life was not without tragedy. His first wife died during the winter of 1850 and was buried on Christmas Day. He remarried quickly, acquiring another four children by 1856. He died at the inn on 25 October 1862, his young widow, Francis, followed him to the grave in March 1863, and the place was temporarily taken over by Harding's executrix, Elizabeth Pearce. In August 1863, the licence was transferred to Joseph Phipps Roynon – and what a transformation he made. Within a year it was being hailed as 'the worst house in the town'!

The Sun in the 1950s

Roynon and his wife Ann, however, were experienced innkeepers from Bath, and he was no doubt used to dealing with the likes of Ann Yerbury, who in September 1863 stole a jar of cider worth one shilling. Ann received 14 days' hard labour in exchange for her illicit tipple. By January 1864, the police were hauling away drunks from the yard, and that month a female customer attacked a prostitute whilst another customer restrained the shady lady so that she could not even defend herself. 'Go at her, Martha, and hit her while you are about it', he cried. No wonder local people had begun to complain about the place.

In September 1864 Frome Band of Hope and Abstainers Union presented a memorial to the annual licensing session requesting that any poorly-run pub should have its licence removed – but the only one mentioned by name was the Sun.

Roynon was summoned before the bench to explain himself. It was inexplicable, he maintained, because he had caused no trouble at all for the police. His licence was renewed, but he was cautioned that he was close to losing it. Roynon did make an effort – he even turned police informer. In February 1865, he supplied the police with information leading to the arrest of thief John Payton. Perhaps he lost business as a result, for by August 1866 Roynon had skipped town owing money.

By the time Benjamin Gunning took over, the seedy reputation of the Sun was firmly established. In the summer of 1872, a 'notorious' lady from Warminster, Caroline Smith, was turned out by the police for drunken and disorderly conduct, having been evicted a week earlier. When she was sentenced to 21 days' hard labour, she attributed all her sufferings to 'Frome beer'! During his time at the Sun, Gunning's first wife died and he quickly wed another, much younger, woman. More children followed, but happiness did not. The pressure of a failing marriage and a business doing likewise took their toll on him, and in 1887 he threw himself out of his bedroom window, with the inevitable result.

The next two licensees had little staying power, and it was not until James Coleman arrived in the early 1890s that any semblance of stability was restored. Coleman was a popular sort – except, perhaps, with the police. In August 1895, he was charged with permitting drunkenness on the premises. The police said they had observed several drunken men in the pub for a number of years. Coleman's lawyers turned the tables on the police, asking why they had waited so long to do anything about it, adding that, 'if it was not the duty of the police, at least it would have been an honest and charitable act to have told the landlord in the first instance'. The case was dismissed, a decision greeted with loud applause in the court.

Like many families in the licensing trade, the Colemans had strong military connections and James' son fought with the 6th Dragoons in the Boer War. In November 1899, Corporal Coleman wrote home to describe his experiences:

> We are camped here on a piece of ground by the station, and it is something awful to be here. It is like being on a desert; it is all sand, and we are nearly blinded. We get sandstorms two or three times a day, and you can't see for hours after. All our food is covered with it as soon as we get it ... We are allowed a pint of beer a day, and you have to pay sixpence for it. If you have not got the money you can't have the beer.

The worst news arrived in March 1900:

> I regret to inform you that your son, No 3703 W Coleman, a corporal in my regiment, who was reported missing is now known to have been killed in action.

In 1903 Coleman left and Frederick John Hawkins took over briefly, followed by Albert Rabbitts in 1906. In May of that year, Rabbitts was charged with permitting drunkenness on the premises. The police claimed to have found a hopelessly drunk

The inn sign in 2012

man in the covered way adjoining the inn that was used as a cart stand. In court it was stated that he had been drinking at the inn with several others for over an hour. Rabbitts and two witnesses testified that, whilst the man was clearly drunk, he had not had any liquor at the Sun. A likely story, and indeed the magistrates were gravely suspicious. Yet in the absence of evidence, the case was dismissed.

The Sun in the 1990s

The Sun in 2013

John Arthur Rogers saw the Sun through the dark days of World War One, after which Joseph Williams, a former manager of the George Hotel, took over. He was lent the money to take the tenancy by George Knibbs, an ironmonger in Bath Street who had just sold his own pub, the Crown in the Market Place. Whilst Williams was a popular landlord, he had a fatal flaw. It was a weakness exploited by a man known as the 'Wizard of Ascot' to whom he paid £6 per tip. By 1923, Joseph Williams was bankrupt. At his public examination his liabilities were £917 8s 11d and his assets £127 6s 9d, leaving him with debts of £790 2s 2d. He had been betting since he took over the Sun and had lost almost £250 since 1921.

Henry Elmer took over once Williams had gone, and was there until 1932, followed by James Singer and then quite a number of landlords through the war years and beyond, before being run by the Watts family for over 20 years until recent times.

Today it is still a free house and a friendly 'locals' pub', much improved by the removal of the render from the lovely honey-coloured stone.

Swan, Badcox

Prior to its demolition, the Swan Inn stood at the junction of Nunney Road and Broadway. Despite its late-Georgian front, it dated back at least to the mid-1600s, the new façade being added in the late 1700s to create an illusion of modernity. This facelift was not the only modification. Originally the White Swan, it dropped the prefix in the 1800s when a new White Swan opened in Vallis Road. From thenceforward it was simply the Swan.

Of its early occupiers, we know Mr Court or A'Court was there between 1663 and 1685, followed by Pearce A'Court until around 1717, and George A'Court until around 1740, although it is unclear whether they were the landlords or simply the

The Swan in 1961

owners. Mrs Allen is shown as paying rates from 1742 until 1753; she also paid rates on the Anchor. Richard Hales was there by 1747, and he was succeeded by James Ford in 1770. Popular during James Ford's time was the rather gruesome 'sport' of back-sword fighting; there was an open-air stage adjoining the Swan for this purpose, probably somewhere in the area where the road is today. Back-sword originated as a form of sword practice before becoming a popular entertainment, often played for large sums of money in the vicinity of inns. Somerset men earned a great name as back-swordsmen and were often national champions in the sport. It was a particularly violent single-stick combat sport, as this public announcement suggests:

> To be played for, at Backsword, at Frome, on Thursday and Friday 15th and 16th Sept, ten guineas each day; likewise, One Shilling to be given for every blood drawn and half-a-Crown to him that draws it. Persons breaking three heads to quit the stage.

In 1786, a prize of ten guineas – five in the morning and five in the afternoon – was offered to back-sword fighters in Frome. The sport certainly drew in crowds and helped make the Swan prosperous, no doubt explaining why James Ford insured the inn and its contents with the Sun Insurance Company for £650 in 1774 – a tidy sum.

John Neal took over in 1793, although Ford retained ownership. When Neal's wife died in 1796 after a long illness, he bravely endeavoured to raise his children alone. The result was tragic. One morning, concerned that one of his children was unwell, he decided to make a poultice from the dregs at the bottom of a large strong-beer cask. He descended into the cask, but was overcome by the fumes and fell downwards, his legs suspended from the ladder. It took a quarter of an hour to retrieve him, the person charged with this task nearly succumbing to the same fate.

Every attempt was made to resuscitate him, but to no avail. John Neal was much respected in Frome as an industrious man, and his death left a large number of orphans. Evidently, the whole sad affair could have been avoided if he had simply followed the well-known practice of throwing a bucketful of cold water into the cask to render the fumes harmless. Not long after this the Swan fell under the control of the Baily family.

Throughout the 1800s, the inn had its share of troublesome clientele. In 1860, Isaac Rich gave his sister-in-law Elizabeth a black eye there, her devoted husband sleeping through the entire fracas. Later, in 1874, James and Mary Ann Knight assaulted PC Kelly, who was removing the drunken duo at the request of landlord James Frapwell. Mary Ann scratched Kelly's face and pulled out his hair whilst James Knight knocked the landlord to the ground. Mary Ann received a month's imprisonment, but her husband got off scot free!

Henry Smith succeeded Frapwell in 1887, but within days had run into trouble when a somewhat intoxicated Thomas Aldridge staged a sit-in at the Swan. His money, he declared, was a good as anybody's. The authorities were unimpressed, declaring Aldridge a 'public nuisance'. Henry Smith left two years later, but the matter of replacing him proved complex.

Thomas Philips applied for the licence and, as an experienced publican, should have been readily approved. Not so. Philips was a man with a tarnished past, namely convictions for selling under-proof gin and permitting drunkenness in his previous pub, the Bell at Banwell. When asked to explain these occurrences, he claimed that the first offence had been committed days after a new licensing law was passed, and copies of the act had not yet reached Somerset. As for the second, he had not been culpable. The licence was granted, but another complication immediately arose. Philips had recently married and his bride, widow Wilcocks, was the landlady of the Crown & Sceptre. This meant that Mr and Mrs Philips now held the licence for two inns in Frome. Ultimately, Mrs Philips was persuaded to relinquish her licence and the couple managed the Swan for a dozen years.

The succeeding decades of the twentieth century proved happily uneventful, though there was a scary moment in 1940 when an unattended lorry crashed into the Swan. Its hungry driver, Frank Perkins of Mells, left the engine running when he dashed off for some fish and chips, and the vehicle careered from Badcox car park into the Swan's cellars, demolishing a wall, window and door. Passer-by twelve-year-old Mary Young had a narrow escape, receiving severe bruising and lacerations.

In 1926, the Swan Inn was sold for £1,800 to the County Council, who intended to demolish it for 'road improvements', and in 1963 a tender was accepted from E C Knight & Sons to carry this out for £563, regardless of its status as a listed building. Also scheduled for demolition were the buildings of the old Swan Brewery, which stood where the car park between Nunney Road and Broadway is today. The Swan was finally razed to the ground in 1965, with some surprising results. As the old inn was being felled, 17 early £1 notes were discovered in the wall, all dated between 1815 and 1820. In the 1813/14 parish survey the owner of the Swan is recorded as James Ford. By 1822 it was William Baily. It is therefore unclear to which of these gentlemen the notes belonged.

The site is now a triangle of grass with a tree and a telephone box!

Tandem, Locks Lane

Known only through a single mention in the local press. In August 1868, James Jelly was granted a wine & spirit licence for 'the Tandem beerhouse in Lock's Lane', despite much opposition from TF Williamson down the road at the Railway. There is no publican named Jelly in the 1871 census and no other references to the Tandem have been found.

Three Swans, 16-17 King Street

The Three Swans around 1850 by WW Wheatley

The passage between 16 and 17 King Street

The Three Swans is one of Frome's oldest public houses. The part with the gabled front, No 17, dates from the 1600s or perhaps even earlier. In the late 1700s, another building – No 16 – was added next door. This half of the pub still shares a chimney with No 15. At some point in the second half of the nineteenth century, 16 and 17 were combined, as is evidenced by the strange elongated storeroom in the middle of the building. Clearly, this was formerly an alleyway between 16 and 17, as it has a 'doorstep' and an external window.

In 1786, when the Three Swans occupied only No 17, Michael Griffin was the tenant landlord, although the building was owned by James Hyde. It was sold that year, along with No 17, which was occupied by a shoemaker called James Vinney. Michael Griffin stayed on after the sale, however, as this entry from the diary of Constable Isaac Gregory reveals:

> 24 September 1818 – Was sent for to the Three Swans late at night – a respectable young man had been drinking there till shut up time, but as he was informed he could not stay

there he grew outrageous … I found him afterwards under charge of the watch, he was bloody and said he had been used ill at the Public-house. I insisted he should go to his lodgings if he had any or I must confine him – he went away and I kept his bundle till the morning when he came for it. He said Mr Griffin had used him ill and he would have the law of him for it.

Little is known about the character of the early Three Swans but it is clear that by the 1800s it had a reputation as a lively house. One evening in 1827, a young man was engaged in the tried-and-tested tradition of doing anything for a bet – in this case eating 193 oysters and drinking a quart of beer. This attracted the attention of the national press.

Yet it wasn't all beer and oysters. In 1850, a 50-year-old painter, Henry Yound, fell out of the malt loft at the Three Swans and was seriously injured. Quite what he was doing up there in the first place is a little unclear, but he died that night. The landlord at this time was Enoch Ham, who ran the pub with the assistance of his wife Mary and niece Sarah.

By the mid-1850s, Robert Eyres had taken over and the inn was beginning to show signs of wantonness. In 1856, a case was brought against Eyres by Superintendent G W Summers, who attested that his attention had been drawn to the house one evening due to the loud singing therein. Inside he found six prostitutes and a group of soldiers, many the worse for drink and all carousing lewdly. 'Do you know you have a lot of bad girls in your house?' he asked. Eyres replied he had no way of knowing if they were good or bad, a response which met with short shrift form the superintendent. He informed the landlord that they were known prostitutes, which did not deter Eyres from continuing to offer them hospitality until well after midnight!

Eyres clearly believed he had got away with it, for the very next night Summers was again drawn to the pub by the hullabaloo there. Inside he found even more prostitutes than the night before, 'one of them in a most disgraceful position', and four of the others absolutely drunk. The landlord claimed to have been in the passage – possibly the now-converted cupboard – and unable to see what was happening in the inn. When the men and women left, most were barely able to stand. Eyres promised to mend his ways if the superintendent let him off this time. No such luck. He was summonsed for both offences and heavily fined.

Remarkably, Eyres kept his licence, but failed to stay out of trouble. The following year he was fined £3 for permitting drunkenness and disorderly conduct in his house after midnight. He did not remain long, however, and in 1859 Jabez Deacon took over.

The Three Swans continued to attract unwholesome characters. Using illegal measures was the most common reason why publicans wound up in trouble in the 1800s, and in 1860 Jabez Deacon was prosecuted for just this offence by the Inspector for Weights & Measures. The case excited a great deal of interest in Frome and Deacon hired a Bristol barrister for his defence. After all the evidence had been presented, the bench decided that, even though Deacon was technically wrong, it was not a case which required severe punishment. He was simply fined one shilling and absolved of any blame in the matter! That same year Edmund Carvill was fined for drunkenness and assaulting a policeman. Yet, when he wasn't busy avoiding strife with the magistrates, Deacon also seems to have done a nice early line in pub grub, one of his 1860 advertisements offering 'Chops and Steaks provided on the shortest notice' along with 'Home Brewed Beer of the Best Quality'.

In 1862 Mercy Newport, a well known character in Frome, was charged, along with her companion Robert Halliday, for being drunk and riotous in Bath Street. They were, according to PC Aaron Burgess, behaving 'in a grossly indecent manner'. Mercy had long featured in the annals of Frome police courts and was sentenced to three months imprisonment, her companion receiving just a small fine. It seems they had spent the evening getting thoroughly drunk in the pub, so the landlord was lucky on this occasion not to have become embroiled in trouble too. It does, however, serve to illustrate the manner of clientele that frequented the Three Swans at this time.

In 1866, Jane Stevens of Woodlands was charged with being drunk and riotous as she left the premises. She was creating a commotion and had attracted a huge crowd around herself. Her release was conditional upon her leaving town. Mr Ames took over after Deacon, although it must have been trickier running the inn without the help of his wife who, in 1869, died from a burst varicose vein.

The next licensees were the Timburys from Beckington who remained there for some time. In 1872, landlord John Timbury had the bright idea of opening at five o'clock in the morning to serve tea and coffee to factory hands on their way to work. He presented a petition to the licensing authorities signed by many local people. The magistrates refused to allow it— if they permitted one

The Three Swans in the 1960s – and an advert from Ronald Hibbard, who became landlord in 1963

Above: The Three Swans in 1992

Below: Boarded up in 2000

Bottom: A pub with no beer in 2013

pub to sell tea and coffee in the morning, who knows where it would end ... John Timbury died in 1881, and his widow Charlotte held the licence until she too died in 1889, allowing eldest son George to take over. His only licensing infringement seems to have been for owning a dog without a licence in 1891!

John Handell became landlord early in 1892. Within weeks he was fined £3 for permitting drunkenness on the premises and had his licence endorsed. The 1872 Licensing Act had codified offences and ensured that they would now be recorded on the licence. Repeated offences would lead to forfeiture of the licence and loss of livelihood for the landlord. Thus Handell's £3 fine, though substantial, was probably less important to him than the endorsement on his licence. Not surprisingly he appealed.

Joseph Holloway stepped in after Handell, becoming a respected licensee in the town and president of the local Licensed Victuallers' Association. He died at the Three Swans in 1916 and Arthur Charles Blackmore replaced him for the next eight years, followed by the Baker family, and then, in 1935, Robert Wordly, who died there in 1943, aged 66.

In 1938, Frome Urban District Council rejected proposals to attach a preservation order to the building, although it is now a Grade II listed property.

Dorothy and Albert Barnes took over in 1959 when their previous pub, the Waggon & Horses in Gentle Street, closed down. Albert Barnes died in 1961, but Dorothy remained there until her retirement in 1963, when Ronald Hibbard took over.

His successor, John Nuth, renovated the pub kitchen and attempted to revamp the pub's image. In the early 1970s you could eat 'pizza' at the Three Swans to the accompaniment of Les Daniels' organ in the renovated 'Tudor Room'. Award-winning publicans Bill and Rita Savage took over in 1972, when John Nuth relocated to the Horse & Groom in East Woodlands. Three years later, Savage won the coveted Watney Innkeeper (West) of the Year award, beating 500 other tenanted pubs to the £500 prize. In 1982, German-born Othold Werne and his wife Sylvia took over, having already run public houses in the Channel Islands. They promoted the pub as dating from the 1300s – it would be nice to know which fourteenth-century documents they had seen!! But all good things come to an end and in 2012 the Three Swans closed.

Fortunately, this was not the end of the story. The following year it was bought by local businessman, Chris Moss, who said he wanted 'somewhere to go for a decent pint', and, after an outstanding refit, the Three Swans opened its ancient doors yet again in January 2014 under the new landlady Helen Rowlinson. Despite limited opening hours and 'not really' doing food, it has become one of the most popular pubs in Frome and has an enthusiastic 'dog friendly' policy.

Trooper, 11 Trinity Street (formerly Trooper Street)

A modern sign above the door states 'The Trooper 1720', but the earliest date we have found so far is 1761 in the church records, when it was owned by John Webb and run by John Little.

Then there is this bizarre story from the *Oxford Journal* for 10 March 1764:

> Bath March 8th: Last Thursday evening about four o'clock two young men and their sweethearts being drinking at the Sign of the Trooper in Frome, one of them (Samuel Laverton, a Cardmaker of that Town) went out without speaking a word to anyone and hung himself in his master's stable. The coroner's inquest sat on the body Monday last and brought in their verdict Felo de fe, whereupon he was buried at the crossroads the same night.

We have not been able to find out any more about this but there must be more to the story and it would be good to fill in the details one day. Rev WE Daniel, in his *Frome Street Names* of 1897, recounts the story of how the pub got its name:

> The Frome Trooper [after] winning much plunder, returned to his native town and settled down to rehearse, to admiring pot-lovers, his deeds of bravery and bloodshed. His inn stood on the south side of Trinity Street, between the Bell and No 4. Its bow window was only removed a few years back, though the sign of the Trooper had not waved there for many years. The street had perhaps hardly yet lost its name, derived therefrom, of Trooper Street.

Nothing has been found to back this story up but it is a good one and deserves to be true. Sadly there is nothing else to say about this cute little pub. There is an entry in the church rates showing that John Little was still there in 1799, and Edmund Crocker's diary records that a Miss Elizabeth Davis of the Trooper got married in 1801. After that the trail goes cold.

It is now a private house, nice and tidy at the front, although marks on the stonework show where the door has been moved and some of the windows altered, as mentioned by Rev Daniel. It would be nice to know more.

The Trooper in 2012

Unicorn, 83 Keyford Street

The Unicorn has gone now but was one of the town's principal inns in its day, and dated back to at least 1770 when its rates were paid by a Leonard Brown. By 1781, it was in the hands of Joseph Cook, who also owned the Cross Keys in Eagle Lane and had some involvement with the Spread Eagle. After his death, his widow Mary seems to have sold the inn, and the landlord at the turn of the century was James Gully. He went bankrupt in 1801 and suffered the indignity of having his goods and chattels – including his bed and wheelbarrow – auctioned on the premises.

Frederick Gane came next, and in 1810 advertised his new 'Posting Concern' in the *Salisbury & Winchester Journal* of 14 May 1810:

> FREDERICK GANE, of the Unicorn Inn, respectfully informs his friends and the public that, for their better accommodation, he has established his new Posting Concern with three pair of neat Chaises, excellent Horses and careful and expeditious drivers; and assuring them that every immediate attention shall be paid to their orders to any part of the Kingdom, he confidently relies on their patronage and encouragement.

This does not seem to have gone too well, as the following year he was – like his predecessor – bankrupt, and the freehold premises were advertised for sale with all fixtures and fittings. What happened next is unclear, but a William Gane bought the inn, so maybe Frederick's son or brother was able to pay off his debts.

No pub is without its trouble makers and, in July 1818, long-suffering Constable Gregory was

> sent for to the Unicorn to stop fighting. I saw a man by the name of Pinchin in the kitchen stript to his shirt with his fists clenched challenging the company to fight. I ordered him to put his clothes on and behave peaceable, he refused and menaced me with his fists for a considerable time so that I was obliged to get assistance to take him to the guardhouse – on the road he made a desperate attack on my person – he kicked me in the leg and made a wound and aimed several blows at me.

Nasty Mr Pinchin ended up with six months' hard labour in Ilchester gaol and a fine of one shilling.

The mid-1820s were tough times for the weaving industry. Strikes and riots were commonplace, and at one point the Frome Justices authorised the breaking down of doors and seizure of goods from home weavers who were on strike. Weavers organised a 'Society for the Suppression of Truck', which was allowed by the local magistrates to hold meetings at the Unicorn every six weeks commencing on 12 August 1823. 'Truck' was a system by which employees were paid in goods at high prices from company stores rather than money to spend as they chose.

William Gane leased the Unicorn to James Baron, who was landlord for some time. His wife, Alice, died in 1832, however, and he was made bankrupt a year later. There does not seem to have been much profit in this inn.

In 1833 Ezra Knight became the landlord, followed in 1836 by John Knight, presumably his son, who is only 25 in the census of 1841, and was living there with wife Alicia and one-year-old daughter Louisa. The Knight dynasty continued for a considerable time, and, by the time of the 1851 census, 20-year-old William Knight was landlord.

By the census of 1861, William and his wife Frances had four children. He continued to run the Unicorn until 1879, when the lease had only five years left to run, and the freehold was put up for auction by the executors of Mrs Read. William bought the freehold for £1,400 and installed his son, William Jr, as landlord, while he presumably continued to run the brewery.

Lads of the Unicorn off on a beano – an undated photograph

Within a year, William went spectacularly bankrupt, owing the bank over £8,000, and had to sell the freehold of numerous properties. The Unicorn was sold privately for £1,000 to Charles Luce after failing to meet its reserve at auction.

William Higgins became landlord in 1884, but, after his wife died in 1901 at the age of 42, he became very depressed, and in December 1902 cut his throat with a razor. Bleeding profusely, he walked across to the ostler who managed to stop the bleeding and called the doctor. His life was saved but it was a close shave, and Frome United Breweries, who now owned it, advertised the Unicorn to let.

Mr and Mrs Bond behind the bar of the Unicorn in its later years

Alfred Watts was landlord from 1913, but had a bit of a misunderstanding with the police over some Army Stores in 1918 and was committed for trial. The affair seems to have been resolved satisfactorily as he continued as landlord until 1948.

Another 20 years and it was all over. The ancient pub and the old stone houses surrounding it were demolished by 1968 and replaced by the new fire station, best described like most buildings of that era as 'functional'.

The fire station on the approximate site of the Unicorn

Victoria, Christchurch Street East

In many respects the Victoria Inn epitomises the Victorian pub. It was founded in the wake of the liberalised licensing laws of the 1830s, which inspired many a tradesman to open up a beerhouse in his humble abode. Not that there was anything humble about the Victoria, its proportions remaining impressive even today. The founder, in the 1840s, was William Gale, a cloth worker from the town's weaving district. It was a rough and ready sort of inn in those times, raising much of its revenue from a large number of lodgers and travellers. These were usually labouring men and women – railwaymen, hawkers, plumbers, carpenters and the like.

William's first wife, Hester, died in 1851 and within months he had married young Mercy Bryant. It was not the easiest or quietest of inns and Mercy must have wondered what she had let herself in for. In 1859, the ironically named brush-maker Will Justice earned himself a five shilling fine for causing trouble at the Victoria. But Justice was not alone in creating chaos. Just a year later, the entire inn narrowly escaped disaster when a hapless lodger set fire to her bedclothes. Ostler Benjamin Cousens raised the alarm and 'extinguished the conflagration'. The lodger escaped injury and the inn was saved. As for the hero of the hour, within a decade Cousens had fallen on hard times and spent much of the remainder of his life in the workhouse.

Trouble persisted and sometimes it was the landlord who caused it! In 1859 William Gale was charged with permitting drunkenness and disorderly conduct in his inn. Superintendent Summers had heard a great furore emanating from the Victoria from halfway across town. Arriving at the inn, he found four prostitutes in the tap room, while in the parlour Mr Gale was quarrelling with a customer – and using the worst language the policeman had ever heard! Mrs Gale herself asked the policeman to remove her husband and lock him up, which he did, and he was later fined. Clearly, this was not the sort of pub one visited for genteel company and polite conversation. In 1862, Henry Rodway smashed all the windows after being ejected for drunkenness and, whilst on this occasion the court took the side of the landlord, it was not always so. In early 1865, Gale was up before the magistrates again, this time for serving beer on Christmas Day, a Sunday, before 12.30pm. He admitted it but said he thought it would cause no harm as it was a holiday. The court disagreed and when, three months later, he was caught again serving beer after hours, he was warned that another slip-up would lose him his licence. He cleaned up his act a little after this. Then tragedy struck, when his three-year-old son was killed in a wagon accident outside the inn in 1863. Gale died in 1868, leaving Mercy to run the inn and raise the remaining children alone.

This was no easy task, and Mercy certainly could not rely on her own family for assistance. Her brother, James Bryant, had already served a two-month stretch for stealing from the inn's till! Not surprisingly, Mercy Gale abandoned the idea of running the Victoria. She and her daughters were temporarily separated, working as servants in various homes around Frome, before relocating together to Sussex. There, many years later at the age of 62, Mercy finally remarried and spent the rest of her days in Croydon with her husband.

Meanwhile, a new family had taken over the Victoria beerhouse. Bristol-born bacon dealer Henry Williams had moved his family to Frome in the 1850s and set up as a fruiterer and fishmonger in Cheap Street. Perhaps living next door to the Albion Inn inspired him, for in 1868 he took over the Victoria. His time there was unremarkable – no doubt a great testimony to his capacity to manage the inn properly and peacefully – and his wife took over following his death in 1882. Henry left a great legacy to the licensing trade of Frome, for no fewer than three of his children went on to run pubs. Joseph Williams managed the Live and Let Live, the Vine Tree and the Great Western; Hester Williams ran the Crown at Keyford; and Sarah Ann Williams also managed the Vine Tree before taking over the Victoria when her mother died in 1886.

The Victoria, complete with petrol pumps, around 1960

Sarah Williams did not have an easy life. In 1868, she married John Stone but before long he had begun to ill-treat her and lead an 'immoral life'. In June 1871, when Sarah and her children visited Frome, her husband sold off all the family possessions and disappeared. After two years patiently waiting for him to reappear, she was granted a protection order, a legal measure giving her control over her own property. Clearly Sarah Stone had plans and wanted to protect her business operations in Frome. She spent the next few years assisting in the Victoria and her brother's pub at Clink before becoming landlady of the Victoria on her own account.

In 1890, John and Thomas Baily took on the lease from the Marquis of Bath for £123 per annum, but purchased the freehold outright later that year for £5,500. Throughout the negotiations, Sarah Stone remained as landlady, and stayed on for many more years.

Even an experienced and respectable publican like Sarah Stone occasionally ended up on the wrong side of the law. The Child Messenger Act prohibited the sale of alcohol to children except in 'sealed' bottles. In 1915, Sarah Stone breached this law. A twelve-year-old child was seen by a policeman coming out of the inn carrying liquor in an unsealed bottle. When questioned, Mrs Stone could only say, 'I did serve the child with a pint of ale, and I forgot to seal the bottle. I am sorry, but I was busy at the time.' Unfortunately, the child then piped up, 'Mrs Stone, you never seal a bottle for me!' By now, Sarah had been at the Victoria for over 47 years and her name was synonymous with the inn. She had a good reputation, so the magistrates applied the smallest possible fine. She died in 1924, aged 79, having run the Victoria right up until her death.

There followed a series of landlords of varying duration, none however matching up to the likes of Gale, Stone or Williams. In June 1932, when John Brown was proprietor, the Lamb Brewery Ltd altruistically conveyed to the minister and churchwardens of St John's church 'all that piece and parcel of ground near Christchurch Street east lying to the north and east of a building known as St John the Baptist Senior School, and now [forming] part of the garden of the Victoria Inn for ever, on trust that the premises be used for education'.

In 1949, landlord Arthur Starr, in an attempt to increase revenue, applied for a licence to sell alcohol both on and off the premises, and the inn also made money from its own petrol pump. During the 1950s and 60s, the licensees did their best to bring the old beerhouse up to date, offering a variety of entertainment. One newspaper advertisement in 1957 proudly proclaimed:

> We have all you want! Darts, Shove Ha'penny, TV, radiogram, Tape Recording Machine (Hear Yourself Talking), Saturday Night Dancing in the Club Room (with Band).

By the 1960s, the Victoria had become an Ushers Inn and in 1965 the licence was taken over by retired Royal Navy Lieutenant Twine. He ran the inn for the next seven years until the licence was taken over by Patrick Curtis, and then by Frank Urch. Under them, the Victoria achieved prominence amongst local skittles and darts teams. In later years a little notoriety was added too. In the summer of 1979, a gang fight erupted outside the pub of such intensity that Frome police had to call for reinforcements. It began when one customer was ejected by landlord Frank Urch. The pair started arguing outside and a crowd gathered, one man even

The Victoria as it looks today

taking off his shirt and inviting all-comers to a fight. When the police arrived there was a free for all and police officers were kicked and assaulted. Just like the good old days when the Gale family ran the Victoria! Plus ça change ...

The old Victoria Inn currently operates as a pet-grooming centre.

Vine Tree, 35 Berkley Road

The Vine Tree was a classic incarnation of the Victorian beerhouse. In 1872, the landlord was Joseph Williams, whose family ran the Victoria on Christchurch Street East. He may have been its first landlord, as we can find no reference to it before that. During his time at the Vine Tree, Joseph was assisted by his sister Sarah, who had been deserted by her ne'er-do-well husband. At some point Sarah seems to have held the licence, but in November 1873 it was transferred to Henry Mason, on account of the house being 'a most disreputable one and ... the means of leading many young people astray'. Henry was soon replaced by Frederick Clark, who in March 1878 was indicted for stealing hay belonging to Mrs Lucy Ann Wilkins. Although he had been seen leaving the field with hay under his arm, he was acquitted. Nevertheless, just a fortnight later the licence was transferred to James Price. Clearly, thus far the Vine Tree had a less than healthy reputation.

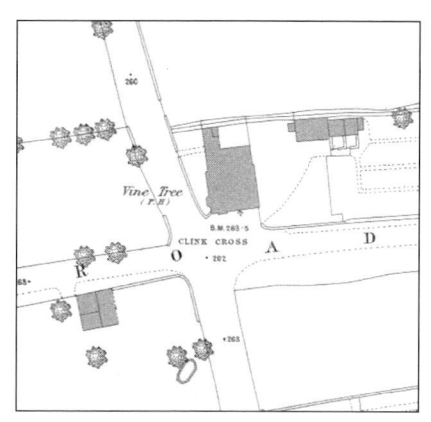

The Vine Tree on the 1886 OS map

James King was licensee for a few weeks in 1881 before William Wells took over. During his decade-long sojourn he managed to keep the pub's name out of the papers, handing over to Thomas Edwards, who ran it during the mid-1890s. The Vine Tree at this time was owned by the Lamb Brewery.

Henry Hayter was licensee from 1897 until his death in 1899, when his widow Sarah Ann took over. Like many landlords' widows, she successfully ran the pub for many years, assisted by her son, Thomas, as manager. He took over completely for a brief period in 1911.

William Stillman was licensee from 1913 for almost two decades and was, for many, the man synonymous with the Vine Tree Inn. Yet even the good Mr Stillman occasionally ran into trouble. In October 1916, he fell foul of wartime lighting restrictions, introduced as a result of the threat of zeppelin attacks, and was summonsed on account of

The Vine Tree around 1900, perhaps with Sarah Hayter beside the horse

Charabanc trips from the Vine Tree in the 1920s. In the photograph above, William Stillman is on the right, holding a dog; in the line-up below, he is sixth from left in the front row.

a light shining from his kitchen window. In court, he was replete with remorse and explained that he had certainly not intended to break the law, and thought he had obscured the errant light. He was fined five shillings, the standard fine for such an infringement.

During the early 1930s, CJ Beck took over for a couple of years until 1935, when Frome footballer Wyndham Haines of Weymouth Town applied for a transfer– not to another team but to the Vine Tree. Prior to his career as a publican, Wyndham 'Willie' Praetoria Haines (1900-1974) was a centre-forward with a long and creditable career. As a youth, he played for Warminster Town, before joining Frome Town in the

158

Western League. From there he joined Portsmouth (1922-28), Southampton (1928-32), Weymouth (1932-38), and afterwards Frome Town again. Whilst at Fratton Park, Haines acquired the nickname 'Farmer's Boy', and Portsmouth fans would often sing a verse of 'To be a farmer's boy' in his honour. His time at Portsmouth saw Pompey move from the Third Division, through the Second, to reach the First Division in 1926-27. In 1928, he moved along the coast to Southampton and rapidly gained popularity at the Dell. He retired from Southampton in 1932 following a spate of injuries, and returned to the Western League with Weymouth. He retired from professional football in 1935 and returned to Frome where he became landlord of the Vine Tree from 1935 to 1949, after which he moved into the dry-cleaning business. Football was never far from his heart, however, and in 1960 he became chairman of Portsmouth Supporters Club. He died in Frome in November 1974.

Wyndham was succeeded in 1949 by T Adams. During his period as licensee, there were regular dances at the Vine Tree with the Madhatter's Dance Band providing the music, and more often than not raising funds for various good causes in the town. There were also frequent talent competitions.

The Vine Tree in 1982 ...

... and in 2012

By the 1970s, the pub was in the hands of Watney Mann, who carried out major alterations, enabling the inn to offer a full range of bar food. It took five years to renovate the Vine Tree, by which time it allegedly had the longest bar in Frome. The managers by then were Bernard and Pat Corrigan. Amongst their most valued customers was 'Prince', a golden Labrador who used to pop in to the Vine Tree every evening for a bottle of Guinness – not for himself but to take home for his owner, Mrs Anne Dolen, former landlady of the Foresters Arms at Beckington, where Prince used to collect the empties. The Vine Tree, a large building with ample parking at a busy crossroads, remains open today and has huge potential. It is currently owned by Enterprise Inns.

Waggon & Horses, Gentle Street

Gentle Street, the cobbled thoroughfare which even today retains much of its old-world charm, is the location for one of Frome's oldest taverns. First mentioned in 1568, some of its sixteenth-century interior is still visible today. In its heyday, this was one of Frome's main coaching inns and derived its name from the wagons or coaches leaving en route for London. This side of the business continued for upwards

The Waggon & Horses around 1900

of a century. It was from Joseph Clavey's yard, known as Clavey's Barton, behind the inn that the Frome Flyer stagecoach would depart for London each Monday at 1pm during the early 1700s, reaching Holborn by noon two days later. The return coach left at 1pm each Thursday and reached Frome at noon on Saturdays, travelling via Amesbury and Warminster. The horses had to be changed at least every 20 miles en route and, for a fare of eight shillings, a traveller could take 14lbs of luggage with them on this arduous journey. The coaching yard is now a small, private car park.

In November 1761 it was reported that

> a Stag was turned out in Long-Leat Park by Lord Weymouth and some other gentlemen, which shewed fine sport for some Miles; when taking into the Turnpike road he ran into Frome, and making into a Public-House, the Sign of the Waggon & Horses, took Shelter in the cellar, where he was pursued, and taken alive under a Butt of stale Beer.

Why would Lord Weymouth have been permitted to extend his hunt onto the premises of the Waggon & Horses? Well, because he owned it – the inn was part of the extensive Longleat Estate and remained so until 1919 when it was auctioned off.

At the time, Gentle Street was still known to many by its far less relaxing soubriquet of Hunger Lane, and several of the properties along it were owned by David and Hester French. By the early 1770s, David French was also licensed victualler at the Waggon & Horses. Although they had had five children, only one daughter and one son lived beyond infancy. Then, in August 1782 tragedy struck when

Revealing the ancient fireplace in the old taproom to show the many forms in which it has been used over the centuries. To the left, at the top, a hole in the wall leads through to a disused stairwell

their only son was accidentally shot dead by a friend while they were out shooting for the day. By the time Hester died in April 1784, their daughter Sarah had, like so many publicans' daughters, married another innkeeper in Frome, Charles Romaine. As they were already running an inn, this meant that, when David French died, the inn passed out of the French family.

James Burt was the next landlord, and during his brief time there gained much respect in Frome. He died on 7 January 1788 and was succeeded by James Cheltenham. By the 1820s, Charles Vincent was landlord, and following his death in November 1826 his widow Eleanor managed the inn for the next decade, until Walter Fussell took over the reins from 1839 to 1842.

The next landlord, William Simms, was there in December 1844 when a fire broke out. Fortunately, he needed some change and went upstairs to fetch it, whereupon he found the bedroom full of smoke and the woodwork on fire. With the assistance of a few customers, he extinguished the fire with minimal damage. The fire had originated in the flue of the kitchen chimney.

An idea of what the Waggon & Horses was like at this time can be gained from a newspaper report of July 1846, after the body of an infant was discovered in a vessel there, which stated that 'the dissipated of both sexes are in the habit of repairing to this inn, which may in part account for the appalling discovery'.

Evidently the bad reputation continued, despite the noble attempts of successive landlords. During the early 1860s, William Pitman was proprietor. He was licensed to sell both wines and spirits, maintained a fine bowling alley and held an 'ordinary' (social dance) each Wednesday. Pitman was also a member of the Frome Volunteers, which evidently did little to earn him respect, for in November 1866 John Holloway, 'a young man of respectable parentage', was sentenced to two months' hard labour for stealing a basket containing vegetables from the Waggon & Horses. By 1868 Charles Knapton was landlord.

Permitting prostitutes to gather in a public house – often euphemistically referred to as keeping a 'disorderly house' – was the cause of many landlords falling foul of the law in the mid-1800s. In February 1868, Charles Knapton was fined for having 'knowingly permitted divers persons of notoriously bad character to assemble in his house'. PC William Lock had found four prostitutes there drinking with five completely inebriated customers. The only defence Knapton could offer was that he had not been at the house long and had not acquainted himself with the local characters. It was not really a good enough explanation and the bench fined him £2, describing it as an 'abominable case' and threatening to impose a £10 fine if he appeared before them again. The police were requested to keep a particular eye on the place in future.

In August 1875, James Harris was charged with assaulting PC Westcott in the execution of his duty. He had been summoned to the inn to eject some parties who were kicking up a row, and on his way down Gentle Street, hearing the terrible commotion there, asked a man called Sheppard to accompany and assist him. He demanded to be let in through the tap-room door, but, as soon as he stepped across the threshold, he was struck on the back of the head by a spittoon and fell insensible in the corner of the room. Harris was later fined £3, but as he could not pay he was locked up for two months in lieu.

The Waggon & Horses in 1957 (above) and 1949 (below)

The rough experiences of the Waggon & Horses' landlords continued unabated. In August 1877, William Phillips, a book dealer, was charged with assaulting landlord Alfred Drew. Unfortunately, the accusations of keeping a disorderly house persisted as well. In February 1883, George Chappell and Richard Ball were charged with drunken and riotous conduct in Gentle Street in the early hours of the morning. They had evidently just left the Waggon & Horses with two prostitutes and were brawling over one of them.

Inns were often used to hold inquests. An altogether convenient arrangement, especially if the deceased was a member of the publican's own family, as happened in 1883 when 55-year-old Mary Summerhayes, wife of the landlord, was found dead in her bed. She had a heart complaint it seems, and it was deemed to be due to natural causes.

The following year, the new landlord, James Maundrell, found a small boy asleep in a wagon in the yard at the back. He took the child, twelve-year-old Herbert Henry Bendle, to the police station where the reasons for his open-air sojourn were discovered. He had truanted from school, and not for the first time. Young Henry was brought up before the magistrates on a charge of vagrancy. The magistrates dismissed the case with a warning that if the boy reoffended he would be sent to the industrial school.

In 1919 the Waggon & Horses, now leased to Frome United Breweries, was finally sold by the Longleat Estate. The sale particulars described it as having a

> Bar, Bar Parlour, Servery, Two Sitting Rooms, Kitchen, Wash-house and Cellar, with five bedrooms, and two Attics over ... In the Yard adjoining, which is approached from Blind House Lane, is a commodious Range of Outbuildings [including] Cart Shed ... Large Wagon Shed ... 4-stall Stable ... 6-stall Stable ... Poultry House ... old Skittle Alley (now converted into Pig sty) ... Large Clubroom and Ante-room approached by separate staircase.

The old place closed as a public house in 1959 and by 1963 had fallen into disrepair with smashed windows and an air of decay. It was converted into flats by Frome Urban District Council and provided social housing until sold at auction in 2012. It has now been turned into a family home, with many of its original features having been uncovered and restored.

Wheatsheaf (or sometimes Wheatsheaves), 22 Catherine Hill

The first name mentioned in connection with this beerhouse is Caroline Harding, shown in the rates as occupier in 1834. Her family were still there in 1841, when the census recorded William Harding – probably her son – as landlord, aged 35, along with his wife Rebecca and four children. The Hardings had gone by the census of 1861 when John Hiscocks aged 60 and his wife Jemima were running the place.

There was a curious case in 1866, when Elizabeth Stokes was charged with stealing a purse from the pocket of Samuel Harvey, a slumbering coal haulier. The principal witness in the case, tap boy William Hiscox, stated that he was entering the room when he saw Stokes take her hand from Harvey's pocket. She then unaccountably gave Hiscox two sovereigns, all of which he had now spent 'apart from 10s which Fanny Lusty (a prostitute) snatched from him'. The learned magistrates could have been forgiven for falling off the bench laughing at this story, and maybe they did, but the report states that the case was adjourned and Hiscox arrested for the theft after a number of witnesses saw him spending the money in the Sun. There was a happy ending, with Stokes being acquitted and Hiscox sentenced to three months' hard labour.

In 1873, landlord James Thick applied for a spirit licence on the grounds that 'it was a great inconvenience that country folks should be unable, (oftentimes coming in very wet) to obtain a drop of spirits at his house'. He added that he had kept the beerhouse for the past seven years, that it had been an alehouse for 40 years and had an excellent character. There were also plenty of rooms for accommodation and, whilst there were no stables, there was room for them. Despite all this, the application was refused.

The former Wheatsheaf in 2013. In early postcards of Catherine Street the pub can just be made out with a gable end facing on to the street. Its removal has given the building the oddly truncated look we see today.

The 'excellent character' claimed for the Wheatsheaf came under question in 1884 when Henry Thick was summonsed for 'harbouring prostitutes'. PS White gave evidence that he was watching the house and found it to be 'full of men and women – at least eleven of the latter being in the tap room'. Thick asked the officer to point out the women he objected to, but he did not, and accused the defendant of having been drinking! Despite a robust defence contradicting the police on several points, and the fact that the house had never had a complaint against it, poor old Henry was convicted and fined £1.

The Wheatsheaf remained in the Thick family until 1911, and in October 1912 passed to Harry Cooper, a blacksmith, who was there until the end.

Magistrates seem to have been on a mission to close as many pubs as they could in the early twentieth century, and the only reason given for closing this one is that there were four other pubs within 200 yards. Even the police witness agreed that the place had a clean licence and was in good repair. Despite objections from landlord and brewery, the licensing committee decided to close it for good in 1924, awarding £885 9s 6d in compensation.

Wheatsheaves / Mansford & Baily / Three Wheatsheaves, 23 Bath Street

The pub we see today in Bath Street, although old, is not the original. The Three Wheatsheaves Inn stood on roughly the same site in a warren of small streets known as Anchor Barton. This adjoined Cox Street or Back Lane, and was cleared away shortly after 1810, when Bath Street was built to improve the flow of traffic in and out of town. The land was owned by Lord Weymouth and a deed in the Longleat archives records that the lease of the Three Wheatsheaves was granted to William Wayt, innholder, for 99 years in 1731. It was described as being in Cox Street, which later became Eagle Lane, and which at the time extended westwards to the Market Place. Wayt had a wife named Mary and a son called Lucas, and he died in the late 1730s or early 1740s. His widow married an attorney called William Whitchurch, whose family owned a large house further down the hill, and who is named as the owner in the church rates up to 1749.

The Wheatsheaves in the 1820s

Whitchurch died in Fleet Prison in 1750, presumably in debt, and Mary, widowed once again, appears in the church rates as 'Widow Whitchurch' until 1780, when a new lease was granted to a tanner called John Stevens. In the 1785 census, J Stevens is shown as the owner and Ann Tapp as the publican, with one man and two women in occupation.

Piecing together what we can from details in the church rates and Crocker's map of 1808, it seems that the original inn lay at the end of Bridewell Barton, a continuation of Anchor Barton, and what is now Eagle Lane. Shown as plot 44 on the Crocker map, it is described as belonging to Lord Weymouth and leased to the estate of the late John Stevens. Ann Saunders, widow of John, is shown as the occupier and presumably remained so until the builders moved in.

The cutting of Bath Street meant that the old building had to go and, when the inn was rebuilt, a new lease was granted to George Porch in 1813. A few years later, in March 1818, Constable Gregory had to have a word with landlord John Hobbs:

> I went round to some of the public houses they were all fast but the Wheat Sheaves – he had a party in the kitchen too far gone in liquor. I told Mr Hobbs it was near 11.00 and he ought to have his house shut as there was several drunken men prowling about, he was very civil and said he would shut up directly. I observed that those men he had in the kitchen was far too gone, and when they leave the public house in that state they was generally very noisy in the streets, and he should be not to keep open past hours – I said this to him because he do not shut up at the proper time.

In September 1821, when the property was put up for auction, it was described as 'the newly built Wheat Sheaves Inn', occupied by George Porch. Porch was an upholsterer who had lent over £1,000 to the Methodist Chapel and had previously held the lease on the Anchor across the road, which he later used as a workshop and warehouse for his goods. He was also involved with the brewery at Welshmill.

In 1825, Porch assigned the lease to Joseph Edward Mansford, a wine merchant who had been trading in Palmer Street or Catherine Hill since 1809. Mansford established the Bath Street Wine Vaults there in partnership with William Griffith. When Griffith died, he took Mr Oxley as a partner but the business was dissolved in 1835. Joseph Mansford had died by the census of 1841, but his widow Mary was carrying on the business with the help of her children. In 1854, she sub-let premises in the yard to Mr Butler, a partner in the Bath Street chemists, who printed his own labels there. This was the start of the firm of Butler and Tanner, once the biggest employer in Frome.

By 1871, Mary Mansford's son, Henry, had taken over, although she was still there, now aged 76. That same year, the lease was assigned to Henry Mansford and Charles Baily. By the 1881 census, Henry was a widower, aged 61, but still in business as a wine & spirit importer. In 1895, the Longleat estate sold the freehold to Charles Baily, the remaining partner, and things carried on in much as before, with the

The entrance to one of Frome's tunnels leading off to Catherine Hill.

wine business being advertised in the local press throughout the First World War and into the Second.

In 1971 a lorry demolished the porch, which was rebuilt, and further modifications to the front were carried out during the 1970s. In 1985, a sealed room was found containing shelves of empty bottles and a bottling machine that had not been used for 40 years.

In the early 1990s there was a serious fight at the pub followed by an even bigger one in 1998 during which CS gas was used. The new millennium saw a major refit and the pub reopened as the Wheat Sheaves Inn and Tavern. Later developments included the opening of 'Diva's Nightclub' upstairs. In November 2014, after it had been closed for some time, it reopened as the Wheatsheaves, with an emphasis on live music, on Friday and Saturday nights only, until 3am. It is owned by Enterprise Inns.

The Wheatsheaves in 2013

Wheelwright's Arms / Lion, 95 Broadway

The story of the Wheelwright's Arms in Broadway is essentially the story of one man – Samuel Joyce. Joyce was a wheelwright by trade, born in Frome in 1829, the eldest son of a wheelwright. In 1857, he married local butcher's daughter, Mary Ann Newport, and the couple set about transforming their home in Broadway into a profitable beerhouse.

Being a landlord of one of the more notorious beerhouses required a certain temperament – if not a certain temper – and Samuel Joyce certainly had that. In 1862, he was charged, along with his father-in-law and two other people, with a violent assault on Frome innkeeper and coal merchant, Thomas Williamson. Williamson had been travelling back to Frome from a local fair when he had the misfortune to stop by the Ring O'Bells where Samuel Joyce and his companions were drinking. One of the group, Henry Wilcox, jumped on Williamson's feet, whilst Samuel Joyce punched him so hard he fell to the ground and was rendered insensible. The gang continued to beat him, tore out his hair and ripped his clothes. In court, Samuel Joyce's solicitor attempted to show that Williamson was hardly a model citizen himself, having started the quarrel by insulting a woman, and that it served him right if he was beaten up! The jury took a slightly less perverse view and found Joyce and Wilcox guilty. They were fined one shilling each. Joyce's father-in-law was acquitted.

It is hard to believe that a man of Joyce's character was ever permitted to open a drinking establishment. In June 1868, he was summonsed for permitting his house to be open for the sale of liquor on Sunday. PC Watts had visited the house at noon on the day in question and found no less than 15 customers there, some with beer glasses in hand, others collecting money for the next round. In court, Superintendent Duggan stated that the Wheelwright's Arms was 'a regular Sunday morning house'. Joyce was fined £1 in his absence, having not bothered to turn up to court.

His bad behaviour continued. In 1870, he was charged, along with Thomas Newport, a member of his wife's family, of assaulting John and Ann Kite in a drunken fight at the pub, which had by now been renamed the Lion. Newport got off but Joyce was fined ten shillings. Three months later, he was brought in custody yet again – this time charged with assaulting his wife. On this occasion he was fined only five shillings. A week later, he was summonsed for using threatening language towards James Kite, and was bound over to keep the peace for two months, paying a surety of £5.

Given all this, it is incredible to think he managed to keep his licence. In September 1873, he was summonsed again for unlawfully opened his house for the sale of alcohol during prohibited hours on a Sunday. PC Maidment described how he had seen a lad named Wheeler coming from the back yard of the Lion with a pint bottle in his pocket, and, when he stopped him, found that it contained beer. Joyce was fined £2 and his licence was endorsed.

That same month, he was summonsed for having in his possession on two 'unjust' tin penny and three-halfpenny measures. Joyce's solicitor maintained that the penny cup was a legal measure, although the three-halfpenny cup was not, and quoted from the new Licensing Act to support his claim. The bench decided to look at the legal issues more closely and adjourned for a fortnight. When the case resumed, they concluded that, although Joyce may not have had bad intentions on this occasion, he was nevertheless guilty and a fine of sixpence was imposed.

The following year, he was summonsed for assaulting a young iron fitter named Thomas Gallon, who appeared in court with his face much disfigured, the result of an attack by a bottle-wielding Samuel Joyce. Surprisingly, the prosecutor applied to withdraw the summons. However, this

The Lion in 1957

was simply because he wished to take the matter to the county court so that the injured party might sue for damages. The application was granted and, when the case was heard in the county court a few days later, the judge described the assault as 'unjustifiable, cowardly, and ruffianly'. Joyce was fined £5 10s.

It was a remarkable string of offences, yet, despite all his court appearances, Samuel Joyce managed to remain landlord of his beerhouse. Indeed, business must have been profitable, for in 1878 he submitted plans to build a cottage in Broadway. The plans were approved and, for a number of years, he seems to have stayed out of trouble – or at least managed not to get caught! Then came his Al Capone moment. Having spent years avoiding the full force of the law, perpetrating numerous acts of violence and rule bending, Samuel Joyce was finally tripped up by an act of stupidity. In October 1882, he was found guilty of stealing two shillings worth of hay! In court, his solicitor ridiculed the idea that a *respectable* man like Samuel Joyce would risk ruining his character for two shillings worth of hay. Several local tradesmen appeared as character witnesses for Joyce, but the jury still found him guilty, recommending mercy on account of Joyce's *previous good character*! He was sentenced to three months' hard labour.

What would become of the inn in the meantime? In November 1882, Joyce's brother-in-law Thomas Newport applied to take over whilst Samuel was away. Not surprisingly, the bench refused the application. The Lion was now leaderless and closed its doors – Samuel Joyce would never again be granted a licence to run a beerhouse.

Undefeated, Joyce returned to Frome following his incarceration and resumed his old trade as a wheelwright. By 1885, he was successful enough to buy himself property in Union Street, valued at £75. Old habits die hard, however, and in 1890 he was summonsed for stealing a quantity of French beans, worth threepence, from William Doel of Broadway. He pleaded guilty. Fining Joyce £1, the judge could not help but comment that Joyce was an old man and ought really to have known better. Old man or not, Joyce lived for another 19 years. He continued working as a wheelwright until 1901 when he retired to his home, 'Rosebank', at 13 Nunney Road. He died there in 1909, aged 81.

White Hart, Market Place and 7 Cheap Street

Before taking over the rather grand and ancient building in Cheap Street, the White Hart was situated in the Lower Market Place almost opposite The Blue Boar, and with a rear entrance in Blue Boar Yard where Scott Street is now. Early owners included Mrs Lock in 1753 and Zachariah Baily in 1775. But it is landlord Joshua Yeomans, a tenant of Zachariah Baily, who interests us most. Yeomans was an interesting fellow and by far the most notorious landlord ever to pull a pint in Frome. He earned this dubious accolade thanks to a corpse discovered in the 'backwater' of the river at Frome on 1 August 1774. There were no obvious signs of violence about the body, nor were there the usual indications of death by drowning, and an inquest jury failed to determine how the deceased had expired.

Nevertheless, rumours began to circulate that the death was somehow connected with the White Hart. If this tells us nothing else, it reveals that it was already an inn of infamy. So what lay behind the rumours?

Lodging at the inn at the time was Jacob Stevens, a dubious character known to deal in contraband goods. Two days after the discovery of the buoyant corpse, Stevens and Yeomans quarrelled. Stevens accused Yeomans of killing the unknown man, an accusation which was overheard and swiftly reported to the constables of Frome. The next day, Stevens and Yeomans were summoned before Justice Horner. Stevens described how, on 29 July, he had been woken in the middle of the night by a disturbance. There was fighting downstairs, followed by a loud discussion as to how to dispose of 'the body'.

Yeomans protested his innocence, claiming that Stevens was merely an embittered lodger, annoyed at not being allowed to gamble at the inn. The justice decided there was no real evidence and discharged the prisoners. The cause of death of the man found in the river was never – officially – determined.

This was not the last time death visited the White Hart Inn. In 1841, William Pearce, a local farmer, popped in for a pint, but before the refreshment could reach his lips he dropped down dead in the tap room. No foul play this time, but the White Hart kept its seedy reputation and customers still received the occasional rough-housing. The building was owned by Richard Strong, who also owned a house on the Bridge, and by 1847 was being run by John Eades and his wife Ann. At the time of the 1841 census, they were living in King Street, with John working as a 'postmaster'. Despite moving to the White Hart, he retained his post, and in the 1851 census is described as postmaster and innkeeper, aged 50. His family were to run the inn for over half a century.

In 1855, Jane Barber had her beer thrown in her face, followed by a swift punch to the same spot and the removal of a clump of her hair by fellow drinker, Ann Yerbury. In her defence, Ann claimed that Jane had been 'speaking lightly of her character previous to her marriage, which had caused some unpleasantness between her and her husband'! She was fined ten shillings.

Around 1857, the White Hart moved from the Market Place to Cheap Street, along with John Eades, his wife and extended family. The move followed the death of Richard Strong Sr, a retired currier, who owned the freehold

No 7 Cheap Street painted by WW Wheatley in the 1840s, before the White Hart moved into the building

of the inn. His son, Richard Strong Jr, sold the property and opened the house he had inherited on the Bridge as the Bridge Inn, but went bankrupt within the year.

Like many licensees at the time, John Eades had to diversify in order to earn a decent living, and, after giving up being a postmaster when he moved, tried a new way of supplementing his income, as this oddly worded advertisement reveals:

> John Eades, White Hart Inn, Cheap Street, Will send out his One-Horse Hearse to any Burial Grounds in this town for 10s 6d. Chops and Steaks at the shortest notice. Well-aired beds at moderate prices.

During the 1860s, both Eades and his daughter Matilda Fricker were widowed and ran the inn together. In 1882, the licence was officially transferred from 81-year-old Eades to Matilda, although in reality Matilda had been the acting proprietor for some years. Even when the Earl of Cork sold the inn to Shepton Mallet solicitor, John Nalder, for £963 in 1889, Matilda Fricker remained as yearly tenant. She held the licence in her own name for two decades until the inn was taken on by 41-year-old ex-Sergeant Major Nation in June 1901.

Albert Nation had been sergeant-instructor of the local company of volunteers, and, after completing 25 years service, had received his discharge with an exemplary character. He only stayed at the White Hart for five years before moving to Bath, where he ran the Britannia Inn.

The licence was taken over by ex-butler Maurice Stock in 1906, although ill health meant his nephew George Edward Stock was effectively in charge from 1907. When Maurice died in 1909, his will revealed he had left neither nephew George nor his own estranged wife Lavinia anything in his will. It all went to a friend, and George Stock left the White Hart a few months later.

In 1910, Frederick Castle and his wife Annie took over. Their stay was brief, for by 1913 George Frederick Roberts was running the pub. After such a long period of stability under the Eades-Fricker family, the White Hart was now going through a period of rapidly-changing proprietors. Like the previous four landlords, Roberts soon left and in 1915 Thomas Herbert Paget took over. He had previously run the Railway Hotel in Radstock and the family established themselves as active residents of Frome. He was a popular landlord and after his death was long remembered in Frome as a billiard player *par excellence*. In January 1919, Paget's 17-year-old son, Keith, raised £1 3s 6d for the War Memorial Fund, compared with only 18s at the Castle and 5s 6d at the Black Swan.

Thomas Paget's time at the White Hart was marred by two events: the early death of his wife in 1919, and the fire which broke out in Cheap Street in August 1923. The fire started in a drapery store and took such a hold that at one point it seemed the whole street might be destroyed. Several people, including a fireman, were injured, and the inn was only metres from the centre of the blaze. One man, Mr Benger, made an heroic and ultimately successful attempt to rescue children from the upstairs and was later operated on for serious burns to his arms and face.

In 1924, the White Hart, by now in the hands of Oakhill Brewery, closed. During the 1970s it became a café, the Crusty Loaf, and in 2011 was divided up into shops.

The White Hart around 1907 ...

... and the building in 2014

White Hart, Vallis Way

Next to nothing is known about this one. The first mention comes in the *County Gazette* for 1840 when a William Read is listed as running a beer shop in Vallis Way. The Churchwarden's accounts between 1832 and 1846 show a John and Sarah Read occupying a house and garden in Vallis Way. William Read does not appear in the 1841 census, but John Read, a clothier, and his wife Sarah, both aged 45, with son Alfred, aged 14, are shown as living in Vallis Way. No other information at present.

White Horse / Bird in Hand, 11 Portway

From the outside, the White Horse Inn was indistinguishable from any of the other buildings on Portway. Only the sign above the door and a few assorted advertisements marked it apart. Inside too there was little difference between this traditional ale and cider house and many of the nearby homes. It was a simple establishment, one room at the front serving as the public bar, with a hatch leading to the kitchen behind which doubled as a stillroom. Structurally speaking, it was created out of two separate abodes, and, like many Victorian beerhouses, was modestly furnished. Such diminutive establishments were numerous in Frome. No doubt the overcrowded conditions experienced by large families crammed into small cottages meant that the pub was a welcome relief, even an escape.

One of its earliest landlords was Alfred Happerfield, who ran the nearby Live and Let Live until 1862. He moved to the Bird in Hand, then described as 'a beerhouse containing twelve rooms, yard, smith's shop adjoining with two cottages at the rear', and almost immediately began complaining that his rates were too high. When Alfred died, his widow took over and managed the house during the 1860s and early 1870s, and also took in lodgers.

There has always been a dark side to public houses. One of the earliest references to the Bird in Hand provides an example of this. In 1865, Charles Whimpey was fined for assaulting William Trotman there. It was a savage attack and Trotman took several days to recover. Licensees too created problems for themselves and in 1875 Lydia Happerfield was fined £1 for serving illegal measures. She left the trade four years later and moved in with her daughter's family in Milk Street.

The White Horse in 1907

In pubs like the White Horse, the landlord or landlady was almost as likely to fall foul of the law as the customers. In April 1879, new landlord Thomas Smith, the man credited with changing the pub's name to the White Horse, was fined for selling liquor out of hours on Good Friday morning. Unfortunately, Smith failed to learn his lesson. Three months later, in July 1879, PC Vincent was passing at midnight when he heard voices in the tap room. The policeman spent an hour and a half trying to peer through the windows – a tricky job since the blinds were down! Eventually, the late night revellers began to depart and were promptly apprehended by the awaiting policeman. In court, the magistrates concluded that, due to the closed blinds, the policeman had probably made a mistake. Nevertheless, at the 1879 licensing sessions the White Horse was singled out as the 'worst pub in town'! The magistrates told Smith they would only renew his licence if he swore to conduct the pub better. He promised to do so and the licence was granted.

The White Horse in the 1960s

Mr and Mrs Sid Barnes, landlord and landlady at the time

In 1892, Sergeant Major Davis, late of the Dragoon Guards, took over, but by 1899 he was dead and his widow Emily fell upon hard times. In 1900, she was summonsed for refusing to quit the Ship Inn and striking a policeman while inebriated. She did not attend court and was fined in her absence.

World War One saw dramatic changes in the pub trade. Under the Defence of the Realm Act (DORA), opening hours were cut back and prices rose; the long pull (pouring oversized measures), treating (buying somebody a drink) and allowing customers to run up tabs were all outlawed. Fear of Zeppelin attacks meant that everyone had to adhere to lighting restrictions, and in 1916, landlady Fanny Morris was summonsed for breaching blackout regulations. Whilst she had carefully screened all her front windows, she did not think aerial attackers would be able to see light from her back windows! The chairman of the magistrates corrected this mistaken idea and fined her five shillings.

Over the following decades, the White Horse prospered, and in 1949 was granted a full licence. In the 1960s, under Sid Barnes and his wife, it expanded to provide bed and breakfast accommodation, but by 1977 it had closed to become a butcher's. It has since been converted into apartments.

The former White Horse in 2014

White Swan, Vallis Road

The White Swan, in what is now Vallis Road, was opened as a beerhouse by Benjamin Ball and his wife Harriet, and lay at the far end of what was at the time called Robin's Lane, just where it joined Kissing Batch. Harriet's family were comfortably-off farmers, her brother Robert Ashby farming land near Vallis Leaze, and her father Edmund Ashby running Vallis Farm.

The first record of it comes in Pigot's 1842 *Directory*, which lists Benjamin Ball as a 'retailer of beer' in Vallis Way. Two years later, his wife's father died and left her the tidy sum of £100, which would certainly have helped them to get the business onto a secure footing. It is first recorded as the White Swan in the 1851 census.

By 1861, Benjamin Ball had died and Harriet was running the place single-handed, taking in lodgers to bolster her income. After she died in 1863, it was taken over by the George family. Like many other beerhouse keepers, Frank George had another job, working as a carpenter during the day. He experienced problems similar to those of other landlords, having to deal with customers like Henry Dix, who in 1874 was summonsed for refusing to leave. Dix not only refused to go but tried to fight the landlord in the tap room, putting his fists right into his face. Not that Henry George himself always stayed on the right side of the law. Opening during prohibited hours was a perpetual temptation for even the best landlords. In 1886. George was summonsed for selling beer on a Sunday morning, after Sergeant White found Alfred Bray hiding in the carpenter's shop, which adjoined the beerhouse, with a bottle of beer in his pocket. George was fined £5 and his licence was endorsed, something most publicans dreaded even more than a fine.

At least his wife Ann was honest, albeit a little too much so on occasion. In 1886, William Coleman was charged with being drunk and disorderly, and calling the constable a ' ******* bobby'. Ann George was called by Coleman to give evidence in his defence. Unfortunately for Coleman, she was a little bit too honest in her testimony and said that, when he left the pub, he had had 'a little too much'. Coleman was fined five shillings but, since he had no money, he was given 14 days' hard labour instead.

The former White Swan in the 1970s

Frank George died in 1892, leaving his widow to spend much of her remaining years in the Blue House, reliant upon charity. She was not the only landlord's widow to fall upon hard times. For such women it was usually a straight choice between making a go of it as a landlady – as did Lydia Happerfield at the White Horse, Matilda Fricker at the White Hart and Mrs Rendall at the Ship – or falling into poverty and ending up into the workhouse, as did Mrs Tucker of the Bridge Hotel. For Ann George, who had been raised as a child by an octogenarian pauper aunt before starting work as a weaver, such dire straits may not have come as such a shock. It is nevertheless sad to see a respected landlady end her days a pauper.

After the George family left the White Swan, Frank Penny took over briefly before handing the reins over to John Bown from Wells in 1893. Initially, Bown was refused a licence because he planned to continue working as a cabinet maker, and leave the day-to-day running of the pub to his wife Julia. The licensing authorities were unimpressed with this display of frankness and Bown had to backtrack in order to get the licence, promising to focus on the beerhouse alone. They did not remain long anyway, moving on in 1895 to run the Wheelwright's Arms in Chapmanslade, where John Bown was able to continue working as a cabinet maker without any objections.

James Philips took over at the White Swan, remaining for just over a decade. As a former policeman in the Bristol docks, he was well prepared to deal with any nonsense, and the pub seems to have been well run during his time. In 1909, it was taken over by another ex-policeman, Alfred Barnes, who had been with the Metropolitan Police before getting a taste for the licensing trade. He and his Wiltshire-born wife took over the London Inn on Mortimer Street in Trowbridge before moving to Frome.

His successor, Frank Urch, a former groom at Whatley House, arrived in 1913 but died within the year, aged just 42. His widow, Alma, stayed on, but she too met an early death in 1918. Between 1919 and 1922 there were three landlords in quick succession – John Patrick Hiscocks, Edward Stickler and Mr Geoffries. Finally, in 1923, some stability returned to the house in the shape of John Herbert Hole.

The Hole Family were the longest-serving publicans of the White Swan. John Hole was landlord for 36 years, whilst simultaneously working as chief clerk at the New Frome Quarry of Messrs Roads Reconstruction Co Ltd. His son, Trevor Sidney Hole, was born at the pub in 1924 and later became landlord. Regulars recall the 'Mucky Duck', as the White Swan was known, as a 'proper cider house – absolutely full of old characters', with farmhouse cider brought up from South Somerset. During Trevor's time, it was granted a full licence, so that wines and spirits could be sold as well. After his death, it passed out of the hands of the Hole family, although in 1967 it was managed briefly by another member of the family – Graham Hole, Trevor's brother. During his time there, he used to tie quarts of cider to pieces of rope and dangle them down from the wall of the adjoining factory, so that night-shift workers could pull them up over the wall and have a drink.

In January 1970, after the landlord, William Harrigan, left for Ireland, the licence was transferred to Richard John Walter, regional manager of Ushers Brewery, but the White Swan closed shortly afterwards. The following year, Frome Urban District Council granted Michael Sellers permission to convert it into an art gallery and coffee bar. It is now a private residence.

Woolpack, Badcox

One of two Frome pubs called the Woolpack. This one was at 4 Badcox and is shown on the 1774 map on a triangle of ground pointing towards Badcox, with Vallis Way on one side and Broadway on the other.

It was first mentioned in the church rates of 1782 as being owned by a William Ford, described as a collar maker (the collars probably being intended for horses). He was there until 1799, after which there is no further mention of it as a pub, and

Above: The former Woolpack on Badcox in the 1920s

Top right: The Woolpack on the Cruse map of 1813

Right: The site of the Woolpack on Badcox today

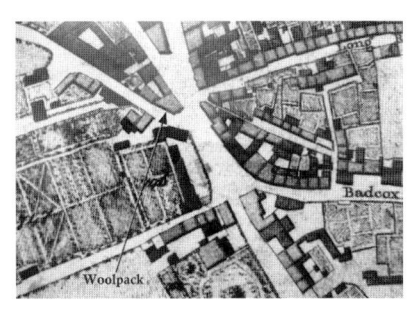

its history is difficult to trace until 1875, when it was occupied by a Mrs Ann Stokes, haberdasher and draper, who interestingly was born in Spain.

She is still listed in directories as a draper in 1883, after which it became Mrs Palmer's Pioneer Tea Rooms, followed by Mrs Plowman's Pioneer Tea Rooms, and from 1920 Mrs Chick's Pioneer Tea Rooms.

The site was cleared in the 1960s and is now a council car park.

Woolpack, 8 Culver Hill

The Woolpack was one of a large number of beerhouses which sprang up as a result of the 1830 Beer Act. First came a malthouse, which was included in an indenture of August 1841 describing various properties borrowed by Thomas Millard Jr from Simon Hoddinot in connection with a £500 mortgage. This was described as 'that building used as a malthouse ... with cart house, dwelling house and other buildings adjoining … built by Thomas Millard the father, on the said piece of garden ground'.

A decade later, when Thomas Millard sold the property to Benjamin Cornish for £302 in an auction at the George Hotel, it was described as

> all that tenement or dwelling house, shop, bakehouses, and outhouses situate at Culverhill, together with the malthouse, cart house and other buildings thereto adjoining and lately occupied by Thomas West but now by Benjamin Cornish ... erected on the lower end of a piece of garden ground known as New Tyning and containing by estimation half an acre.

The Woolpack was probably opened by Benjamin Cornish shortly after he acquired the property. He had not been there long when, in November 1851, his wife Sophia was called as witness in a murder trial involving the death of a young girl and three accused men who had been drinking in the pub.

It was certainly a lively place, as an incident from 1859 demonstrates. One October evening, PC Roe of Frome went to the Woolpack to serve a summons on George Thorne. As the policeman entered the pub, a man rose and swore at him, saying 'Yes! You -----, I am George Thorne, get out you ----- and your summonses too.' In fact, he wasn't George Thorne at all, but a man called Richard Jelly. As PC Roe was walking away, Jelly grabbed him and knocked him to the ground, shouting 'You are the ----- that shopped Follett.' Jelly was later sentenced to two months' hard labour.

Benjamin Cornish was not a man blessed with much good fortune. In 1861, he was given forged money by William Bushe, who owed him £14 for groceries purchased from the pub. In April 1866, Job Orchard obtained a quantity of pollard oak from him under false pretences. In September 1866, he was summonsed for selling beer during illegal hours, but, since the beer was poured out in the workshop adjoining the beerhouse, he escaped punishment.

The Woolpack on Culver Hill in the 1960s

Clearly, Cornish was a man often taken advantage of, so it should come as no surprise to find that by 1867 he was so short of money that he had to borrow £350 from local builder James Greenland. This probably only made matters worse, for two years later he was bankrupt, owing over £1,000, and all his property and belongings were confiscated. In an attempt to get back on his feet, he moved to the Midlands, spending long periods away from his wife and large family, working first as a carter and then in a brewery. He was unable to put his troubles behind him, however, and, one morning in June 1883, 60-year-old Benjamin Cornish, by then employed at the Ash Inn Brewery in Stockport, stabbed himself in the stomach six times and threw himself into a beer vat, with predictable results.

During the 1880s, Herbert Henry Bound was licensee at the Woolpack. There has always been a huge variety of games played in and around pubs, and bound up with the love of games was a passion for gambling. One evening in 1887, PC Mason was passing the pub one night when he heard a young voice from inside say, 'I've lost three-ha'pence'. The upshot was that Herbert Bound was fined £1 for permitting illegal skittling at his beerhouse. Two months later, he gave up the licence and Isaac Thomas Derrick took over.

Being a landlord wasn't all beer and skittles, as Derrick discovered one evening shortly after he took over. It was around 10.30, and he had just refused to serve Henry Short. The irate tippler's response was that, if Derrick would not serve *him*, then he would not be serving *anybody*! Derrick endeavoured to remove him from the premises and they went outside together. Minutes later, Derrick staggered back into the pub with his ear hanging off. His attacker was sentenced to two months' hard labour.

One of the major trends in the pub trade in the late 1800s was the increasing number of pubs taken over by breweries. After Benjamin Cornish's financial woes, builder James Greenland bought the Woolpack, later selling it to Eliza Baily in 1873 for £900. She in turn sold it on to J&T Baily in 1884 for £1,100 and thus the Woolpack joined the properties owned by the Lamb Brewery.

Thomas Derrick was followed by a series of short-lived tenants, until John Nightingale arrived in 1900. He ran the inn with his wife Anna, and, by and large, they avoided trouble – until one afternoon in 1904. That day, three likely lads – Harry Neighbour, George Lambert and Oliver Screen – were drinking at the Woolpack. After they left, Anna Nightingale noticed that a bottle of rum was missing from the bar. Man of action John Nightingale immediately jumped on his tricycle and peddled after the rogues. He caught up with them and quizzed them about the rum. 'No, we know nothing about it. We haven't seen the rum,' said Harry Neighbour, with a bottle of rum clearly sticking out of his pocket! In court, Neighbour produced a ten years' exemplary character reference from the army, on account of which his punishment was reduced to a mere 14 days' hard labour.

The Woolpack's latter years were largely uneventful. In 1960 the Lamb Brewery was taken over by Ushers, who closed the pub the following year and sold it to Kenneth Fudge and Victor Cuff of the Albion Garage on the Mount. The sale was subject to a covenant stating that the property was not to be used as a club or for the sale of intoxicating liquors, 'to protect the company's other property at Frome', namely the Beehive and the New Inn.

The former Woolpack in 2013

Prior to the Woolpack's closure, part of the premises was in use as an off-licence and grocer's. Following the closure, there was a long and enthusiastic campaign by local residents for the grocer's to reopen. In May 1971, Pamela and Donald Scott moved in and applied for permission to open a small grocer's shop, supported by a petition signed by 150 local residents. The application was declined, but Mrs Scott appealed successfully and the grocer's opened in 1973.

Today the premises are the office and showrooms of Klear Water Systems and the authors are very grateful to Mr Longhurst for allowing access to his deeds.

Wyredrawer's Arms, 17 Portway

This first appears in a deed from 1761 as 'all that tenement or dwelling house at Garston Style occupied by George Mees as tenant and called by the name or sign of the Wyredrawer's Arms'. It is described as having a garden measuring 45 feet by 33 feet, and being 'bounded in front or the south by the roadway leading from Frome to Warminster'. It was owned by John Smith of Stoney Littleton, who also owned the Black Swan and went spectacularly bankrupt in 1771 owing over £16,000. The property was leased to a dyer called Robert Meares, who also held the lease of the Black Boy at Wallbridge along with much other property in Frome. Its unusual name came from the woollen industry, referring to the process whereby a thick piece of wire was pulled or drawn through a narrow hole, making it thinner and longer. In this case, the finished product would probably been used for making teeth for the wool cards.

The Wyredrawer's does not appear on the town plan of 1774, indicating it had closed by then. However, the map shows an inn called the Horse & Groom on roughly the same site that the Wyredrawers had occupied (see separate entry), and this may have been a renaming. A deed of 1812 also records that John Smith, who owned the Wyredrawer's Arms in 1761, had also owned what later became the Horse & Groom. However, entries in the church rates from 1790 to 1799 refer to William Baily owning property described as 'late the Wire Drawers'. This suggests that, over 20 years after the building had been the Wyredrawer's Arms, it was still being referred to by its former name rather than as the Horse & Groom.

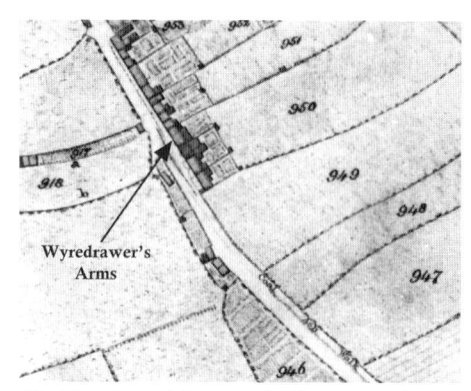

The Wyredrawer's Arms on the Cruse map of 1813

The building today

There are more unanswered questions than usual with the Wyredrawer's Arms and the Horse & Groom, and further research may well come up with a somewhat different story, but it is a suitably intriguing mystery on which to end our survey of Frome's historic inns.

Bibliography

These are the publications that have proved most useful in our research. Many are in print and obtainable from Frome Museum:

Belham, Peter, *The Making of Frome*, Frome Society for Local Study, 1985
Gill, Derek, *Bath Street, Frome*, Derek Gill, 1992
Gill, Derek, *The Sheppards & Eighteenth Century Frome*, Frome Society for Local Study, 1982
Goodall, Rodney, *The Buildings of Frome*, Frome Society for Local Study, 3rd ed., 2013
Haydon, Peter, *The English Pub: A History*, Robert Hale, 1994
Leech, R, *Early Industrial Housing: The Trinity Area of Frome*, Royal Commission on Historic Monuments, 1981
McGarvie, Michael, *Crime & Punishment in Regency Frome: The Journals of Isaac Gregory*, Frome Society for Local Study, 1984
McGarvie, Michael, *Frome Place Names*, Frome Society for Local Study, 1983
McGarvie, Michael, *The King's Peace: The Justice's Notebooks of Thomas Horner of Wells 1770-1777*, Frome Society for Local Study, 1997
Miles, Mary, *Perfectly Pure: A Directory of Somerset Brewers*, Brewery History Society & Somerset Industrial Archaeological Society. 2006
Swift, Andrew & Kirsten Elliott, *The Lost Pubs of Bath*, Akeman Press, 2005
Ware, Len, *Shepton Mallet Mine Host: A Record of Shepton's Pubs*, Shepton Mallet, 2008

NEWSPAPERS

Somerset Standard, 1886 to present day
Somerset & Wiltshire Journal, 1855-1886
Frome Times, 1859-1886
North Somerset Independent, 1931-33

There are some original copies in the Frome Museum but they are getting a bit fragile and it is probably best to use the microfilmed ones in Frome Library, which has a more complete collection.

MAPS

There are no readily available modern maps of Frome that show the town in any detail. There are helpful free copies from estate agents and the Red Books series but they are very basic and do not show everything. Mendip Council has a website with O/S maps updated frequently, see below.
Historical maps which have proved most useful include:
The Jeremiah Cruse Survey of 1813. A wonderful map with good detailing, which covers the whole district and is available at www.gomezsmart.myzen.co.uk. There is a close-up version of the town centre available to view at the Frome Museum in 17 sections. The original is now at the Somerset Record Office in Taunton.

The Ordnance Survey produced a very detailed set of maps in 1886 at a scale of over 10 feet to the mile. Frome Society for Local Study has combined some sections to produce an excellent map of the town centre available from Frome Museum either as a folded map or as an expanded version on CD.

The John Ladd Survey of West & East Woodlands, 1744. This consists of a very large map detailing the rents of property owned by the Marquess of Bath. The original is at Longleat House and the survey book is available to view at the Wiltshire Record Office in Chippenham on microfilm. This helped us to locate a couple of lost pubs.

The 1840s tithe map is on microfiche at Frome library

Census returns are on microfilm at the Frome Library and the years 1841 & 1861 are available online at www.freecen.org.uk.

DOCUMENTS

The deeds from pubs owned by the Lamb Brewery, which was absorbed by Ushers and then by Watneys, are at the Wiltshire Record Office in Chippenham.

WEBLIOGRAPHY

Frome Museum: www.frome-heritage-museum.org.

Ordnance Survey maps are viewable online at www.mendip.gov.uk

Picture Credits

Akeman Press: ii, 15 (bottom), 36 (bottom), 38, 54 (both), 73, 93 (bottom), 98, 112 (top), 130 (both), 142, 162 (top), 170, 181; Trevor Biggs: 128; Frome Museum: x, 8, 11, 14 (bottom), 19, 20 (centre & bottom), 23, 27 (top), 30, 32, 35, 36 (top), 37 (all), 39 (all), 47, 51 (left), 53, 56, 57, 62 (top), 65, 67 (both), 70, 71, 72 (both), 76 (bottom), 88 (top), 89, 91 (bottom), 94 (top), 105 (bottom), 108, 109, 111 (top), 114, 115 (bottom), 120 (top), 125, 126 (top), 131 (top), 135 (top & centre), 144 (top), 145, 147 (top), 149, 150 (top), 153 (top), 153 (bottom), 155, 157 (bottom), 158 (both), 159 (top), 160, 162 (bottom), 164, 167, 169, 171, 172 (top & centre), 173, 175 (left), 176; Frome Reclamation: 16, 106 (bottom); Colin Hamilton: 110, 136 (top); John Peverley: 106 (bottom); Diane Rouse: 80 (top), 92, 111 (top), 127; E&G Saner: 10 (bottom); Colin White: 105 (top). All other photographs and illustrations are the property of the authors.